LOST

IN

CHINA

LOST
IN
CHINA

A Memoir of World War II

JENNIFER F. DOBBS

Peach Pit
PUBLICATIONS

Published by Peach Pit Publications, Memphis, TN
www.lostinchinabook.com

Edited and designed by Girl Friday Productions
www.girlfridayproductions.com

Cover design: David Fassett
Project management: Kristin Duran and Laura Dailey
Image credits: cover © Shutterstock/Arthur Balitskii, iStock/zenink

ISBN (paperback): 979-8-9858883-1-7
ISBN (e-book): 979-8-9858883-0-0

For Daddy—and all the daddies lost to war.
We miss you. You left too soon.

F.E.L. Dobbs, Ted, Daddy (1900–1941).

This is a story about a little girl who, although she lived in war-torn China, felt her world was much like the worlds of *Winnie-the-Pooh* and *The Wind in the Willows*: warm, safe, essentially predictable, and fun. Most of the story is true. What isn't true was invented to make sense of the true parts.

CONTENTS

PART II: THE USA

AUTHOR'S NOTE

All the dialogue in this book between Chinese speakers and between Dobbs family members and Chinese speakers, although rendered in English, can be assumed to have taken place in Chinese. Everyone in the Dobbs family spoke Mandarin Chinese; it was my mother's, my brothers', and my first language. My maternal grandparents, Katie and John McGregor Gibb, as well as Katie's parents, who came to China from England in 1878, all spoke Mandarin. English was reserved for school, children's parties, and our parents' friends.

影攝國歸師牧瞿送錢生科天年二科頒月五年八國民華中

訏毛赫聶袁周劉何劉劉周宋馬田
景叔金雨洞級彼比崇振顯紹辰
雲身貴潤天禮得應齊義名任賢午

John McGregor Gibb (1882–1939), my grandfather, front and center, surrounded by his English language class at Peking University in about 1910.
Peking University, established in 1898, is considered the second-best university
in China, and its sixty-eight-acre campus is considered the loveliest. In addition to teaching, John McGregor devoted himself to campus beautification—
he supervised the construction of buildings and brought to the campus
many large pieces of decorative marble, including a pair of columns bearing
dragon reliefs, from the ruins of Empress Dowager Cixi's Summer Palace.
The palace had been demolished in 1860 by French and British troops
during the Second Opium War (1856–1860). John McGregor thereby pre-
vented the lovely carvings from being chipped up by scavengers and sold as
garden rock.

My grandmother, standing at the right end of the middle row with a group of Western ladies invited to tea by Empress Dowager Cixi (1835–1908), seated front row and center, and her court, Peking, 1903. Although she was one of many concubines, Cixi rose by cunning and manipulation to control the government of China, initially because she bore the emperor a son and she could read and write Chinese. During the forty-seven years she controlled the government, China rose from a medieval to modern country; she banned foot-binding (thus initiating women's liberation), outlawed barbaric punishments, modernized the military, and reformed the education and legal systems.

It should be noted that Chinese does not mimic the grammar and syntax of English, and therefore in translation, it's somewhat difficult to render a sentence's meaning with the same colorful, often nuanced, flavor. The written language is not constructed from individual words but from ideograms, or characters, each a collection of images developed from a stylized picture or symbol. For example, the ideogram for a "happy household" is made up of three parts: symbols for a lady and a pig under a roof. Furthermore, Chinese has no need for verb tenses. One knows when an action takes place by the word/character selection: *now*, *yesterday*, or *next week*, for example. Finally, word order is important. Changing the word order in a sentence can change the sentence's meaning entirely.

To add to the complexity, spoken Chinese characters are uttered in one of four "tones" or vocalized inflections: level; rising; dropping; or dropping followed by rising, as in a V shape. Thus, the same written character can have a different meaning depending on how it's pronounced. For example, the sound *ma* can be pronounced in four different tones, and each tone affects the sound's meaning. When pronounced with a level tone it means "mother"; when pronounced with an ascending or rising tone it means "linen"; a descending or dropping tone means "scold"; and a dropping/rising V-tone means "horse." This is not a totally unfamiliar aspect of language to English speakers; consider the various ways the word *oh* can be pronounced; it might be an exclamation, a declaration, or a question.

In addition, since there were/are many local dialects in China, foreigners (whose work required frequent travel) often resorted to a language known as pidgin: a simplified, improvised, bare-essentials language that arose (in many cultures) when there was an urgent need for those who spoke different languages or dialects to communicate—for example, for purposes of trade. Chinese pidgin in particular first developed in 1634, when English-speaking traders arrived in Canton and Macau; it is believed the name is derived from the Chinese interpretation of an English word for "business." By the 1830s, Chinese pidgin had spread north to Shanghai and the surrounding cities.

PROLOGUE

January 2021
Memphis, Tennessee, United States

A crash of thunder shook me awake at dawn. I pulled the quilt
from around my ears; rain had fallen steadily all night, and heavy
drops splatted against the driveway outside. The curtain flapped
against the window frame. It was the sort of morning that made
me want to stay snugly in bed. But I couldn't. A little twinge,
an unrelenting whisper of "It's time, it's time," beat like a metro-
nome in my head, nagging me into action. It was the same whisper that had called me to go into the attic the night before and
carry down a wooden box—the size and shape that rifles were
shipped in—and place it on the red leather seat of a chair in the
dining room.

Just when the box had been nailed shut, I didn't know, but it
was long before it came to me. It had arrived on my doorstep in
Philadelphia when my grandmother died. Relatives said it only
contained old papers. No one wanted it. Stained and nicked, it
had then traveled with me when I moved south more than fifty

years earlier, and it had been sitting in a dim corner of the attic ever since. It went unnoticed except in January of every year, when I placed my box of holiday ornaments back on top of it.

I'd often planned to pull out the rusted nails and open the box, but some minor interruption distracted me every time. Perhaps I'd let myself be distracted, because my feelings toward the box were ambivalent. Everyone had said its contents were valueless, yet I'd kept it for all these years. Had I been afraid of what memories might scramble out if I opened it?

I clicked on the dining room light. When I approached the grease-stained wood, I felt oddly apprehensive. With the hammer that I'd retrieved from a kitchen drawer, I set to work. Surprisingly, the first three nails slipped out easily. The next two were harder to dislodge. And the last three were decidedly obstinate; the lid cracked and split lengthwise. Slowly I lifted the three boards that I'd pried loose and placed them against a table leg. I reached into the box with both hands and lifted out a yellowed manila folder. The rubber band around it crumbled; hard, dry bits fell onto the carpet. Below it were two more thick folders and a fourth slimmer one. Each had been labeled in my mother's neat hand:

SHANGHAI

CHUNGKING

BURMA ROAD

HONG KONG / STANLEY POW CAMP

As I lifted the last folder, a scrap of paper fluttered to the floor—a tattered bit of yellow newsprint, a clipping. It was from the *Philadelphia Inquirer* and dated January 24, 1943. Slowly I read it and reread it twice more.

Youngsters Fly Half-Way Around World
War Widow Reunited with 2 Children After Year

At an unnamed American airport a few days ago, a young mother rushed out to a big plane and tearfully embraced her young son and daughter, whom she had not seen since before Pearl Harbor. The children, John Dobbs, 6, and Jennifer, 8, had just flown more than half-way around the world, from an interior point in China to rejoin their mother, who had been taken prisoner when the Japs[1] captured Hong Kong.

The mother, Mrs. Alice Dobbs, now lives at [518] W. Beech Tree Lane, Wayne. Her husband F.E.L. Dobbs, a member of the English Department of China's Salt Tax Administration, lost his life in the Jap invasion.

CAPTAIN HAROLD A. SWEET of Pan American Airways, who revealed the happy reunion yesterday at New York, recalled that during the children's long flight they invariably "gave a lift" to the American soldiers they met in India, the Anglo-Egyptian Sudan and other points where their plane stopped. "Doesn't it seem good to see American kids?" a private at one foreign field remarked to Captain Sweet. At another overnight stop officers argued for the chance to give up their beds to the children, Sweet said.

But the children's principal thrill, of course, was meeting their mother at the journey's end. They had last seen her early in December 1941 when she and their father left their home at Kunming, China, for Hong Kong to do some Christmas shopping. But the Japs struck while the couple was there, killing Dobbs and capturing his wife.

After months in a prison camp, she was released and reached this country last August aboard the prisoner-exchange ship *Gripsholm*. Learning her children were safe inland she arranged with the State Department, the Army, Pan American Airways and the China National Airways, a Pan American affiliate, to bring them home.

What a joyful reunion it described.

But it hadn't happened like that at all.

NOTES

1. In dialogue throughout this book, the Japanese people are re-
    ferred to as "Japs." The word was commonly used as an ethnic
    slur during World War II by Westerners as well as the ethnic
    Chinese who were at war with Japan and to whom the Japanese
    were the much-hated enemy.

PART I

CHINA

1

Tentacles of War

September 1, 1939
Manila Bay, The Philippine Islands

The luxury liner RMS *Canton* rocks gently at anchor in Manila Bay,[1] a scheduled stop on its route from London to Shanghai to take on supplies and allow the passengers to step ashore for a little respite. On board are people returning with their families from home leave in England, or going out to assume their first postings in the Far East: missionaries, businessmen, doctors, nurses, civil servants, teachers.

The "children's parade" on the deck of the RMS *Canton*, 1939. Teddy, center, holds my hand; Amah carries John; Mummy, wearing dark glasses, stands close to the ship's railing.

This morning, as usual, the passengers' lounge on the ship's top deck is transformed into a playroom. And this morning Mummy wants to go shopping in the city, so she leaves my little brother, John, and me to play with the other passengers' children, with an English nanny there to watch us. We have lots of toys and coloring books to choose from. My brother Teddy is happily off in some other lounge with his nose in a book. He scorns the playroom—he's nine years old.

Nanny is busy distributing coloring books and pencils to the other children when we hear a crackling sound. It's the ship's loudspeaker, and it means only one thing. Nanny steps out of the cabin, and a maid Nanny must have found to replace her bustles in. A few minutes later when Nanny slips back into the playroom, she looks flustered. She probably hopes that none of us children have noticed her absence. I look around the room; sunlight streams over our heads. Everyone's busy drawing, coloring, or playing on the deck between the tables with wooden pull toys or tops, or miniature metal trucks, cars, or airplanes.

Nanny straightens her long white apron and scans the room.

"Boys and girls, please listen," she begins hesitatingly. "Today is a very sad day." She smooths her ruddy hands over her apron again and tucks a strand of dark hair under her white cap; then she pauses and scans the room for the umpteenth time. "Our captain has just announced that Germany has invaded Poland." Nanny sighs softly. "We're at war."[2] The unspeakable said, she gathers her courage and continues. "And because Germany has done this terrible thing, the captain has asked everyone on the ship to throw overboard anything that was made in Germany."

We children stare at her blankly.

Straightening her shoulders, Nanny addresses the first child her eyes fall on. "Jennifer, can you read?"

"Yes, I'm five," I chirp. "My brother can't, though. He's only three." I turn to look at the chubby toddler sitting beside me.

"Those children who can read, please help the younger ones." Nanny's voice descends to a growl as she turns and prints MADE IN GERMANY on a blackboard. "Look for this," she says.

I return to snipping around the head of a paper Shirley Temple, careful not to cut off her golden curls. I have no idea what Nanny's talking about. I brush my bangs out of my eyes, look up, and realize that Nanny is no longer her usual starched self. Then, to my surprise, I see that she has tears in her eyes. *Did*

Nanny fall and scrape her knee while out on deck, like I sometimes do?

Snap! John closes the lid of the flat tin box on the table in front of him.

"Look, Ferfer," John says, calling me by the nickname our Shanghai amah had given me when she had trouble pronouncing "Jennifer." He points to the shiny surface. The words BUNTSTIFT, MADE IN GERMANY jump from the case. They're printed in small black letters below the outline of a castle and mountain.

The older children stop what they're doing. The trucks, airplanes, and pull toys roll gently back and forth between them.

Several children now hurry over to inspect the yellow box on John's table and then return to their seats to hunt for their own offending words. Wooden lambs, pigs, ducks, and horses are turned upside down, metal fire engines and tiny cars and milk trucks hastily overturned and inspected. When a little boy recognizes the words MADE IN GERMANY on a green pencil, the other children scramble through the boxes of colored pencils and crayons on their tables. Crayons and colored pencils scatter. Some fall to the deck.

"I found one."

"Here's one."

"Look, here's one."

The voices echo shrilly around the cabin.

John bends over his collection of pencils, then suddenly turns to me. "Where's Daddy?" he asks.

"Out there," I reply, pointing toward the large windows that open onto the starboard deck where two deck chairs stand close together. "When Nanny's not looking, go and look. I'll tell you when."

But there's no time.

Nanny says crisply, "Are you ready, children?" Then, "Follow me." She turns, crosses the cabin, and with an exaggerated motion steps over the high sill, through the narrow doorway, and onto the deck. She lowers her head to duck under a lifeboat suspended overhead as she crosses to the railing. The wind catches her broad apron and it billows out in front of her like a spinnaker sail.

One by one we follow in single file, stepping high over the sill and onto the deck. Each of us clutches a toy or fistful of colored pencils in one hand. The only sound is that of the wind whistling around the ship's single black smokestack. The sweet smell of bougainvillea—bright-pink masses climbing over the gray stone mansions that line the shore—drifts across the water and mingles with the briny fragrance of the bay. Flags snap on the ship's two tall masts.

Nanny waves to direct us to line up along the handrail. We each reach out with our free hand to grab a lower rung. Far below, white wavelets lap and bare their glistening teeth.

"Can I go first?" asks a redheaded girl with pigtails and buckled shoes, and without waiting for a reply, she selects a yellow pencil and aims it toward the water.

Next a little boy chooses an orange stub from his handful and tosses it overboard.

"I like green and purple," John yells as he extends his arm between the rails. One by one, he tosses each pencil overboard. Each cuts the water without a ripple, bobs back up, and settles into a trough between two wavelets. "Good," he says in a satisfied tone.

I look over his head and sniff the air. Deep in the tips of my toes I know something is terribly wrong, something I cannot describe, not even to myself. Something I can only feel. Little do I know that this is the opening salvo, the prelude, to the dark days and years to come.

After thinking about it for a moment, I choose a red pencil and toss it. One end of the pencil hits the railing, and it somersaults as it drops into the water. I select another.

One by one the colored pencils fall. When there are no more left, we stand silently watching the tiny armada floating toward the ship's stern.

"Look, look!" John waves his arm wildly between the railings. "Look, Nanny, look."

A bluish blob of jelly floats below. Long pink-and-purple strands fan out and undulate on each ripple. Black filaments swirl about.

"It's going to eat our pencils, Nanny," John wails.

Everyone stares as a massive jellyfish bobs on the steady rise and fall of the waves. Its tentacles reach out, circling, twisting, engulfing the tiny colored sticks now almost lost to view in the sea.

NOTES

1. RMS *Canton* was built in 1938 in Glasgow, Scotland, for the P&O, the Peninsular and Oriental Steam Navigation Company. Equipped with six holds, she had considerable cargo capacity as well as room for 257 passengers in first class and 221 in second. Her sumptuous decor included fine timber, carpets, and drapes in the cabins, lounges, promenade deck, smoking room, dining room, ballroom, and Verandah Café.

   At the outbreak of World War II, RMS *Canton* was converted first into an armed vessel and then into a troopship. After the war she was converted back into a passenger liner, but her postwar career was short, both because of the increase in popularity of air travel and because she was not air-conditioned. She was retired from service in 1962.

2. World War II is generally considered to have begun when Germany invaded Poland in September 1939. However, China and Japan went to war with each other much earlier, in July 1937, when the Japanese manufactured an incident at the Marco Polo Bridge, near Peking (now Beijing), that they used as a motive to attack Chinese soldiers.

2

Cholera, Diphtheria, and Typhoid Fever

Early June 1940
The International Settlement, Shanghai,
Jiangsu Province, China

My younger brother and I live with our parents, Ted and Alice (Mr. and Mrs. F.E.L.) Dobbs, at 43 Tientsin Road in Shanghai's International Settlement.[1] For most of the year, my older brother, ten-year-old Teddy, is at school in Chefoo,[2] one thousand kilometers (621 miles) away by coastal steamer, but at four and six, John and I are too young for boarding school.

Our comfortable Western-style brick house accommodates servants and their families in their own quarters across a side courtyard. The house is in a tree-lined street about twelve blocks from Shanghai's Bund,[3] the waterfront embankment lined with massive Western-style buildings, where the majority of Shanghai's international commerce takes place and where our father's office is located in the Custom House.[4] Tientsin Road is not far from the Huangpu River, which flows into the Yangtze River, and Suzhou Creek, and thus is prone to flooding each spring.[5]

We are in China because after graduating in 1924 from Clare College,[6] Cambridge University, in England, Daddy was recruited by the British Foreign Office to come here to work for the Salt Gabelle,[7] part of China's Department of Finance. His first posting was in Peking. As a salt mine inspector, he travels widely in north and west China and so far has also held posts in Chefoo, Hankow, and now in Shanghai.

Mummy was born in China, in Peking in 1908, to John McGregor Gibb, a chemistry professor at Peking University, and Katie Gibb. Mummy's parents met Daddy while playing tennis shortly after Daddy arrived from England. Mummy was off at boarding school in Chefoo at the time. With the Christmas holidays, Mummy came home to Peking, and she met Daddy when her parents invited him to join the family for Christmas dinner.

Alice, nicknamed Girlie, in the living room of her family's Peking house, 1927. The black-and-gold lacquer cabinets came to America with Katie and remain in the family.

Bamboo scaffolding erected around a marble column in preparation for moving it to the Peking University campus, about 1910. Note the men standing in the top scaffolding.

The two marble pillars that John McGregor had moved from the decimated Summer Palace in about 1910 still decorate the Peking University campus.

My father in the 1930s, China.

Although Mummy and Daddy wished to marry shortly after she graduated from high school, her daddy, John McGregor, asked her to go to college first. So, Mummy dutifully sailed to America to attend Wilson College in Chambersburg, in central

Pennsylvania. Two years later, John McGregor relented and Daddy went to America to meet her. They were married in a church service in Bryn Mawr, Pennsylvania, in May 1928, surrounded by Mummy's American relatives. Following their honeymoon, Mummy and Daddy returned to China and Daddy's new posting in Chefoo. In 1930 Teddy was born there. I followed in 1934, in yet another posting, Hankow, and John in 1936, also in Hankow. Then, after a home leave in England in 1938–39, we moved to the comfortable big brick house at 43 Tientsin Road in Shanghai's International Settlement.

The house in Hankow, where we lived when John and I were born, 1933–37. One morning our family awakened to find hundreds of Chinese soldiers camped in the fields around it. Teddy watched the soldiers parading until our father told him to stay away from the windows.

Ranch in Rosario, Argentina, where my father was born. His dad went to Argentina to breed Irish ponies with Argentine ponies in hopes of developing superior horses for the sport of polo, 1904.

My father, Ted, seated in front of his father, Francis (Frank), and beside his older brother, C. Eric Stewart, at their ranch in Rosario, Argentina.

Alice Gibb Dobbs, just married, Philadelphia, Pennsylvania, 1928.

Like all foreign households in China at the time, ours is run by a staff of live-in Chinese servants. Ping San (which means the third person named Ping) is the head houseboy, and he supervises the cooks, Da Shu Foo (Big Cook) and Er Shu Foo (Number Two Cook); a houseboy, who keeps the house clean and tidy; Amah (Maid), who takes charge of us children; and Wash Coolie, *coolie* being the word for "laborer" in China. In most cases these beloved and loyal staff members are the children of the men and women who work for our maternal grandparents, Katie and John McGregor Gibb. This second generation of Katie's servants came to work for our parents when our parents married. A gardener is shared with another Western family, and a chauffeur is provided by our father's office when he's in Shanghai.

My grandmother Katie, left, and guests take tea in the garden of her Shanghai house on Avenue Haig in the French Concession, 1939.

In addition, each spring and fall a tailor (called Mr. Tailor, in Chinese) sets up his treadle machine in front of a big window in the upper hallway to turn out Western-style clothes for Mummy,

John, and me. Mr. Tailor is a guest in the servants' quarters for the two or three weeks he needs to stitch the re-creations of pictures that Mummy selects from magazines. My only store-bought clothes are my school uniforms, which are ordered from Lane Crawford in Hong Kong. Daddy's suits come from Savile Row in London.

***

The front entrance of our house on Tientsin Road leads directly into a bright, spacious foyer with doors opening into the kitchen; the living room (with windows that open onto a large back garden); Daddy's study; and the dining room. The large square kitchen opens onto a side courtyard, beyond which are the servants' quarters. We're allowed to go there only when invited.

First portrait of my father and us children, Shanghai, 1937.

Directly opposite the front door a carpeted staircase rises, comes to a landing, and makes an abrupt left turn as it continues to the upper floors. It's on this landing that we children like to lie, faces pressed against the banisters, to watch what's happening below—to spy, unseen, as Ping San answers the doorbell and Mummy and Daddy greet guests in the foyer. Like actors walking across a stage, men in dark suits and others wearing high-collar olive uniforms or dark silk gowns move between the front door and archway into the living room. Sometimes the men are accompanied by ladies in flowery dresses or bright satin *cheongsams*.[8] It's not the conversation in both English and Chinese that draws our attention; it's the swirling kaleidoscope of red, gold, green, black, navy, and olive fabrics that fascinates us. Amah knows. Sometimes during our bath, she whispers something like, "Cook tells me there's a party tonight. Do you want to see the ladies in their pretty dresses?"

Today I sit on the top stairstep just below the landing. I squirm. The carpet is prickly through my cotton shorts. "John . . . John. Where are you?" I call down the stairs.

John pops out from the dining room, a toy truck in one hand. He's probably been crawling around under the large dining table, a favorite hiding place of his.

"What are you doing? Where's Mummy?" I say.

Amah appears at the top of the stairs. She's wearing her usual black cotton pants and crisp white jacket, and her glossy black hair's smoothed over the top of her head and twisted into a small bun on the back of her neck. "Missy's gone to play cards at her friend's house," she says.

I slide down a step toward the foyer. "John, let's go and look at the street."

The Yangtze is flooding, causing its tributary, the Huangpu, to overflow its banks. For the past several days, dirty brown water's been rising in Tientsin Road, inch by inch, and now it entirely covers the asphalt. Only the steep curb holds it back from flowing over the sidewalk and into the neighborhood courtyards and gardens.

Amah looks out the hallway window. "Outside's bad; it's raining," she says.

John looks through the dining room window. "It's only raining a little, Amah."

The conversation is quite enough to convince us that this is the perfect time to explore the street in front of the house. Amah, who has apparently realized that she'll be unable to dissuade us, hurries to get our raincoats and boots from the hall closet and arrives in time to catch us at the front door. As she goes out, she grabs a large black umbrella from its stand.

Amah supervises as John and I muck about in the flooded street in front of our Tientsin Road house, Shanghai, 1939.

I sniff the air. Muddy, smelly water swirls and flows beside the curb. Sticks, leaves, and unidentifiable debris sweep by. John and I watch, fascinated. Amah quickly puts her hand over her nose. She opens the umbrella.

John picks up a stick and pokes a mass of leaves and twigs that have lodged against the curb, causing a small dam. As the mass breaks loose, something floats up from under it and slides away. We step back and look at each other. "What was that?" I exclaim.

Amah looks horrified.

"A rat?" I ask.

All three of us watch the hairy object as it is swept along in the current, tangled among dead leaves and other debris, and then frees itself.

"Can it swim?" John asks.

"No, it's dead," I say.

"Oh!" John replies. The rat drifts out of sight, propelled by the current, and we fall silent as we gaze into the water with its many surprises. An endless parade of interesting objects glides by: a clump of dead insects, an old straw sandal, more twigs and leaves.

"Look, there's a spoon," I say, as a large wooden kitchen spoon floats past.

John picks up three sticks, breaks them into different lengths, and drops them into the water. He watches intently as they drift away. "Will the long one go faster?" he asks. Then he pokes at a brown gooey mass that's lodged nearby. It divides into bits and slips away.

A rickshaw splashes by, churning up the water. My hand jerks up to my nose. "Let's go in and look at a book."

Before John has a chance to reply, Wash Coolie emerges from the gate that opens between the servants' courtyard and the street. He's carrying a large round white metal basin. "I don't need this today," he says as he places it in the water in front of John and me and holds it so it won't float away.

Amah shifts her umbrella to her other hand. "That's a bad idea," she says and frowns at Wash Coolie, as John steps into the makeshift boat.

***

An hour later, Mummy arrives home riding in a rickshaw.

We run into her bedroom, where she's changing out of her silk tea frock. John and I can hardly wait to tell her of our adventures. Amah stands hesitantly in the doorway. She doesn't seem as delighted as we are when Mummy speaks to her.

The servants don't like it when Mummy's like this, I think.

"Amah." Mummy's voice is stern. "The water in the street is very bad, very dirty." She pauses. "There could be cholera, diphtheria, and typhoid fever in it." Mummy looks out the window, then back at Amah. "The children should not play there," she says.

I hope Mummy doesn't sound too scary to Amah.

"Add this to kidnappings, the high crime rate in Shanghai, and the Japanese . . . ," Mummy says to herself, and shakes her head. "I wish my bridge partner hadn't been quite so graphic."

***

Later that evening on the landing, I hear Daddy's and Mummy's footsteps as they move from the living room, where I'd pictured them sitting close together drinking out of pretty little glasses, to the dining room. I hear Daddy pull out a chair for Mummy. It scuffs softly over the Chinese carpet under the dining table as they sit down to dinner. Ping San lights the candles—a matchstick scratch. They glow in silver candlesticks. Lying on our stomachs in our hidden perch, we can see the candlelight's reflection flickering on the paneling in the foyer. For once, our parents are eating alone and at home. I picture them sitting side by side at one end of the table. They dine late, at eight thirty.

We children have our meals early, in the kitchen. Sometimes Er Shu Foo chops vegetables at the other end of the big wooden table where we sit. Often Amah sits with us, darning a sock or mending a popped seam.

We listen intently, and I realize that Mummy has waited until the entrée is served to tell Daddy about our activities in the flooded river water.

There's a long pause. I picture Daddy looking at Mummy and maybe shaking his head slowly as I've seen him do. "Are the children's inoculations up to date?" I hear him ask.

"I'll check with Dr. Mosse's office in the morning,"[9] Mummy says in a soft voice, followed by another long pause.

The next morning Mummy scolds us for playing in the floodwater and tells us of all the nasty diseases that we might have caught and still might come down with. I look at John and John looks at me, and I know that like me, he's remembering the fun we had, especially when Wash Coolie brought the big basin to us to use as a boat. But then I think of Amah's face when Mummy was scolding her. Silently I admit that I feel sorry, just a little, that Amah got a scolding because of us. I will have to be extra good and help Amah for a while. And remember to tell her when we hear Mummy say anything about her or any of the other servants.

The next morning at breakfast, Mummy tells us she's made an appointment to take us to see Dr. Mosse. I know he'll probably give us a nasty needle prick, but the candy he keeps in the silvery box shaped like a duck on his desk will make up for it. I look across the table at John and know he's thinking the same thing. I hope Dr. Mosse has some of the toffee from England. It's the best!

NOTES

1.   As a result of its defeat by Britain in the First Opium War (1839–
     42), China was forced to relinquish Hong Kong and five treaty
     ports to the British: Shanghai, Canton, Ningpo, Foochow, and
     Amoy. Previously, Western trade and therefore Westerners were
     allowed to enter China only at the southern port of Canton. In
     addition, in 1843, China granted Britain most-favored-nation
     status and the privileges of extraterritoriality—immunity from
     China's jurisdiction. These privileges were also granted to the
     United States and France in 1844.

     The Shanghai International Settlement, or the Settlement,
     was a union of the British and (short-lived) American Settlements
     in Shanghai and, along with the French Concession (the terms
     "settlement" and "concession" are interchangeable), consisted of
     about twenty-three square kilometers (8.75 square miles) with-
     in the city. Having been granted extraterritoriality meant that
     each of the two areas was governed by its own municipal council
     of local (foreign) residents; ran its own utility service; collect-
     ed taxes; and maintained its own police force, judicial system,
     and volunteer army. Since those living in the Settlements were
     not controlled by Chinese laws and benefitted from their own
     protective forces, both foreigners and Chinese considered it very
     desirable to live there.

     The Japanese Army had occupied the city (other than the two
     Settlements, which had remained neutral) for years before the of-
     ficial beginning of World War II. Japan invaded the International
     Settlement and the French Concession only after it attacked
     Pearl Harbor in the United States. The International Settlement
     and French Concession were dissolved by treaty in 1943.

2.   Chefoo School, also known as the China Inland Mission
     Boarding School, was named after the town on the north China
     coast where it was established in 1880 by the interdenomination-
     al Protestant China Inland Mission to educate the children of
     foreign missionaries, businessmen, and diplomats. The school
     started with just three children, but the student body quickly

grew to the hundreds. The children of the Inland Mission workers alone numbered more than two hundred in 1894. The staff of the Chefoo School were required to be members of the Inland Mission, and the curriculum followed the British educational system so that graduates could continue on to British universities such as Cambridge and Oxford. The school competed in such sports as soccer and rowing. Boarding students were taken at as young as six years of age, and it was not unusual for students of the missionaries working in far-off corners of China to leave their children there for long periods of time.

3. The Bund was the waterfront area mainly within the International Settlement (a segment called the French Bund lay within the French Concession) that, prior to World War II, was the powerful center of the foreign establishment in Shanghai. Although the buildings' functions have changed since the war, the buildings themselves remain largely unchanged.

4. With its imposing eight-story structure and eleven-story clock tower, Shanghai's Custom House is the tallest building on the Bund. Built primarily of gray granite in 1927, it has four tall columns across the front and an octagonal dome. The four-faced clock, bells that chime hourly, and mechanism were manufactured in and shipped from London. The main lobby has marble columns and is decorated with gold leaf and blue, green, white, and brown mosaic murals depicting Chinese junks in full sail.

5. China's east coast rainy season, known as the plum rain, lasts for about four months from late spring to early summer every year. In 1931, extreme weather overwhelmed the Yangtze River, which drains one-fifth of China's land area together with her tributaries; this, coupled with poor river management, caused extensive flooding in Shanghai. Terrible flooding occurred again in 1935, and exacerbated by famine and social turmoil, it caused tremendous suffering. With the government of China's attention elsewhere—political infighting and war, for example—this situation continued to a lesser or greater degree every year; 1940 was an exceptionally high flood year. Annual springtime flooding was not adequately addressed until the 1990s, when the massive Three Gorges Dam was built in the Yangtze River.

6. Clare College, Cambridge University, the second oldest of Cambridge's thirty-one colleges, was founded in 1326 and named after a granddaughter of King Edward I (1272–1307). Ted was a member of the class of 1924. It's now considered a diverse and welcoming institution.

7. Salt has been taxed in China since 300 BC; in fact, the salt tax was the main source of revenue for the construction of the Great Wall of China. The modern Salt Gabelle, or Salt Administration, was an arm of the Department of Finance. It did not concern itself with the sale of salt or the collection of taxes on its sale, but rather with gathering those taxes to repay loans made to China by foreign banks. Under the settlement of the Boxer Rebellion (1900), China was required to employ a few dozen foreigners (French, German, American, or English) to improve efficiency, reduce corruption, and guarantee that a percentage of the revenue actually went to the foreign governments as specified.

8. A *cheongsam*, or *qipao*, is a traditional Chinese formfitting women's dress made of almost any fabric. This garment has a high, fitted collar and closes with matching or contrasting frog-buttons that extend from the collar and run across the upper right and down the right side of the dress. Sleeves can be short or long, as can the skirt's length and side slits. Occasionally a matching jacket is worn over the *cheongsam*. It's very pretty!

9. Pediatrician Carl E. Mosse, of 592 Amherst Avenue, Shanghai, is fondly remembered by us children for the duck-shaped metal box that stood prominently on his desk and from which he'd offer a candy to sweeten each office visit. Our parents paid him a monthly fee to care for the family. Early health insurance?

3

Lola Arrives

Mid-June 1940
The International Settlement, Shanghai,
Jiangsu Province, China

One evening two weeks later, John and I nestle together on the landing in our pajamas. As we savor the aroma of baked chicken floating up from the dining room below, we hear the swinging door between the kitchen and foyer swoosh open, followed by the unmistakable tap-tapping of Ping San's leather shoes. Ping San is the only servant who doesn't wear the customary black cotton slippers made by Amah, their soles fashioned from multiple layers of fabric salvaged from outworn clothes. Daddy brought back the black oxfords from England, a gift for Ping San's years of faithful service. Ping San endures the discomfort of Western shoes both because Daddy gave them to him and because he knows that the servants of other Shanghai households envy him enormously. This we know because John and I once overheard Ping San tell Amah that when he'd gone to the Andersons' to borrow some fish knives for a party,[1] the Andersons' cook had eyed his shoes admiringly.

In the back garden with Amah, Shanghai house, 1939.

Tonight our parents are dining alone. The dim reflected glow of only four candles on the foyer's walnut paneling confirms this.

"Ping San, please tell Da Shu Foo that the roast chicken was absolutely delicious," we hear Mummy say.

"Yes, Missy," Ping San replies. He tap-taps a solemn circle around the table, exits across the foyer, and re-enters, interrupted only by swooshing door sounds.

"Darling," Mummy says, "would you like some pudding?"

"Dessert!" I whisper into John's ear.

We hear a spoon softly click against the side of the serving dish.

"I think the children are getting too old for an amah," Mummy says. "Perhaps we should hire a nanny." From her tone, I know she's thinking about John and me, our arms up to the elbow in muddy river overflow.

I worry for a moment, picturing our beloved Amah's velvet skin and glistening black hair, a dinner-roll bun at the back of her soft neck. I love to watch her twist and pin her hair in place when she lets me visit her room. John loves her too. Then I realize that because Amah is Da Shu Foo's wife, even if we get a nanny we can still visit Amah in the servants' quarters. I know from visiting my friends who have nannies that the nanny's room would be in the house near our room.

Amah and her children, 1940.

"In fact, I met Mrs. Kadoori while lunching at the Columbia Club yesterday," Mummy says. "She asked after the children, of course, and then if we would consider engaging a nanny for them. You know how civic-minded she is."

The intoxicating aroma of vanilla pudding entwined with Darjeeling wafts gently between the banisters.

"The Jewish Refugee Committee is seeking places for the new arrivals from Austria and Germany," Mummy continues. "Mrs. Kadoori says there're thousands of refugees arriving this very week."

"Yes, I read in the *Shanghai Times* this morning that since New York closed as a free port, we're the only place left for the refugees to escape to," Daddy says. His tone reflects his concern.

"It would introduce the children to another culture, and I would very much like to help," Mummy says.

"Yes, of course, it's an excellent idea."

A look of excitement darts between John and me. A nanny, and from where? I want to ask John but am afraid to whisper for fear of giving away our hiding place. Besides, Daddy and Mummy's dinner is almost over, so we creep back to our beds before they move out of the dining room.

⁂

The following Saturday afternoon, John crawls around under the kitchen table, guiding a toy boat between the legs of the tall stools, while Da Shu Foo chops chicken livers for the servants' dinner and Er Shu Foo busies himself at the sink washing vegetables in permanganate.[2] I'm admiring a bouquet of pink peonies the gardener has just brought in from the garden when I look up to see Wash Coolie come through the back door with an armful of dry sheets. He always smells of soap, that's how I know when Wash Coolie is there. I don't have to even look his way.

Sometimes Wash Coolie gives us a teacupful of water from his tub. We take the soapy water to our room and use it to blow bubbles with little clay pipes. It's fun to bounce the bubbles on my bed. But when the bubbles fall on the floor they pop. John says the bubbles that fall on the bed don't pop because the blanket's soft.

Once while we were driving in the country, we saw a very old lady sitting on the side of the road smoking a pipe that was just like our little white clay bubble pipes. The lady's face was so wrinkled she looked like a dried-up apple. But what was funny was that the lady's tongue was curled around the stem of the pipe. When I try to curl my tongue in the same way, it's very hard to do, impossible. I can't even do it if I try and try. Daddy said the old lady had to hold the pipe like that because she'd lost all her teeth. She looked so funny! We laughed and laughed when we told Amah and Cook about it.

Ping San comes in the back door and leans over to look under the table. "Children, quick. Go and look. Some ladies are coming," he says.

John and I scurry up the back stairs and arrive on the landing just in time to hear the doorbell ring. We quickly flatten ourselves on the landing.

Ping San appears below wearing a long white gown with frog-buttons—the gown he puts on for visitors. He always answers when someone rings the doorbell; it's one of his regular duties because he's the only one of the servants who speaks English. He can also read and write in both English and Chinese, important if someone delivers a written message.

I lean my head against the balustrade and think about Ping San. Every weekday evening at eight o'clock, when Daddy tunes the radio to station XMHA for Carroll Alcott's program,[3] Ping San goes out into the garden, leans against the wall near the living room window, and listens. He has a very good memory; he remembers all the news he hears and then repeats it to the other servants. Daddy says Ping San is very intelligent.

Daddy also says that Mr. Alcott's brave. He has to wear a bulletproof vest and have a bodyguard with him all the time. Daddy says he does this because the Japanese want to kill him. After he told me that, I asked Daddy if the Japanese want to kill us too. Daddy said no, because the Japanese are at war with China and not at war with us. It's very confusing. Mr. Alcott's not Chinese. Anyway, I like to listen to Daddy's news program because they always play special music at the beginning.

Ping San steps aside. Two ladies enter the foyer.

"*Whar-tze*," I whisper to John, as I have often heard Amah say when referring to a pretty lady as a flower.

"Good afternoon, I'm happy to meet you. Frau Julius, Fräulein Julius." Mummy leads the ladies across the black-and-white-checkered marble floor and into the drawing room. "Please sit down."

A familiar creaking tells us that the guests have chosen the long, squishy sofa with the rose-patterned slipcover, which stands against the windows that open out onto the stone terrace and lawn below. Mummy must have selected the pale-blue stripy easy chair across from the sofa because we can't see her. But we hear her so we know she's there.

"May I offer you some tea?"

I picture Ping San nodding in response to Mummy's quiet instructions.

"Frau Julius, we have three children," Mummy continues. "Teddy is ten. He's away at boarding school most of the year. Jennifer's in kindergarten at the Girls' Cathedral School,[4] and John is four years old."

I listen for the rustle of Ping San's starched gown and the tap-tap of his shoes as he passes below and picture him carrying the large oval tray into the living room and placing it on the low table. After a few minutes I see him return across the foyer carrying just the silver tray. I know he's placed all the cups and dishes with little sandwiches and cakes on the table.

"In addition to looking after them at home, I would like you to take Jennifer to school in the French Concession," Mummy says. "You can go in a rickshaw. Do you think you can do that?"

I imagine the two ladies sitting close together on the pink-and-white-rose slipcover I love, close together because that's the only way one can sit on the soft sofa. The light from the large windows would be outlining their silhouettes.

"Of course, Amah is here to help," Mummy adds.

A heavily accented voice says, "*Ja*, Frau Dobbs, Lola very good about children. Lola *liebt* children."

"Please tell me about yourselves. When did you and Lola arrive in Shanghai?"

"We come from Wien," Frau Julius starts. "First, we go to Italy on the train. We go to Genoa, Italy. Herr Dr. Julius very thankful he gets tickets for us on the ship *Conte Biancamano*."[5] A light sigh. I turn my head to try to better understand the thick accent as it rises and falls.

"First we get small place in Hongkew,"[6] Frau Julius continues. "We share with three other families."

"Is it agreeable?" Mummy asks.

"It's crowded in Hongkew. Now I find work with a room." Frau Julius's voice sounds firmer. "I assist doctor in hospital." Frau Julius pauses. "I hope for safe place for Lola now."

"And how old are you, Lola?" Mummy asks.

When we stretch far to the left, we little spies can just see Lola sitting close to her mother, her eyes fixed on the pale chrysanthemums that border the white living room carpet. Lola is wearing black stockings and a black dress with a row of tiny black buttons, like freshly shelled peas, running up from its hem. Her round, smooth face is surrounded by a mass of dark, thick, wavy hair that brushes the edge of her white collar.

Silently John points to the reflection on the polished paneling of the living room doorway, and I can just make out Frau Julius. She wears a fedora with a plume of feathers that bounces like a puff of smoke as she moves.

Frau Julius turns and looks at her daughter. *"Achtzehn,"* Frau Julius says.

That evening while we are eating dinner in the kitchen, Mummy tells us about Lola and her mother's visit and that she's eighteen years old.

***

The following Saturday, Lola arrives in a rickshaw. She carries in one hand a tan leather suitcase girded by a wide belt with a large brass buckle, and in the other a small black cotton handbag. This time Amah, John, and I are in the foyer to greet her when Ping San opens the front door.

※※※

One evening two weeks later—following a chapter of *Alice in Wonderland*, several good-night kisses from Daddy, and a half hour of trying to stay awake by pinching ourselves—John and I wait until we hear the clink of dishes being passed around the dinner table. Dinnertime. We slip out of our beds and tiptoe down to the landing.

"Ted, Lola's so shy," we hear Mummy say. "She just nods when I speak to her. I think she's afraid of me. Am I that formidable?"

"What's *formidable*?" John asks softly.

I put my finger to my lips.

"Oh, she'll be fine," Daddy replies. "It must have been awful for her, forced to leave her country, her home, family and friends, everything she knew, and to travel so far to a land where everything's different. She'll start speaking to you soon—I'm sure of that."

John and I look at each other. Mummy doesn't know that Lola can't speak English! We can hardly keep from bursting with laughter. Pop-cheeked, we rock back and forth, giggling silently. Then we crawl back up the stairs and return to bed.

※※※

Two weeks pass before Mummy realizes that the only English Lola knows is "good morning" and "thank you." And that Lola uses one or the other of these two phrases whenever she realizes she's expected to say something.

Every time Mummy gives Lola instructions, such as which sunsuit I should wear or that we should brush our teeth in the morning, John or I take Lola by the hand and show her exactly what Mummy wants her to do. But only after Mummy has left the room.

NOTES

1. In Shanghai in those days, it was understood that if the head houseboy of one Western household needed additional silverware for a dinner party, he could borrow it from another household. Thus, it sometimes happened that a newcomer to Shanghai might be surprised to see his own monogrammed forks and spoons on his host's dinner table.

2. Potassium permanganate is a purple liquid that was widely used to disinfect fruit and vegetables.

3. Carroll Alcott (1901–65) was an American war correspondent and newsman in Shanghai. It was said that the Japanese had a contract out on him because of his vociferously anti-Japanese broadcasts, sentiments that he published in his 1943 book, *My War with Japan*. Every evening Alcott's news broadcast opened with the "March of the Wooden Soldiers" from Tchaikovsky's *Nutcracker Suite*.

4. When I attended the Girls' Cathedral School, it was located at 273 Avenue Haig on the western edge of the French Concession. The British built it for the children of the British residents of Shanghai as the sister school to the Boys' Cathedral School. Our uniforms were very pretty: a mauve dress with a flared skirt that buttoned up the front in summer and a navy-blue jumper with box pleats worn with a white blouse in winter.

5. The SS *Conte Biancamano* was an Italian ocean liner built in Scotland in 1925. She had all the modern amenities of the time. She carried 180 passengers in first class, 220 in second, 390 in economy, and 2,660 in third!

    The *Conte Biancamano* had a long and colorful career, initially sailing for her Italian owners between Italy and the United States, then between Italy and South America. In 1935, she transported Italian troops and armament to Eritrea in East Africa in preparation for the invasion of Abyssinia (Ethiopia), and in 1936, she sailed between Italy and the Middle East. In 1939, she made several crossings between Genoa and Shanghai, including one that carried the last group of European refugees just before the war's outbreak. On entering World War II, the United States seized the *Conte Biancamano* and converted her into a troop-ship capable of carrying up to seven thousand men.

In 1947, the ship was returned to Italy, where she reclaimed her original name, was refitted as a luxury liner, and again be-gan to travel between Italy and South America. She made her final trip in 1960, having completed 364 ocean crossings. When she was scrapped, her bridge, several first-class cabins, and the large ballroom were dismantled and reassembled in the National Museum of Science and Technology in Milan, Italy.

6. Hongkew is a district of Shanghai, about 23.3 square kilometers (nine square miles) in area.

4

Ping San

Early August 1940
My Imagination

Ping San strides along the brick walkway that runs between the main house and the servants' quarters, a frown on his normally placid face. It's early evening. The sun is nearing the horizon but it's still warm. Amah sits on a tall stool she's pulled out from the kitchen and is darning the heel of a long navy-blue stocking, which matches my winter school uniform and is stretched over a napkin ring. Ping San looks at her approvingly. He knows that Amah's responsibilities have diminished since Lola's arrival and is glad that Mummy has asked her to help the other servants rather than dismiss her. This evening she's working on a pile of mending.

With Lola Julius, our nanny in Shanghai, 1940.

"Ferfer runs, runs, she's always running," she muses, smiling to herself as Ping San approaches.

"I don't understand Master and Missy. Their behavior is very strange," Ping San says, ignoring Amah's mutterings as he leans against the doorjamb opposite her.

Amah looks up at Ping San and nods. Her weak eyes water as she leans over the fine work. She's finished darning the stocking and moves on to replace a missing button from one of John's shorts. She bites off her thread in the dimming light.

"It's as though Master and Missy think the Japanese bombs cannot hurt them," Ping San continues. "They think they're safe because they're Western. I don't think Jap bombs know the difference between Chinese and Western people." He puts his hand through the slit on the side of his long white gown, draws a pack of Cannon cigarettes and a box of matches from his pocket, extracts a cigarette, and lights it with a wooden match. He slumps against the door frame.

"I'm worried," Amah says. "Cook told me that you're going soon to Chungking with Master and Missy, and . . ." Amah's voice trails off.

"Every night when Master and Missy listen to the radio, I listen too," Ping San says. "The news is very bad. And still Master does not act afraid. I don't understand." Ping San taps his cigarette against the door frame. "But he looks tired when he comes from his office."

"Maybe he doesn't want Missy to know that he's afraid," Amah says.

Ping San looks at Amah thoughtfully.

"Maybe being afraid and tired looks the same," she adds.

Da Shu Foo, Number One Cook, leans out the window above the door of the servants' quarters. He holds a metal washbowl. Jokingly, he pretends to toss water onto Amah and Ping San, then gasps as if to catch himself before dousing them. Ping San and Amah grin at Cook's antics.

"Cook, I forgot to tell you that Missy said she and Master are taking dinner at the club tomorrow night," Ping San says, then adds, "They go out so often these days." And to himself mumbles, "They go out too often."

"Where are John and Ferfer?" Amah asks.

"Lola took them to the park today," Ping San says. "They were very tired so they went to bed."

"And what will Lola do when Master and Missy go to Chungking?" Amah asks.

"Lola told me that Missy has a friend that wants her because his wife is expecting a baby," Ping San says.

"Missy is nice, she'll find a new position for everyone when she leaves for Chungking."

"I don't like all the staff to leave. It means that Master and Missy are not planning to come back to Shanghai," Ping San says.

"When I go to market I chat with the cooks from the other houses. Some Western folk are bad to work for," Cook adds.

Amah nods and looks at him. "Missy knows a lot of people. She'll find a good position for you. She'd not want you to go to a bad household."

"Why are you going to Chungking, anyway?" Amah asks, turning to Ping San. "Don't you like Shanghai?"

Ping San rubs his chin. "I like it here but I've worked for Master and Missy for a long time. And before that, my father worked for Missy's father for many years. Now I worry about them. I want to make sure the family is safe. English people, sometimes . . ." Ping San's voice trails off and he turns to look over the wall into the treetops.

Cook disappears from the window and reappears at the door a few minutes later, carrying a stool. Ping San offers him a cigarette as he joins them in the blue-gray light.

"All China's in terrible trouble," Ping San says. "Not only are the Chinese fighting the Japs, but they are fighting each other."

Amah and Cook nod in agreement. Cook shuffles his feet as he settles onto his stool and draws deeply on his cigarette.

"Japs capture Chinese and make them fight other Chinese," Ping San says.

"And Chinese make Jap prisoners fight Chinese," Cook adds. "It's very confusing."

Amah pulls another stocking she's repaired off the napkin ring, over which she'd positioned the hole she just darned, and places it on top of her sewing basket; it's getting too dark to see the tiny stitching. "The Japs say they want China for the Chinese but, at the same time, they drop bombs on us. How can they say they want to help our people and, at the same time, drop bombs on China?"

The three old friends look at each other and nod their heads. Life is certainly confused and baffling. Comfort seems to exist only within the confines of their courtyard.

A light tapping sounds on the gate.

Ping San looks at Cook and Amah. "Are you expecting some-one?" he asks, looking back and forth.

"No," they both say in unison.

Ping San draws on his cigarette, and the tip glows red in the twilight. Tap, tap . . . a little more insistently. Ping San looks at the gate as if his sight could penetrate the thick oak.

Silence. The heavy rasp of cicadas in the locust trees behind the house seems louder than usual. A few muffled street sounds slip over the courtyard wall; pedestrians, rickshaws, a car. With gas scarce there are few cars these days.

Ping San forces himself to concentrate. No one comes to the gate at this time of night . . . and after dark. Perhaps it's a thief. Or perhaps it's a person who's lost, or who has made a mistake and will eventually move along.

Amah shifts her weight on the stool. Ping San knows that she certainly would not answer the knock at the gate; he's the head houseboy and responsible for taking care of things like this, in any case.

The tapping is repeated a third time. Ping San decides he cannot ignore the sound. He takes a few steps toward the gate. Reaching it, he draws the heavy metal bolt and pulls the gate toward him. He hesitates, then places one foot so that the gate can swing open only a few inches. Listening, he hears the sound of breathing and peers through the opening into the shadows. He sees the lower half of a long blue gown, the hem muddy.

"Is this number forty-three?" the stranger asks.

"Of course, the number's on the house." Ping San can smell the stranger more than he can see him. *He's not from Shanghai,* he thinks. *Yunnan or Sichuan, maybe. They eat different food, use different spices.*[1] "What do you want?"

"I want to talk to Ping San."

"Why?" Ping San whispers.

Cook calls out, "What does the person want? If it's a beggar, tell him to go away."

"I have news for Ping San," the stranger says.

"Give me the news. I'll tell Ping San," Ping San says.

"No, I can only give the information to Ping San."

There's a long pause. A car horn beeps in the distance.

"Give me twenty-five Mex,"[2] the stranger says, abruptly.

"I am Ping San," Ping San says, his normally placid voice tinged with annoyance, "and I don't have any Mex. Go away."

"Ahh, Ping San, I see that you are an intelligent man. And I know that you want to help your master," the man says, drawing in his breath with a hiss. "I also know that your master works in the Custom House on the Bund and that your master's children go to the park in a rickshaw with a foreign lady." The man pauses, then adds, "I'll come tomorrow. Have the Mexes ready tomorrow."

Ping San hears the man shuffle his feet. *I wish I could see his face,* he thinks.

"I'll only come once more," the stranger says. He abruptly turns and walks into the shadows.

Ping San's eyes follow the stranger, straining to see his profile. The man limps on the left side. Ping San wonders if he's seen that gait before. He pushes the gate closed and bolts it, slowly.

"What did the man want?" Cook asks.

"Oh, he's a friend from my village," Ping San lies. "He just wanted to talk to me."

"Well, if he was a friend, you should have asked him to come in and have a cigarette with us," Cook says.

"He's not a good friend," Ping San replies. He kicks at the thin grass that grows along the edge of the walkway and takes the packet of Cannon cigarettes from his pocket, extracts one, and, shaking the packet, offers the last cigarette to Cook.

Ping San looks up at the main house windows. "The light's on in Lola's room; Master and Missy are out; the children are in their beds; all's well," he says to himself under his breath.

Ping San goes to his room in the servants' quarters to look for some Mex. He knows he will not sleep that night, worrying about the stranger and what he should do. He wants to be ready the following evening. "And, where have I seen that limp before?" he asks himself over and over.

***

Ping San dallies in the servants' courtyard. The time that the stranger came by the previous evening comes and passes. Ping San shuffles his feet on the path. His Western shoes pinch. He shakes one leg and then the other, tries to relax. He's wrapped the Mexes in a piece of newspaper and folds the little wad into a copy of the *Shanghai Evening Post and Mercury*.[3] He clutches the paper under his elbow and feels the lump of the silver coins.

After a sleepless night, Ping San has decided to buy the stranger's information, no matter what it is. Even if it turns out to be nothing—a trick to get some money—he'd feel better. It's unsettling that this stranger knows so much about his master and the family's movements. Why is he interested? And why did his strange gait seem familiar, and why does he smell like he comes from faraway Sichuan Province? There are so many strange happenings around Shanghai, he thinks. People disappear. Things happen that are hard to account for. He's heard many strange stories from other servants. Strange stories when he goes to the market. Strange stories about Western people.

Cook sticks his head out of a second-floor window in the servants' quarters and calls to Ping San to come to bed. Ping San replies that he has a headache and the night air makes him feel better. He leans against the doorway and closes his eyes. He doesn't usually stay up this late.

Tap, tap, tap. Ping San hurries to the gate before another tap alerts the other servants. Again he uses his foot to restrict it, but the stranger doesn't try to push the gate to swing further.

"Money," the stranger whispers softly, his voice a velvety hiss.

Ping San passes the newspaper through the open space, making sure the lump of coins touches the stranger's fingers. The thought of bargaining to reduce the price had occurred to him, but he'd quickly dismissed it, not wanting to draw added attention to the stranger at the gate.

"Ah, I see you are an intelligent man," the stranger says.

"Why are you interested in my master?"

"Let me read the newspaper first." Reaching for the newspaper and ignoring Ping San's question, the man steps out of the shadows and under enough streetlight for Ping San to see what he's doing. He unfurls the paper, just a little.

In the dim light Ping San sees the man's chiseled outline and that he's well dressed. *He's not a peasant,* he thinks.

The man steps back to the gate. "Your master should be careful," he says. "And he shouldn't go to work in Chungking," he adds, dragging out the last word, then quickly hisses, "Ping San must stop Master from going to Chungking." The man turns abruptly, tucking the furled newspaper under his arm.

"Work, what work?" Ping San whispers. "Who are you? Master inspects salt mines. That's not dangerous work." But by the time Ping San finishes muttering, the stranger has shuffled down Tientsin Road and out of sight around the corner. *Master works for the government; it's not dangerous,* Ping San says to himself. *Perhaps working for Chiang Kai-shek is not wise.*[4] Ping San looks at his feet and his handsome shoes. *But maybe he also works for the English? I remember seeing a British officer at the house. I showed him into Master's office.*

Ping San realizes that the street is silent. Even the cicadas are still.

He closes the gate, bolts it, and goes to bed.

NOTES

1. Sichuan was and is a province in Western China. At the time of this story, its major cities were Kunming and Chungking.
2. A Mex was a Mexican silver dollar, one of the many currencies circulating in wartime China. My father was paid in Mexes.
3. The *Shanghai Evening Post and Mercury*, an English-language newspaper representing the interests of American commerce, was started in 1929 by American businessman Carl Crow. There was a Chinese-language version of the newspaper that the Japanese tried to shut down in 1937, but they were unsuccessful because of the paper's American ownership. On December 8, 1941, when the Japanese entered the International Settlement and successfully shut down both versions, the Chinese version of the paper had a circulation of forty thousand.
4. Generalissimo Chiang Kai-shek (1887–1975), Chinese politician and military leader, headed the anticommunist Chinese Nationalist Party from 1928 until the Communists drove him to flee to Taiwan. Although purported to be working with the Chinese Communists against the Japanese during World War II, he actually siphoned off American aid and armaments to stockpile for use in the civil war against the Communists to be fought after Japan's surrender in 1945.

5

Minor Terrors

First Week of September 1940
The International Settlement, Shanghai,
Jiangsu Province, China

Amah places a pebble between the kitchen door and the door-jamb. A light breeze ruffles the edge of the tablecloth that's spread beneath John's and my breakfast places.

"It's too hot for the winter school uniform," she mutters, shaking her head and looking at me. I am wearing a navy-blue jumper over a white silk shirt and navy-blue knee stockings.

"Is it time to call the rickshaw?" Amah asks, as she does each weekday morning.

John looks up from what is left of his soft-boiled egg, an empty shell fitted into an eggcup resembling a tiny rooster. He turns the eggshell over. Da Shu Foo, standing at the other side of the table, grimaces broadly, protesting what appears to be an un-eaten egg, the joke a daily routine. John rights the empty eggshell to muffled giggles.

"Mummy," John calls, "why did Dorothy's house in *The Wizard of Oz* go . . . ouch, Ferfer, you kicked me!"

I did kick him. I'm angry that he's going to the cinema today, now for the eighth time, and I'm not.

"Children, please don't fight," Mummy says, coming into the kitchen.

"But Ferfer kicked me!" John glowers across the table as I concentrate on applying a thick layer of marmalade to a piece of toast.

"Ready?" Lola comes in with our raincoats over her arm and carrying the small tin pail and spade we take when going to Jessfield Park.[1] It's good she has the raincoats just in case there's a shower, since this is the rainy season. Brushing unruly hair from John's eyes, Lola helps him into his raincoat as I slip into mine.

My father and we children visit Jessfield Park, Shanghai, 1938–40.

A rickshaw stands on Tientsin Road beside the high stone wall topped with broken glass that encloses our back garden. Glass shards and broken bottles have been set into cement, the local deterrent to intruders. They glisten in the early sun like candles on a birthday cake.

The rickshaw coolie is a young man Mummy noticed loitering in front of the house for days, ready at any hour. She suggested that the scrawny youth become our regular rickshaw coolie, boarding with us. It took weeks of meals for him to gain a little weight and lose his pallid look.

John and I cross the sidewalk, climb into the rickshaw, and settle snugly into the black leather seat; Lola sits in the middle between us. She hands John his pail and spade.

"Lola, is there a sandbox at the cinema?" I say.

The rickshaw coolie tucks his elbows close to his body, places his hands firmly on the bamboo shafts extending from each side of the vehicle, and throws his weight into launching the rickshaw forward. He moves into the flow of traffic. He turns left off Tientsin Road, goes one block, and turns right onto Nanking Road.

As the rickshaw picks up speed, a penetrating whiff of garlic floats back from the coolie. It catches my attention for a moment before it merges with Shanghai's more pungent street smells. The rickshaw coolie, scrawny after years of hard labor on Shanghai's streets, wears a thin blue cotton jacket, loose matching trousers, and the straw sandals that his mother must have made for him before he left home. His black unkempt hair juts straight out in all directions from under a wide-brimmed straw hat.

"Girls' Cathedral School," Lola says. "Avenue Haig. Haig Lu." Although Lola knows that by now the coolie knows the school's address, she often repeats the English and Chinese words.

I glance up at Lola, fascinated by her throaty attempt to pronounce the English and Chinese street names. I think it must be hard for her to learn English and Chinese, too, all at the same time.

As the muscles of the coolie's thin arms bulge and ripple, the rickshaw lurches into the jumble of muted browns, blues, and grays of the street. Sharp sounds and smells stream from the donkeys, trolleys, cars, bicycles, wheelbarrows, handcarts, and pedestrians as we speed along.

John snuggles under Lola's arm and studies the stenciled animals circling his metal bucket. Nanking Road becomes Bubbling Well Road.

"Is the duck going to bite the pig?" John asks, ignoring the street activity whirling around us.

Lola glances at the cartoon characters—a duck, pig, goat, pony, and cow chase each other around the toy pail in a continuous circle above red, white, and blue stripes. "*Nein, Liebchen,* animals play. It's a farm," Lola replies in her soothing, accented voice.

"Oh," John says, turning the pail around in his hands.

The rickshaw travels past hotels and shops for several short blocks. Then a wide expanse, tree-lined along the curb, opens up on the left—the Shanghai Racecourse. I glance up at the tall elegant clock tower that, for a few moments, fills the skyline as it looms over the massive clubhouse and grandstands below it.

We turn right onto Bubbling Well Road. We pass a police station, country club entrance, and the YWCA as we continue on. A massive portrait of Generalissimo Chiang Kai-shek looms over the sidewalk, his cold eyes echoing the message that extols his people to resist the Japanese written in large red characters down the side. Next to this poster, an advertisement in English states "For Safety, Comfort and Dependability Come to Cathay Motors, Ltd. 271 Medhurst Road" above a picture of a black sedan. Lola stares at the words as we pass by.

Lola knows a lot of English words, I think. *She learns more every day. Maybe her daddy has a car like that one, the one in the poster, at home in Austria. English. Chinese. Speaking. Reading. How can Lola learn so much? She must be very clever.*

Just past the Shanghai Racecourse, the rickshaw coolie slows. A Sikh policeman, stiff white oversleeves gleaming on his arms, directs traffic from a raised circular platform in the middle of the intersection. He wears khaki shorts, a matching jacket with silver buttons, and a matching turban.

I lean forward to look around Lola. "The blue part on his turban means that he belongs to the Shanghai Con-stab-u-la-tory." I struggle to pronounce the word. "Daddy says that means 'police.'"

John says nothing. He's busy admiring the sturdy black belt that circles the Sikh's waist and crosses his broad chest. Dark hairy knees show above the navy-blue puttees buckled over heavy black boots. The glint of a silver whistle on a chain catches John's attention. As they speed past, John twists around to look over the rickshaw's furled hood, but I can only see that the policeman has become part of the blur of vehicles and pedestrians receding behind us.

A bicycle glides past; packages of freshly washed laundry wrapped in brown paper are tied to the rack over its back wheel. A second boy with a large tray of dumplings—carefully formed and stacked in neat rows, ready to be steamed and served— passes by on the other side of the rickshaw. A third delivery boy, partially hidden under a giant horseshoe of red and white carnations that he carries over his shoulder, catches up with them as they near Seymour Road. Wide red ribbons with gold paper characters glued to them flutter from the top of the wreath. For a few minutes the rickshaw and bicycle move along parallel to each other, until the bicycle suddenly turns left into a narrow alleyway. *Is it going to a party or to a funeral?* I wonder.

I look down a narrow alleyway as we speed past. Along the curb, chattering housewives squat on their heels over red, yellow, and green plastic basins, scrubbing the daily wash between their knuckles. Babies tied into blue cotton squares bounce up and down on the ladies' backs, nodding beneath bright-pink caps. The vivid caps remind me of one of Mummy's stories, about Chinese mothers who dress their boy babies in girls' clothes and even call them by girls' names. The mummies do this to trick and protect the boy babies from evil spirits. *What do the bad spirits do with the babies if they get them?* I think.

As the rickshaw hurries along toward my school, the concert and kaleidoscope of the street wax and wane around the muffled drone of pedestrian feet and chatter, the tinny beep-beep of car horns, the clang of an occasional trolley, and the echo of the street vendors' cries. It's the sounds of Shanghai that I love most about the city.

"*Tong-hoolers, tong-hoolers,* get your delicious *tong-hoolers* here," calls the candy man. Above his head bob sugar-coated haws, each the size of a chestnut, strung like beads, four to a stick. A dozen of these candy-sticks bristle from a layer of straw matting tightly bound around one end of a pole that the tong-hooler man carries over his shoulder. I gaze longingly at the sticky red fruit, tasting their sweet-sourness in my mouth. I know not to ask Lola for some. Mother has strictly warned Lola against buying any food on the street.

I think about the time I persuaded Lola to buy some *tuck,*[2] dried plum candy, from a man in the park—I'd convinced her it was safe because each piece was individually wrapped in newspaper!—and I didn't get in trouble, because Mummy never found out. Tuck is almost as good as tong-hoolers. I wonder if Da Shu Foo gets his tong-hoolers from this tong-hooler man. I'll ask Da Shu Foo to fix the dessert that's made with tong-hoolers and orange sections formed into a little circular wall, covered with melted sugar, and filled with whipped cream. Delicious!

"Jew-ar-dee, jew-ar-dee, jew-ar-dee. I'll mend your broken cups and cracked dishes as good as new," sings the artisan who repairs broken crockery. With a foot-pedal drill he makes little holes in the damaged bowls and dishes and then puts tiny metal staples through those holes to fix them. Mummy has said that many a teapot and cup has lived on for unanticipated years in Shanghai pantries after the jew-ar-dee man's masterful work.

Along the curb, steam rises from a line of sooty woks, each set over a fire. The fires jump and leap from charcoal piled in the bottom of a fifty-five-gallon steel drum.

I look at the huge metal drums knowingly.

A week ago, while John and I rode in the back of our father's car, he'd told us a story about these metal drums. He said that they were made in faraway America to bring gasoline to China— fuel for the airplanes that are fighting against the Japanese. He said that, first, the drums come to Rangoon by ship. They're then loaded onto trains and taken to the border between Burma and China. Then elephants load them onto trucks. The trucks take the fuel drums over mountains—dangerous mountains, mountains so high they rise above the clouds. Or sometimes the fuel is flown over the mountains by American or Chinese pilots. These pilots must fly so high that there's not enough air, so they have to breathe air from tanks. Then, when the fifty-five-gallon drums are empty, people find all sorts of different uses for them, because nothing goes to waste in China. Many are made into stoves. The stoves are even made to be portable. At the end of each day the street cooks put two poles through the holes that they've cut into the side of the metal drums, lift them to their shoulders, and carry them home.

Before Daddy told us all about the fifty-five-gallon drums, I hadn't paid much attention to them when I'd seen them on the street. Now I eye the pock-scarred metal containers with more respect. They help fight the Japanese.

Delicious aromas turn my thoughts back to food. Each street chef advertises his specialty in his own way—announcing, cajoling, describing, and tantalizing the passing pedestrians. *Low-bing* (fried bread), *congee* (rice gruel), *mein* (noodles), and . . . and . . .

At the corner of Bubbling Well Road and Ferry Road a man stands behind a mound of rice dough oozing on a large wooden board. Using a small bamboo rake, and starting at the top of the wobbly mass, he carefully scrapes around and around, in ever-wider circles, until he's reached the base of the dome of dough. In this way he shaves noodles off the mound, places them, hot and steamy, into bowls, and passes the bowls to the breakfast-ers waiting patiently in front of him. If there's a pause between servings, he puts a warm, wet towel over the mound of dough. In addition to keeping the dough moist, the towel restricts the flies to buzzing only around the dome's base.

Across the street, vendors offer noodle soup. The aromas of

chicken broth and pork broth dance above each steaming pot and mingle in the light breeze, more inviting even than the tantalizing descriptions that rise, singsong, from the vendors' lips. Another vendor sells strips of marinated pork skewered on bamboo sticks.

A group of Chinese children on their way to school gather in front of a man pushing a thick rolling pin over a ball of dough, then dropping the flattened *low-bing* into a pot of bubbling oil. The oil pops and spits as each batch of moist dough slides into the cauldron and is quickly spooned out again with a bamboo ladle—puffy, crisp, hot, and golden, in just a minute or two.

I glance up at Lola.

"Lola, why do I have to go to school when you and John are going to the cinema?" I ask. "And he's already seen *The Wizard of Oz* many times, but I . . ." My voice trails off.

"I think *Mutter* take you and John soon," Lola replies.

"I like the part where Dorothy throws water on the bad witch the best," John says. "And then the witch turns into a puddle."

"You're so lucky, John. Just because Lola doesn't know English . . ."

A stream of children, carrying schoolbooks, cross Hart Road in front of us. The last little boy jumps aside as the rickshaw almost runs over his foot. Then the rickshaw careens close to the sidewalk to avoid a wheelbarrow carrying four young ladies in bright flowered dresses, two sitting on each side of its big central wheel.

"*Man-man-dee, man-man-dee, quai-quai-dee,*" Lola says, concern in her voice. Go slowly, go slowly, more quickly.

At that moment a small, shriveled man leaps out of the crowd on the sidewalk and jumps into the rickshaw's path. The coolie pulls up abruptly. The rickshaw's two brass carriage lanterns jerk forward with a clatter. Lola stiffens her legs, braces her feet against the floorboards, and clamps a plump arm around each of us.

The shriveled man grabs one pole, paralyzing the rickshaw. He springs between the poles, lunging in front of the coolie, who jumps aside, leaving the shriveled man standing in his place.

Swiftly, silently, the bandit slips a short knife from beneath his shirt. My eyes are immediately glued to it; I see nothing else.

"Dolla'sss, dolla'sss," the thief hisses through his toothless gums.

Although the words are drowned out by the hubbub of the street, I hear nothing else. Lola gasps. Her usually rosy cheeks drain to white. I feel her body stiffen for the second time that day.

The bandit's coal-black pebble eyes quickly look Lola up and down. Spying the cotton purse dangling from her wrist, he snatches it, pricks a hole in it with the tip of his knife, and slits the soft fabric. A few small coins land on the rickshaw's floorboards between Lola's feet. The bandit glowers; it's a meager prize. Then I see him spot the garnet ring on Lola's left hand. Seizing her palm, he tries to jerk the ring off her finger. It does not budge.

A crowd of onlookers has now gathered around the rickshaw coolie, who stands on the sidewalk wringing his hands. *"Aye ya, aye ya,"* he wails.

The bandit tugs roughly at Lola's finger, desperation in his eyes. He steps closer to Lola and leans forward, pulling her hand, pulling it toward his black and rotting teeth.

John and I cower under Lola's viselike elbows, unable to move. Frozen. Terrified.

The thief bites, bites hard. Bites Lola's finger with all his strength.

Lola gasps. Blood spurts. She pulls her hand back, wide-eyed. Red drops slide down her finger and drip onto her lap, forming a tiny puddle. Teeth marks form, red and purple, around the ring. It's still on Lola's finger.

The thief turns his head—left, right—stares intently at me for a second, then at John. Abruptly, he lunges toward the little pail, knocking it off John's lap. Unsuccessful in his attempt to grasp the pail, the thief bolts into the crowd and is lost among the gawkers jostling each other on the curb.

The pail clatters to the gutter.

A street urchin jumps from the curb, grabs it, and runs.

NOTES

1. Jessfield Park was established in 1914. Although the fifty-three-acre park lay outside the boundaries of the International Settlement in northwest Shanghai, it was administered by the Shanghai Municipal Council, which governed the International Settlement.
2. The word *tuck* is Shanghai dialect.

6

Major Surprises

The crowd of gawkers standing on the sidewalk melts away.

"Why did that boy take my bucket?" John asks indignantly.

I wiggle loose from under Lola's firm grip and see that her finger has begun to swell and turn purple. Teeth marks outline the bite, and a dark lump, oozing red, is forming on one side of her finger. I twist around to look at her face. Lola's closed her eyes.

"Why did the man bite Lola?" John asks.

Tears slip slowly down Lola's cheeks, now bright pink.

No one replies.

***

"Lola, when we get to the police station, please tell the officer exactly what happened," Daddy says. Mummy'd telephoned him as soon as we got home, and he'd rushed over right away. Now Daddy, Lola, John, and I are in the back of the car that comes to get Daddy every morning. John calls it a 1939 Buick Roadster.

Daddy pats Lola on the shoulder. "Mrs. Dobbs told me how marvelously brave you were and how you protected the children. It must have been terribly frightening, but everything's fine now. I'll help you."

"Daddy, the policeman brought us home in a big, shiny red fire truck," John says.

"A van," I correct. I think it was the Sikh policeman we'd seen this morning.

"Yes, Daddy—a van. And it had shiny brass all over and a big brass cannon on top."

Daddy says again, "Lola, when we get to the police station, I want you to tell the policeman everything that you remember."

"*I* remember," I say.

"Yes, Mr. Dobbs," Lola says.

"I remember too," John says.

Lola looks at Daddy, then she turns to stare at the back of the driver's head. He's a driver from Daddy's office, a little man with not much hair and a pudgy neck.

"Yes, you children will be a big help to Lola, I'm sure," Daddy says.

"Daddy, will the robber keep my pail?" John asks.

I look at my brother and realize I'm just as muddled as he is. Everything happened so fast. I remember that it wasn't the robber that took the pail.

Daddy looks tired, although it's early in the day. "It's the war, son. It's the war" is all he says.

The driver turns the car onto Bubbling Well Road.

Glancing at Lola's hand, Daddy says, "Does your finger feel any better?" Mummy had washed it and put iodine on it while we waited for him to come to take us to the police station.

"Daddy, why did the robber bite Lola's finger?" John asks.

The driver pulls up in front of the Bubbling Well Road Police Station, a two-story stone building with four archways on the ground level and a long balcony on the second. We all get out; the driver helps John and me. I look at the ivy that grows up the front of the building and see that it's trained to climb up along pieces of string in the shape of the letter *X*. Six of these huge X-shapes of ivy shade the ground floor, and there are more between the windows of the second story. Catching up with Daddy, and clearly undaunted by not having received answers to his earlier questions, John asks, "Will the policeman at the station have my pail?"

"John, darling son, we'll talk about all this later when we get home. Now we have to tell the police officers what happened."

The Sikh policeman who'd helped us stands by the station door and motions for us to enter. We walk between two young men in baggy uniforms who stand solemnly on each side of the heavy door. I smile at one of them but he ignores me.

"Ni hao, ni hao," says an officer seated at a desk just inside: How are you, how are you? I look around the room and see the usual large portrait of Chiang Kai-shek hanging on the wall behind the desk, with the Generalissimo standing with his hand on the back of a wooden chair. I hear footsteps. The door bangs

shut. *Why did the Sikh policeman leave?* I think. *He knows what happened.*

Daddy explains to the officer at the desk why we are here. The officer motions for us to go down a long, dimly lit hallway leading toward the back of the building. The shiny pea-green tiles look slippery, and I stretch out my hand to touch the wall. Daddy gives me a quick glance. I know he's telling me not to touch.

At the end of the corridor, we pass through a set of double doors and enter a large, sparsely furnished room. My eyes adjust to the light and my nose to the odor. Then Lola, John, and I gasp. Opposite the entrance are two large cages. And in the cages—standing or squatting on their heels—a crowd of men and boys. I realize that some of them are not much older than my brother. *It's terrible!* I think. *Small boys in cages! Where are their daddies? Their mummies? And look at their clothes!* What the men and boys have on look more like rags than shirts and shorts or trousers. Those who are not barefoot are wearing straw sandals. I can hardly bear to look at them.

Another officer gets up from behind a desk. He greets us with a strong Shanghai accent and bows slightly as he motions toward a pair of straight wooden chairs positioned in front of his desk. Daddy tells Lola to sit in one of them, and John and I stand on either side of her.

Daddy now repeats the account he's just given the policeman in the outer office and then translates the policeman's reply to Lola. "The officer wants you and the children to look in the two cells and see if you recognize the bandit who attacked you," Daddy says. "Please look very carefully."

Lola gets up, taking John's and my hands, and we walk up

close to the nearest cage. Some of the men look at us sullenly, but most of them ignore us. They smell like the street. I'm anxious to be finished with this. I look around for Daddy but he's talking to the officer.

We examine the bedraggled group. *They don't look very sorry for the bad things they must have done to get here*, I think. *I wonder what will happen to them.* I gaze quickly at the men and more slowly at the boys, stopping here and there to check a well-placed safety pin or an interesting belt or hat. I step away from Lola's side to get a better view of a short man squatting at the back of the cage. John reaches behind Lola to tug at my sleeve and points out a worn leather belt around the waist of a boy of about ten. The once-elegant belt looks incongruous holding up a pair of baggy and torn shorts.

After a few silent minutes we walk over to look into the second pen. Two of the men in this cage start talking to each other. The policeman calls for them to be silent. They turn their backs to us, and the policeman steps from behind his desk, walks over, and prods one of the men with a cane that he's pulled from under his arm and slid between the bars of the cage. I make a slight grimace at John, trying not to be noticed. I feel like crying. When the officer rattles his cane against the bars, I want to run. I look at the floor, then at Daddy.

"All men look the same," Lola says as she leads us back toward the desk. "I very scared when the robber bite me. It hard to remember."

I force myself to think about the thief. What did he look like? How was he dressed? I want to help the policeman but all

I remember was the color of his teeth . . . and his smell. These cages smell like that man. I think I can't say that, so I say nothing. Instead, I think about the horrible dirty smell and how everything happened so fast. It's hard to remember. I close my eyes. I can see the thief's broken, black teeth. I can see his cold, hard stare. He looked at John and me for a quick moment. He looked at me just before he tried to grab John's little sand pail. I realize those are the only things that have stuck in my mind. How can I explain this? I open my eyes. There's no way to explain this. So, I say nothing.

What I think is that Lola's very brave. She didn't cry—at least, she didn't cry very much. I also think that although rings are nice, they are not as nice as dolls, and toy cars, and teddy bears. Still, I'm glad Lola didn't have her ring stolen. I'm glad the bandit didn't bite Lola's finger off! I realize my imagination is beginning to run away with me.

A door opens and the Sikh policeman enters. "Would the young master like to see our horses?" he says to Daddy, as he looks at my lucky little brother. "I can take him around to the stable while you and the lady speak with the officer."

"That would be splendid," Daddy says. "I know John would enjoy that very much. Thank you for suggesting it."

I look over at Lola as John and the policeman leave by the same door. Lola looks as though she wishes she were going with them.

"John will tell us about the horses when he comes back," Daddy reassures us.

The policeman tells Daddy that he needs to get more

information from Lola, so Daddy asks that another chair be brought for me.

I wish I had been invited to see the horses, though.

***

Mummy is waiting at the door when we arrive home.[1] She says that she heard the scrunch of the car's tires and is anxious to hear everything about the police station.

"Mummy, they didn't have my pail!" is the first thing John says. "And the big horse tried to bite me." John is breathless. "And his name is Dick." John tugs at Mummy's skirt. "The horses puff steam from their noses and Mr. Policeman said Dick marches in all the parades." John is so excited, no one else can say a word.

Daddy looks at his wristwatch. "I'd better go back to the office," he says.

"John, please tell us later," Mummy says and looks at Lola. "Lola, how was the visit to the police station? How do you feel?"

"Better, Mrs. Dobbs."

I don't think Lola looks better at all.

"The horses at the police station are very big and shiny, and they smell warm and like grass," John says.

"Can't you stay for tiffin?"[2] Mummy says to Daddy. "You must be famished." She turns to Ping San, who's just come into the foyer. "Ping San, please ask Da Shu Foo to fix Master something quick. Anything that's ready will be fine." Then she adds, "The children, Lola, and I can eat after he leaves."

"No thank you, darling, I must get back. I'll see you this evening." Daddy hurries out to the waiting car.

John and I rush to the kitchen ahead of Ping San and Lola. We want to tell Amah and Cook about our adventures at the police station.

Ping San comes into the kitchen just as John starts talking about his visit to the stable. "Amah, it was so exciting," John begins. "A real Sikh policeman—he even wore a turban—took me to the stable. When we first went in, we walked between the stalls. Each stall had a huge black or sometimes brown horse in it. All the horses looked at me with their big brown eyes. The officer told me the name of each horse as we passed, but I don't remember them all. I remember the one named Dick. He said that Dick always leads the parade on special occasions like the Queen's birthday or when the American Marines march in Shanghai."

John continues, "The nice officer asked me if I wanted to sit on Dick's back. Of course, I said yes right away. So the officer lifted me up and put me on his beautiful shiny fur. He had stiff fur on his neck. And then suddenly, Dick reached back with his big white teeth and tried to bite me. I jerked my leg back just in time. The policeman thought I was scared but I wasn't. So he lifted me off Dick's back and put me on his own shoulders. Then we walked out of the stable and I saw two Chinese ladies with big yellow sponges giving baths to two horses. They were wearing big, shiny wellies.[3] Other ladies were carrying buckets of water and food into the horses' rooms. The horses . . ." He trails off.

I see that John's tired. We had a very exciting day, and it's only lunchtime.

Mummy comes into the kitchen. "I was planning to take you two to see *The Wizard of Oz* tomorrow, but since it's too late for Ferfer to go to school today, shall we go after tiffin?"

"Oh, yes, could we please?" John and I say at the same time.

"And Lola, take the afternoon off, as well as the weekend," Mummy says. "I'll call your mother and tell her. She'll be anxious to see you after your adventure."

***

After our baths, John and I creep to the stair landing. As we snuggle down, yawning, I hear Daddy say, "I had a big surprise at the police station today."

"Oh?" Mummy says.

"The police form asked for Lola's age."

John and I wait, holding our breaths. But there is silence from the dining room below.

Then we hear Daddy say, "Lola's fifteen."

NOTES

1. In 1998, I traveled to Shanghai and tried without luck to find our house on Tientsin Road. The area no longer appeared to be residential, and in fact, there was an auto repair shop at or near the address. I did find the Girls' Cathedral School building, which had become a nightclub called the Marco Polo Club. There was a large wooden cutout of a train on its roof. What that had to do with Marco Polo was a mystery, since trains had yet to be invented in his time.
2. "Tiffin" was the word commonly used for lunch.
3. Wellies, or Wellingtons, are tall rubber boots that originated in England.

7

Chungking

October 1940
Shanghai, Jiangsu Province, China, to
Chungking, Sichuan Province, China

AUTHOR'S NOTE

A memoir is by its very nomenclature fashioned from memory. And memory is a fickle thing. Some things are remembered because they're scary and some forgotten because they're too scary.

In reality, there was no railway service between Shanghai and Chungking in October 1940. The Japanese battlefront lay between the two cities. And although a thin, yellowed document in Chinese with three photos glued to it—a pass ("for Mrs. Dobbs and 2 children—one boy and one girl," it states) to go through

all military checkpoints between Shanghai and Chungking—
confirms this trip, the trip is mostly forgotten. I do remember
riding in a truck (but there were so very many trucks), but what
other alternative modes of transport were used (possibly a coastal
steamer or car or donkeys), I don't remember.

***

One night as Mummy is tucking us into bed, she tells us that we
will soon be moving to Chungking.[1] Ping San is coming with us,
leaving in advance to prepare the house for our arrival, but the
rest of the servants are going to stay behind in Shanghai.

Our last Christmas in Shanghai. Mummy and her brother, Tom (headmaster at the Shanghai American School), made the dollhouse (every room lit
by a tiny flashlight bulb in the ceiling) and all its furnishings. Western-style
toys were not available in China at the time.

"Why?" I ask. "I love my school here."

"Well," Mummy says, "Daddy's office has moved there."

"But I love Lola and Amah," John says. "I don't want us to go."

"Generalissimo Chiang Kai-shek—the president—moved the capital to Chungking to get far away from the Japanese," Mummy says. "So now we have to go too." Mummy gives my blanket an extra tuck around my shoulders, gives us each a good-night kiss, and turns out the light.

Mummy leaves me thinking about Cook and Amah and Wash Coolie, and then I remember a recent telephone conversation I'd overheard her having that, I now understand, was about them. She was speaking with Gran, my grandmother, telling Gran that Cook, Amah, and Wash Coolie needed new households to work for. I hadn't paid much attention to the conversation, it wasn't very interesting, but now I do remember her saying that Lola was going to be a nanny for a baby. *Lola will like that,* I think. *A baby!*

My mind slips into thinking about Gran. I picture her sitting in front of her low Chinese dressing table, combing her long hair. She's so beautiful. Her hair's so long that it reaches to the floor when she sits to comb it. Gran is special to me. She talks to me and sometimes tells the tailor to make dresses for me from the pretty fabrics left after they make dresses for brides. She once let me watch while she told Mr. Tailor where to put pins into a lady's dress while she was wearing it. Gran called it a fitting. I think about the ladies that I've seen at Gran's house, who were there to have dresses designed. Of course, Mr. Tailor sews them on a big machine. Gran even showed me how to dance. Sleepily I imagine Gran twirling around in circles beside my bed and smiling at me. She loves to dance.

***

A week later, we find ourselves on the train to Chungking. In the compartment with us are six suitcases and a Hong Kong basket of sandwiches.[2] This is the last meal Cook made for us before all the servants, except for Ping San, said goodbye in the front hall of our house in Shanghai.

The first two of the nine hundred swaying, clanking, rumbling westward miles to Chungking pass quickly because Daddy tells John and me stories about the city where our new home will be. He tells us that Chungking is built on top of tall stone cliffs located between two rivers—the peaceful, gurgling Jialing and the ferocious Yangtze, which the Chinese call a yellow tiger. Daddy tells us that Chungking is very different from Shanghai. They both have rivers, but Shanghai's port river, although important, is only a small part of the industry and commerce of the city. Chungking's two rivers are everything—the life and breath of the city.

I close my eyes and picture the Yangtze's mighty water leaping and clawing at its banks as Daddy continues to describe the dangerous swirls and eddies. I think about other stories he's told me about how boats were brought up from Shanghai to Chungking, dragged against these churning currents by hundreds of river coolies, trackers.[3] I hope we see some trackers.

After he pauses to snap pictures from the train window with his Leica, Daddy continues his story. Most of the streets in Chungking are very narrow and so steep that every few yards they change into stairs. These stairs vary from pathways, where only two people can pass each other, to broad staircases where hundreds of people run up and down all day. He says the people in Chungking do not measure the distance between their houses and their offices in city blocks, as we did in Shanghai, but by the number of steps they have to go up or down as they walk to work.

"If the streets are made of stairs, how do the rickshaws go?" I ask.

"Well," Daddy says, "there are no rickshaws there." He pauses. "And there're not many cars and almost no bicycles," he continues. "The people walk everywhere, and carry everything; what isn't brought in or out of the city on one of the two rivers must be carried. Even people are carried."

John looks up. "People are carried!" he exclaims. "How?"

"Sedan chairs, mostly," Daddy replies. "You'll see because we'll get some when we get to the station."

John hardly hears Daddy's reply. Soothed by the rocking of the train, he dozes off.

"Why are we going again, Daddy?" I ask.

"We are going there, Jennifer, because the Japanese soldiers have seized many cities over the past three years—cities in the north and along the seacoast. They even captured the capital, Nanking, where the Generalissimo had his headquarters. So, Generalissimo Chiang Kai-shek moved the capital to Chungking. And you know that I work for him."

"Oh," I say. After a moment I ask, "Will the Japanese take Shanghai?"

"I hope not, but we don't know," Mummy says. She'd been silent for a long time, gazing out the window as the countryside sped by in a blur of grays, blues, browns, and pale greens against the blue sky.

"What will happen to Lola, Amah, and Cook if the Japanese come to Shanghai?" I ask. I am worried about my friends.

"They'll be fine," Mummy says. But the tone of her voice does not reassure me. She looks at me and sighs. "Well, the truth is, darling," she continues, "it's complicated. Sometimes when the Japanese capture a city, they put the people in prisoner-of-war camps—where they get food and a place to sleep—but mostly they let the people stay at home. . . ." Mummy's voice trails off.

"Will the Japanese capture us? Will they put us in a camp?" I ask. This question really bothers me. What would become of us if we were captured? I'm shocked when I think about this possibility, and all of a sudden I feel very glad we've left Shanghai.

"No, Jennifer, the Japanese are not at war with us. They're fighting the Chinese."

"Why aren't they at war with us, Daddy?" I ask.

"Because we're English, Jennifer," Daddy replies.

There's a long pause. *Ping San says that bombs cannot tell the difference between an English man and a Chinese man,* I think.

"Is Mummy English too, Daddy?"

"Well, she is, yes. She's English and American."

"Oh." Ping San didn't say anything about Americans. Maybe Mummy's safe.

"Jennifer, the Japanese aren't at war with the English or the Americans. Don't look so worried."

I don't want to talk about this anymore, so I look out the dust-streaked window at the green rice paddies as the countryside rushes past. Our soft-class seats are so comfortable;[4] I fight to keep from falling asleep.

I feel someone pulling my legs out straight and spreading a

blanket over me. Opening my eyes momentarily I see that it's Mummy, Mummy taking care of me like Amah. Clickety-clack, clickety-clack, clickety-clack; the train rattles and sways rhythmically on its way to Chungking. My head's full of pictures of cliffs and steps and Ping San's voice telling Daddy that Japanese soldiers are coming to Shanghai. I wonder if Lola, Amah, and Cook will get captured. I hope they are safe. I yawn as I try to stay awake so I can hear what Daddy and Mummy are talking about. As I fall asleep, I hear Daddy say, "This is an unusual opportunity." *What does that mean?* I ask myself.

***

Eighteen hours later the train jerks, rattles, and jerks again to a stop. Mummy and Daddy have climbed down from the upper bunks in the carriage and folded the extra blankets back into a Hong Kong basket. Mummy nudges me and then John.

"We're here. This is Chungking," she says.

"But it's the middle of the night!" I exclaim. It's pitch-black outside.

"Yes, it's two in the morning," Mummy says. "Get up. We've arrived."

I don't mind. I'm ready for this new city after the long train ride.

Daddy steps off the train and helps Mummy get down from the high step onto the platform. I lean as far as I can out the window and look up and down. Is this the station? All I can see are two pairs of tracks running into the distance behind and in front of the train and two stone platforms on each side of us. A thin sliver of light seeps from around the window of a low brick building beside the farthest platform. There are no streetlights, so I can just see Mummy and Daddy standing outside. As my eyes adjust to the dimness, moonlight peeps momentarily through the clouds. I watch Daddy climb back onto the train, lift John from the seat beside me, and carry him down to Mummy. Other passengers get off the train. Mummy asks a porter to help with our six cases and they are piled together on the platform.

Now John and I stand close together, close to the suitcases, as Daddy goes off to talk to some men. Down the tracks I see a group of young tired-looking soldiers stretching their bony necks and stiff legs. They pull their limp uniforms straight and readjust their packs as they form two lines.

As I drowsily watch the Chinese soldiers, an unusual scraping noise attracts my attention. A man steps from behind the group of soldiers, dragging one foot.

"Are we home yet?" John asks, blinking.

"Almost, precious son," Daddy calls back to us.

A group of coolies squat or stretch out on the grass at the edge of the road that runs parallel to the platform. The aroma of hot peppers and garlic floats above them. As the first passengers begin to jump off the train, some members of the group jump up, jostling each other as they hurry toward the platform calling, "*Wha-gar, wha-gar,*"[5] in screechy tones. Sedan chair, sedan chair.

In the dim light, I see that each of the coolies who approaches the train has a partner squatting next to a pile of bamboo rods, slats, and strings on the ground beside him. I try to look beyond the squatting men.

It's very dark. I smell mud, mud like paddy fields.[6] We must be in the country. I squint to see farther, past the train station office. There're no taxis. No rickshaws. Not even any buildings.

The passengers who've been on the train with us, in other carriages and compartments, melt into the darkness. All I can see are a dozen or so tattered coolies.

Mummy pays the porter who took the suitcases off the train.

One of the coolies approaches Daddy. He raises a wiry arm and flexes a muscle, trying to impress Daddy with his strength. The piles of bamboo sticks on the ground beside the other men don't look like they could carry anything, let alone Daddy.

Daddy beckons to the coolie to come closer. "We'd like three chairs," he says. "What would you charge to go through the city, across the river, and up the other bank to the houses that belong to the Canadian hospital?"

I see the chair coolie shift the weight of his scrawny frame from one foot to the other.

"Do you know where the Canadian hospital is?" Daddy adds.

The coolie nods.

I listen intently as I hear the coolie tell Daddy that it's about three kilometers (1.86 miles) to the first houses in the city and another three kilometers through the city to the river's north bank. Then I see Daddy nod. They must have agreed on a price.

The men on the grass chatter among themselves. The way these coolies talk sounds different from the way the coolies in Shanghai talk. They smell different, too. Not just dirty, like the Shanghai coolies, but spicy-dirty.

With the negotiation complete, the chair coolie gestures to his associates, and five men hurry up to us carrying their disassembled sedan chairs.

The head coolie motions to us to get into the chairs. First, Mummy gets into a chair to show us how it's done. She steps between a pair of poles as two men lift the chair up under her. Two men, one at the front and the other at the back, lift the ends of a pair of poles. Thus, a slatted seat swings freely between each pair of poles; three sedan chairs materialize out of what had looked like a crumpled pile of bamboo. There's even a swinging bar for her feet to rest on. Then a man with a scraggly beard lifts John and me into the second chair. All the suitcases are piled into the last chair, and a coolie ties a rope around the suitcases so none will fall out. Daddy says he doesn't need a chair—he'll lead the way on foot with his big flashlight.

The coolies waggle their shoulders—to adjust our weight on them, Daddy says. Mummy tells us not to wriggle, because that could throw the coolies off-balance.

The coolies take a deep breath, and we're on our way. We go single file—Daddy first, on foot, then Mummy in the first chair, then John and me in the second chair, and lastly, all the suitcases piled in the third chair; a little procession, in the darkness. It's two thirty in the morning.

As the coolies set the pace, they begin a singsong chant that jumps back and forth between the three men at the front of each sedan chair and the three men carrying the back of each chair, a singsong chant that matches their swinging, bouncing gait.

"Mummy, why are the men singing?" John asks, wide awake with the adventure of this, his first sedan-chair ride. His question, lost in the hubbub, floats into the dark, unanswered.

Leaving the side of the platform, the lead coolie approaches a flight of chocolate-brown stone stairs that I'd not noticed before.

Daddy shines his flashlight up the long flight. The end of the beam melts into the darkness at the top. I hear Daddy take a deep breath as he starts off.

Up, up, up the chair coolies climb, following the beam of light, a bright white tunnel slicing through the blackness. The chairs feel wobbly, and I hope the chair coolies don't drop us. Bounce-bounce, bounce-bounce; the bamboo-slat chairs swing in a rhythmic pattern matching the coolies' stride and chant, the bearer at the front of each chair calling, *"Ho-ho,"* and the bearer at the back of each chair answering, *"aayyaaah."* The sedan chairs tip back on the steep stairs. The men strain to keep them level. Sweat begins to collect and run down their necks and arms between their bulging veins. Bounce-bounce, bounce-bounce, bounce-bounce, bounce-bounce, *ho-ho, aayyaaah, ho-ho, aayyaaah.* Even Daddy, who's only carrying a flashlight, begins to puff.

By the time we arrive at the top of the brown stone stairs, I've counted 193 steps. Gingerly, I lean out to look around Mummy and over Daddy's head. Complete darkness stretches out in every direction except where Daddy flashes the beam of light. At that moment, the clouds part and a sliver of moon appears. I can just see that we're entering a narrow valley; on each side, tier after tier of rice paddies curve around the face of the mountainsides, nestled together like long, narrow stairsteps.

The rice paddies extend as far as the beam of light allows us to see. The young plants in even rows look like black sprigs, but I know they're really green. And I know that there's always a narrow pathway between each paddy field, each path about twelve inches wide. In the dim light the pathways are a honey-comb extending from the top of the stairs in all directions; paths lead off to the left, zigzagging up the mountainside, and others go to the right. The lead coolie nods toward the path that goes straight ahead into the valley, and Daddy flashes his light in that direction.

The mud smells especially muddy. I hear frogs singing, a choir of frogs. As the coolies step away from the top of the stairs and adjust the chairs to the level ground, John points to the silhouette of a huge wheel with a narrow rim and thin spokes that's silhouetted against the dim sky.

"Do you see that big bicycle wheel up there?" John whispers in my ear.

"That's a waterwheel." I feel very smart to be able to tell John this.

"I know," John says. "Let's ask Daddy to bring us here to see it tomorrow."

"It takes water from a low paddy field to a higher field so the rice can grow," I continue, undeterred.

But John already knows. "Sometimes a little boy sits on top of the waterwheel and makes it turn by pedaling with his feet," he says. Then after a pause, he asks, "Do you think it's fun?"

Daddy flashes the light over the dark paddy fields on both sides of us, takes a deep breath as he continues along the narrow path that runs straight ahead. The chair coolies follow: bounce-bounce, bounce-bounce, bounce-bounce, bounce-bounce. The soft mud in the rice fields smells rich and creamy, a warm, comforting perfume.

Soothed by the coolies' rhythmic gait, John soon falls asleep against my shoulder. The frog chorus is louder. *How beautiful the froggy song is*, I think. *The frogs take up the birds' job at night when they're tucked into their little nests.*

Daddy's footsteps now plod along ahead of us. They sound heavy and unsteady against the coolies' soft, confident strides. I close my eyes; the sedan-chair coolies are like the rickshaw coolies in Shanghai; they know their way, every path and pebble is familiar to them. Daddy once told me that chair coolies work in mountainous places all over China. They carry lots of people—old people when they visit temples, people who need to cross shallow rivers where there are no bridges, brides to their weddings. Lots of things are carried, too. Daddy told me that he's seen men carrying large round slabs of salt on their backs—not in a sedan chair but with only a leather strap across their forehead. Daddy saw this when he visited a salt mine, and he said he'd take John and me to see it one day too.

Bounce-bounce, bounce-bounce, bounce-bounce, bounce-bounce. I stretch my neck and look far ahead, past the coolies in front of me, around Mummy's head and Daddy's silhouette, but I see mostly darkness. Bubbles pop softly as frogs splash into the wet paddy fields, disturbed by our passing. We approach a place where another path crosses the one we're on. Daddy flashes the light back and forth. More frogs, caught off guard, jump into the water. We don't turn. We continue on.

Daddy's beam of light catches a clump of tall grass growing beside the path. The grass is pressed flat into the mud. The trampled spot's too large for a dog; it was probably a water buffalo, sleeping. Once we drove out into the countryside outside

Shanghai and saw water buffalo plowing the rice fields before the little shoots were planted. I remember their smell; water buffalo have a peculiar smell that is all their own, hot, wet, muggy. I sniff the air but there's no distinctive buffalo odor there or clinging to the grass. I don't dislike the smell of the countryside, of the things that are used for fertilizer. It's something I've gotten used to. It's collected in the villages and spread on the fields. Nothing goes to waste.

Ahead there's a faint glow; it must be the city. As we come closer, the odors that hang in the air are less of mud, urine, and animal dung and more of hot oil, spices, and unwashed human bodies. And there's another odor—strong, pungent, unfamiliar, smoky. Like charred wood and burned oil; like hot metal. Perhaps it's from trucks that have been driven for too long.

Now the paddy fields glisten, reflecting the glow of the city. Bounce-bounce, bounce-bounce, bounce-bounce, bounce-bounce; on and on the coolies stride. They've abandoned their singsong chant. I think they're too tired to sing; I can feel that their bouncy steps have lost some of their springiness. Bounce-bounce, bounce-bounce, bounce-bounce, bounce-bounce; the hypnotic pace continues without a pause. The city's glow makes the sky above us look blacker in contrast. My eyes close.

Splash!

"Damn!"

The light beam is gone. Total blackness.

Squish. Squish. Splash. I hear a slow gurgle, a sucking sound from the side of the footpath. Daddy's knee-deep in mud; his foot slipped off the path. He stands in the murky water, one hand hanging on to a tuft of grass.

The lead coolie lets out a whoop. All six coolies stop abruptly, probably not because they cannot see, although now the path is lit only by dim moonlight, but because Daddy, on one knee, is blocking the path. The two coolies who are carrying the suitcases put their burden down. The other men squirm, trying to redistribute the weight of Mummy, John, and me on their shoulders.

"Darling, are you hurt?" Mummy calls.

"No, no, I'm not, just twisted my ankle a bit. I'll be fine in a moment."

The two suitcase-carrying coolies stride forward. They place their hands under Daddy's armpits and pull; with a loud sucking noise Daddy is out of the mud and the water. But he's lost his shoe. Without a word, Daddy reaches toward the water where his flashlight fell, luckily still lit. But before Daddy's hand touches the water, one of the coolies jumps into the paddy field, plucks the flashlight out of the mud, and feels around for Daddy's shoe. He finds it and holds it up. It drips lumps of mud.

Daddy's left trouser leg is thick with muck. He pulls great lumps of sticky goo off the fabric and flings them back into the water. Then he squeezes his trouser leg and shakes it, wrings his trouser cuff, and rubs and flexes his ankle while the coolie holds his elbow. Daddy has a little trouble getting his wet shoe on but finally manages it and stands up straight. The coolie uses his shirtsleeve to carefully wipe mud off the flashlight. He hands it back to Daddy.

The two coolies who'd rescued Daddy from the paddy field squeeze back past us and return to the end of the line to take up the sedan chair carrying the suitcases again. Without saying another word, Daddy takes the lead. *Poor Daddy*, I think. *He's so brave.*

***

After another twenty minutes of steady walking, we reach a steep, narrow street; we're on the outskirts of the city. The stench of communal outhouses rises like a wall. I'm so glad I live in a Western house with a real bathroom. The odor of burned oil and burning wood is stronger now. *I wonder what makes all these odors?* I think. *I'll ask Daddy. He'll know.*

Low houses, each joined to the next, line both sides of the desolate, twisting earthen street. It's still very early; everyone must be in bed. Only a dog's bark and the tap-tapping of Daddy's footsteps break the silence as we walk along the road and up or down an occasional flight of stairs. I peer down narrow cross streets and alleyways as we pass them. Every alley is lined with one-story bamboo-frame houses, and each house has a large clay pot standing in front of its doorway.[7]

Dawn breaks as we arrive at the top of the mountain, the center of Chungking. The coolies start down the other side, their pace now slower as they continue along the downward-sloping streets and lope down the stairs that will end at the Yangtze River. Our direction is entirely downhill, sometimes down a broad set of steps, sometimes down a tiny path. I look to the left and right as we pass and see more paths, more steps. Some paths lead to a single, tiny house clinging to the cliff face. Broad or narrow, the steps are all steep.

Now that we're in the city and the sun is coming up, Daddy falls back to walk next to Mummy and then next to me. We've come to one of the wider roadways that must be a main street, and I see a gaping hole in the embankment. "What's that?" I ask.

We pass another of these caves. I look in as we pass. It's pitch-black inside.

"That's an air raid shelter," Daddy says.

"Oh," I reply.

Bounce-bounce, bounce-bounce, bounce-bounce, bounce-bounce. We continue through the still mostly deserted streets. The coolies sweat heavily.

Suddenly I catch a glimpse between the houses of glistening, swirling black water. It's the Yangtze River. The coolies tip the chairs, sure-footed on the shiny, now slippery granite steps. I can see that Daddy is walking carefully. His leg must hurt. I look down at the steps; they look very hard and unforgiving. *I hope Daddy doesn't slip*, I think. *The stone steps look very hard.*

"It's about three hundred steps down to the river," the lead coolie says. We come to the top of the last set of stairs on the river's north bank. Again, the coolies have to tip the chairs to keep us level as they descend the last stone stairway.

When we reach the riverbank, I see lights bobbing up and down on the water. "What are those lights in the river?" John asks.

"They're lamps on the sampans," Daddy says. "We're going to take a sampan to cross the river. You and John can see for yourselves."

Finally, after almost three hours of fast, steady jogging, the coolies reach the river's edge. John rubs his eyes as Daddy lifts him out of his spot next to me and the coolies lower the chairs so Mummy and I can step out. I'm a little stiff. It's hard to sit still for a long time, even if it's fun to travel by sedan chair. I look at the coolie who'd shown his muscles to Daddy and who carried

Mummy; he's rubbing his shoulder. I notice that he has a long scar on the back of his weather-worn neck. I'm glad that the coolies finally have a chance to rest.

One of the coolies knows the owner of a sampan and calls to him across the water.

I stare down into the dark river. When we were on the train, Daddy said that the Yangtze would be dark and swirling. Now I see what he meant. It's very swirly. Scary.

The coolies load our suitcases onto the sampan, then help Mummy step into the boat. It heaves up and down gently. Mummy turns and grasps my hand as Daddy helps me get aboard, then lifts John. The coolies have collapsed the three sedan chairs and carry them on board.

The sampan owner, the oarsman, stands in the back of the small boat and uses a long oar to row us across. The current must be strong; I see that he's steering against it, leaning heavily against the single oar. But I also see that he knows exactly how to get us to the landing place on the south bank. After disembarking everything, and after Daddy has paid the sampan owner, we assemble into the chairs again. This time Daddy says he'll take John on his shoulder, at least for a while. I notice that the coolies have switched around so that different coolies are carrying Mummy and me. We start off up the hill along sometimes wide and sometimes narrow paths and more stairs.

In half an hour of steady jogging, we arrive at our new home. Ping San is waiting, standing beside a tiny house, just one room, that's built into the wall beside a gate. Daddy pays the chair coolies, and I look around as Daddy and Mummy talk to Ping San and the gatekeeper, a hunched little man who looks like an ogre, who'd emerged from the gatehouse when he heard us arrive. The ogre-man opens the gate. Inside we see three large Western-style houses around a big lawn, each house sharing this large front garden. I want to explore our new house but I'm much too tired. Tomorrow I will look at everything!

The sun rises over the trees as we walk up the path that leads to the closest house, the one on the left; Daddy and Ping San carry the luggage. As we go up the path, I hear Daddy say to Mummy that the house belongs to a nearby hospital and that the hospital was built by a Canadian charity. Then Daddy says that the Gray family, our friends from Shanghai, is staying in one of the houses across the lawn.

Even in my exhaustion, I remember that Mr. Gray, who works with Daddy, has a daughter named Penelope. Penny went to school with me in Shanghai and often came to our house to play. She has red hair and lots of dolls! She also has two brothers, so John and I will have children to play with.

We're so tired that when we enter the house, we head right upstairs. Mummy tucks us into the beds that Ping San has readied for us in our new spacious bedroom.

As Mummy turns out the light I hear Ping San's voice, saying, "Missy, Master, would you like some tea? I'll bring it to you in the living room?"

And as I close my eyes, I hear Mummy reply, "Thank you, Ping San. I think something just a bit stronger is very much in order."

NOTES

1. Chungking (now called Chongqing), a southwestern Chinese municipality bordering Sichuan Province, is a major commercial center and now the most populous city in China. It's built on a high bluff overlooking the place where the Jialing River flows into the Yangtze River. During World War II, Chungking served as the country's capital. Gen. Joseph Stilwell, an American war hero, was headquartered there.

2. Hong Kong baskets were made in Hong Kong of woven bamboo and were shaped like suitcases and even hatboxes. Extremely popular, they came in many sizes and shapes.

3. Trackers were coolies who, attached to boats by long ropes, pulled the boats—sometimes against the current—as they walked along a narrow path on the riverbank. Hundreds of trackers could be tied to one boat. Trackers no longer pull boats up riverways in China, although the pathways they wore into the riverbanks are still visible.

4. "Soft class" was the term commonly used for first-class seating in train compartments. Second-class seating was made of bare wood and called "hard class."

5. The word *wha-gar* is Chungking dialect.

6. Paddy fields, ubiquitous in China, are fields that are flooded for young rice to grow in.

7. The large clay pots that sat in front of the houses were used for cooking and were fueled by coal or wood.

8

War Arrives

.

A Few Days Later in October 1940
Chungking, Sichuan Province, China

"Hurry, Ferfer, John," I hear Mummy call, as she hustles us out the front door and around to the back of the house. "Not again," she mutters as she stops to adjust the strap of the snakeskin T-strap sandal on her left foot. We hurry because the air raid siren's screaming.[1]

When the siren began, I was in Mummy's room, helping her pick out a frock to wear to a tea dance on the deck of the USS *Tutuila*,[2] which, she says, is moored at the American embassy on the Yangtze's south bank. The dance is in celebration of the gunboat's arrival from Shanghai. Daddy enjoys visiting the ship to chat with the officers, and everyone loves hearing the latest songs the ship's bo's'n has brought from America.[3]

We like our new house. Since Ping San came a week early to arrange everything, it didn't take us long to settle in. He hired a cook and a wash coolie and stocked food, including some big cans of Klim, a white powder that Mummy mixes with drinking water for us every morning, using an egg beater—it's thick and frothy.[4]

We also like the big, comfortable compound where we live.[5] It's surrounded by a ten-foot brick wall, the top three feet of which are decorated in brick latticework, and it's this wall—and Mr. Ma, the ancient gatekeeper—that holds back the noisy, smelly, busy Chinese city that churns all around us. Mr. Ma guards the only entrance, admitting visitors at his discretion through the carved wooden gate. Our house is on the left as you enter. Mr. and Mrs. Gray and their children, Brice, Brian, and Penelope—called Penny—live opposite. Three Western doctors who work at the hospital live in the third residence, but we never see them.

A broad stone veranda in front of the drawing room windows extends across the front of our house. I think ours is the nicest of the three buildings because there's a very wide view of the river and the city from the second-story back windows; John and I often stand on chairs to look at it.

But today I'm not thinking about the view as we scramble after Mummy down the embankment behind our home. We hurry, slipping on the loose earth. The air raid siren wails: hooooOOOOoooo, hooooOOOOoooo, hooooOOOOoooo. Simultaneously, a gigantic red balloon is hoisted up a flagpole on the north side of the river. I see that it's the second balloon on the flagpole. The balloons must be gigantic because we can see them from across the river, miles away.

Mummy pointed out the red balloons weeks ago, the first time we heard the air raid siren. From our house, they're tiny red dots against the skyline. Mummy told us that men—radio operators, probably soldiers—hide in the hills all over free China to alert us of a pending air raid. Daddy told us that these Chinese spies watch the Japanese airfields through binoculars, downriver from Chungking, in Hankow, and send a radio message to Chungking when they see the bombers leave the airport. That's the signal for our air raid wardens to raise the first big red balloon. Then, when our wardens get a second message sent by other, closer spies telling them the planes are ten minutes away, they raise the second red balloon. When they raise the third balloon it means the planes are over the city. I think that third balloon is silly. When the planes are here, everyone can hear and see them.

On the day of our first air raid, Mummy pointed to a long line of black cars snaking along a mountain road on the other side of the river. She said these were the cars of government workers going to the countryside, where they would be safe. She said this was a sure sign that the air raid was not a false alarm.

When the second air raid sounded a week later, Mummy took us to a shelter in the Canadian hospital basement, just a short walk from our gatehouse. She was unhappy with it, though. I heard Mummy telling Daddy that at the hospital shelter, the patients were brought down from all the upstairs wards on stretchers and placed close together along the basement walls. So, Ping San and the new wash coolie dug into the sandstone hill under the back of the house to open up a small cave that was already there. John and I watched as they filled burlap bags with sandy earth and used them to build a wall in front of its entrance.

Now, close behind us, Ping San says, "Missy, aren't you going to the hospital today?"

"No," Mummy says. "I don't think it was such a good idea. When we went last time, we saw all the patients—their stretchers placed side by side along the basement walls, all the different diseases—there, together." Mummy looks at me and half-smiles. "The hospital shelter may be more dangerous than the bombs." Mummy slides sideways around the sandbag wall and into the cave that Ping San and Wash Coolie had built.

John holds on to Mummy's dress and I hold his other hand. Mummy carries a small oil lamp; *Treasure Island* is tucked under her arm. She bows as she enters the low opening. John slides in next. The scratchy burlap brushes against my shoulder as I round the baffle after him. Daddy says the burlap baffle should keep the wind that the bombs make when they fall from blowing into our shelter. I didn't know bombs make wind.

The cave is dark and clammy. I shiver and feel sorry I didn't bring a sweater. I think about going back to get one, but I don't go. I don't think Mummy would like me to go now that the second balloon has been raised. Anyway, I think, the air raid will be over soon. It's not so cold. I can wait.

Ping San strikes a match as my eyes adjust to the dim light. A strong smell penetrates the still air. The lamp's cotton wick sputters and flares as Ping San touches the match to it. The brown clay oil lamp is shaped like a little squat teapot; the wick comes up through its tiny spout.

Mummy, John, and I sit on three little round wooden stools Ping San has placed in a circle in the middle of the cave—away from the walls, which constantly drip sand and water and provide a home to spiders and ants. Our knees are touching. I find that reassuring.

"Did Cook go to the basement?" Mummy asks Ping San. Ping San replies with a nod. "Under the stairs is also a safe place from bombs," she says to us.

I glance at Mummy. She looks apprehensive. Is she thinking about the planes, or about Daddy at work? Every day Daddy and Mr. Gray share a sampan across the river to their office on the north shore, and they usually come back together in the evening. Mummy has said we're safe, because the Japanese don't bomb this side of the river. But what about Daddy? His office is on the other side.

"Mummy, does Daddy have a bomb shelter at his office?" I ask.

"Daddy's safe, don't worry." But Mummy's voice sounds wobbly, and I see her reach for and take John's hand for just a moment. Is she scared?

Mummy opens *Treasure Island* at the bookmark and bends over the book. She begins to read. The lamplight is dim and shaky.

Outside we hear the far-off hum of engines, the sound of the planes that Daddy calls Zeros. I've learned they come in waves, like in the ocean on the beach, and I listen carefully so that maybe I can tell how many groups of planes there are. Silently, I count. Number one, wave number one. I can just barely hear the low hum, still very far away. I wait and listen. The hum grows louder. The hum changes to a buzz, the buzz becomes a roar. Mummy keeps reading, but I can't hear her, even though her lips are moving. The roar gets louder, then louder still. The roar turns into a screech.

I've heard this screeching sound before, far away. When I

asked Daddy what the sound was, he said it was the sound of bombs falling. Now I wait, and boom . . . boom . . . BOOM, almost simultaneous explosions—too many booms to count. I know that each boom is followed by a puff. I can feel the puffs even though we have a sandbag wall in front of our little shelter and cannot see them. Today they feel like one long pufffff. The earth around our cave rattles and sand sprinkles down from the ceiling. The tiny flame of the oil lamp flickers and hisses. I try to follow the words that Mummy is reading, reading tenaciously. Reading in a stiff hard voice. I look at my brother. He looks captivated by the story. I wait for the next wave of planes.

I can't stop wondering whether Daddy is in an air raid shelter on the other side of the river. Tonight, when Daddy returns from work, I will ask him to come home when there's an air raid. "Mummy, why doesn't Daddy come to our cave?" I ask.

Mummy turns the page. "Don't worry, Ferfer, Daddy's office has a very good shelter. He's safe."

I watch as John leans over and reaches a hand toward the hard, sandy floor. His index finger gently touches the packed earth. A small red spider crawls up his finger, then up his hand and onto his sleeve.

I count to myself; number two. The second wave of planes flies from the northeast. Again, the hum gets louder and louder and turns into a roar. I know the planes come from far away. Daddy told me they come from a city halfway to Shanghai and that it's easy for them to find Chungking because they can see and follow the Yangtze since it flows through both cities. It's just like driving along a road. *Daddy knows everything; I can ask him anything. He tells me the truth.*

Today the drone of planes seems endless. I wish Daddy were here. Sometimes he doesn't come home until late, until after dark. Whenever I ask Mummy why Daddy hasn't come home, she says he has to wait until he's sure no more planes are coming before he leaves his office. It's more dangerous to cross the river at night, I know. I've heard Ping San talking about the logs and pieces of broken boats that float in the rough water and how it's often hard for the boatmen to see what's floating in the water at night. He's heard that boats are hit by big pieces of debris and sink and no one ever knows what's happened.

Mummy's voice drones on. She starts a new chapter, when BOOM—there's a thunderous, deafening noise. Then, a few seconds later, wind whistles around our sandbag wall and sucks the air out of our cave.

Sand falls from the ceiling.

The oil lamp goes out.

Treasure Island snaps shut.

"It's all right, children, don't move," Mummy says.

I hold John's hand.

"Ouch! Don't squeeze my fingers!" John exclaims.

I close my eyes and think about the all-clear siren, which I hope will sound very soon.

I don't know how long we wait in the dark until it does, but finally, there it is: a long, level blast, hooooooooo, hooooooooo, hooooooooo, repeating over and over. All clear, the siren says. You can come out of your shelter.

We squeeze back out of our little cave, like toothpaste out of its tube. Mummy, John, Ping San, and I.

I look across the river and see billows of smoke drifting

skyward. Long fingers of red flames stretch up from the billows of tarry black smoke. An oily stench floats across the river, carried on the wind. The popping and crackling we hear is the sound of the bamboo houses burning, Mummy says; bamboo houses burn quickly. The bamboo canes are made up of many small airtight sections that explode with the heat. Since we can hear it when we're so far away, the popping and crackling must be very loud where Daddy is.

I think about the morning after each air raid, the sky gray with wisps of smoke still rising, the strong smell of burned wood and oil. On the wide steps along the riverfront on the north side of the river, hundreds of coffins are lined up like matchsticks in a row, waiting to be carried downstream by sampans and barges for burial. John and I watch from the upstairs back window as families dressed in white gather around the coffins of their loved ones, heads bowed, shoulders slumped, waiting for their boxes to be loaded up. Sometimes the family goes on board too. We watch the boats float downstream, followed by swirling paper flowers, until they're out of sight around the bend in the river. Sometimes at night we see little lights twinkling on the river, candles in paper saucers floating behind the boats.

One morning after an air raid, Ping San passes as we're watching this sight. "Why is everyone so quiet?" I ask him. I know that a proper Chinese funeral has lots of firecrackers, wailing mourners, and the crackle of paper play-money burning. Sometimes, when the wind blows from the north, we hear mournful wailing, but mostly the funerals are silent.

"Because even the birds are sad," Ping San says.

Then he adds that many people are so poor, they can't afford to hire mourners, set off firecrackers, or burn play-money for their dead family members. Sometimes, he says, they can't afford to go with the coffins to the cemetery or even buy white mourning clothes. In that case, they just tie a strip of white cloth around their foreheads.

After seeing this sight once, it's hard not to picture it again and again while crouching in our little sandy cave with the sound of bombs overhead. Mummy doesn't talk to John and me about the things we see from the upstairs back window. We have lots of questions but don't ask.

NOTES

1. The Japanese bombed Chungking mercilessly from 1938 through 1943. Much of the city, including 18,600 buildings, was destroyed, and ten thousand civilians were killed.

2. The river gunboat USS *Tutuila*, assigned to the Yangtze patrol, plied the Yangtze River from Shanghai to Chungking from 1928 to 1941. She was the only American gunboat in Chungking during its heavy bombing by the Japanese, and she survived many bombing attacks. When she was unable to depart the city because the Japanese occupied the river below, her crew of twenty-two enlisted men and two officers was ordered to depart by plane, and the gunboat was turned over to the Chinese government under the terms of lend-lease.

3. "Bo's'n" is an abbreviation for "boatswain," a ship's petty officer in charge of the deck crew.

4. Klim was a fortified dried milk product widely used by non-Chinese people in China during this period because cow's milk or the milk of other animals was not available. Chinese children didn't drink milk once they were weaned.

5. I returned to Chungking, now called Chongqing, in 1998. The railway station was new and modern, but the chocolate-brown stairs were still there. I hiked to the top; vendors lined it on each side, and at the top, streets and houses stretched out in all directions as far as the eye could see. The city's famous stairs no longer seemed as ubiquitous, somehow—not commanding as much pedestrian attention, although still there.

   I looked for, and found, our old compound on the south bank near the Canadian hospital. The gatehouse and brick-lattice wall had not changed, but the big lawn had become a barren, earth-packed soccer field, devoid of all grass, and the lane in front of the gatehouse was lined with butcher shops with slabs of meat hanging in front of them. I was invited into our old house; every room was now occupied by a family or a single person. The woman who graciously invited me to her room served me a cup of hot water, the customary refreshment when tea is not an option—the hot water implying that the water has been boiled, and is therefore free of bacteria.

9

Snow

Third Week of October 1940
Chungking, Sichuan Province, China

"What happened to your doll?" I ask. Penelope and I are sitting on the front steps of her house.

"Oh, she was out in the rain," Penny says casually.

I look at the sky. It's beautiful and clear now. "You can ask your amah to make some new hair for her," I say.

"It's all right," Penny says. "My daddy will get me a new Shirley Temple if I ask him." Penny twists a strand of the doll's straggly hair around her finger.

John comes across the wide lawn. "Where're Brice and Brian?" he asks. "What are they doing?"

"They're upstairs, I think," Penny says.

When we came to Chungking, John and I had to leave our toys with Mummy's things in a godown in Shanghai.[1] Mummy said that after the war we'd go back and get them. Now we play with all kinds of different things. When she's finished with them, Mummy gives us the tins from her Craven A cigarettes to play with.[2] We chop up nasturtiums and other flowers and leaves we pick from the garden and make play food for John's teddy bear and my doll.

"Good morning, Mr. Gray," I say as Penny, Brice, and Brian's father comes down the steps. He's on his way to our house to meet Daddy. Every morning he and Daddy walk down to the riverbank and take a sampan across the Yangtze together. I don't say anything, although I know that this morning Daddy will not be accompanying him. Daddy has to stay in bed because he has a stomach ulcer, and this morning it hurts so much he's not going to work. Mummy says the next time we go to England Daddy will have an operation. For now, Mummy makes special food for him that she presses through a sieve.

While I'm playing with Penny, the air raid siren sounds. Leaving her on the steps of her house, I run across the lawn and call to John, who's digging in the garden with Brian, "Come, we have to go home."

Mummy, Ping San, John, and I hurry to our shelter. We slide behind the sandbag baffle. As usual, Mummy carries a little oil lamp. Today I carry the book—we've finished *Treasure Island* and are now reading *Robinson Crusoe*—and Ping San is ready with the matches.

"Is Daddy coming with us?" I ask. I wish he would. It would be so nice.

"No, he's going under the stairs with the servants," Mummy says. "There's more space there."

Mummy holds the lamp as Ping San strikes a match. I notice that Mummy's hand shakes. Ping San strikes a second match before the wick catches fire. We sit in our usual places on the stools—I have my back to the doorway—as Mummy opens the book and begins to read. The story's very exciting. We've come to the part where Mr. Crusoe finds footprints on the sand and realizes he's not alone on the island. Then I hear the planes flying low overhead.

I don't know whether I should listen to the story or to the planes. Daddy told me the planes are always far away from our house. I decide to concentrate on *Robinson Crusoe*. If I look as if I'm listening to the story, John won't know I'm scared. I don't want him to be scared too.

I can't help it; I listen to the planes, but nothing happens—no whistling, no explosions. That's strange. The only sound I hear is the planes flying low, flying in big circles, then flying away, leaving, and then returning.

Mummy stops reading. Silence. I'm scared. I don't know what'll happen now. I look at John and Mummy. *Are they scared too?* I wonder. I turn and look at the entrance. If there's a huge crash, I'm ready to put my hands over my ears. But the drone changes to a hum. Then the hum fades away. The planes are gone. The all-clear siren sounds, and dogs all over the city start to howl. They don't like the sirens any more than I do.

I jump up, ready to leave the cramped shelter. Mummy puts her hand on my shoulder to make me stay, but I slide out from under it and look around the baffle.

I stand, astonished. "Snow!" I call. "It's snowing!" Everyone pops out of the cave.

Across the river, clouds of little white flakes flutter down from the sky. People run back and forth catching the flakes. Instead of bombs, the Japanese planes have dropped scraps of paper all over Chungking.

When a few of the papers fall on our side of the river, I see that they are leaflets. John and I rush to catch one, but the breeze blows them over the compound wall, where they disappear. As we look hopefully toward the sky, one lands in the garden, caught in the bushes next to the wall. Ping San pushes the branches aside and retrieves it.

Mummy's gone back into the house, so Ping San hands the slip of thin, yellowish paper to John.

"It has funny pictures on it. Look," John says to Ping San. Pictured is an Oriental soldier attacking a Western man with a bayonet;[3] the man being stabbed is screaming in Chinese. John points to the Chinese characters in the little blob coming from the man's mouth. "What does it say, Ping San?"

Ping San takes the slip of paper and studies it. "The Japanese planes drop paper snow to say that the Chinese should join the Japanese and fight against the Western people, that we can't win the war." Ping San crumples the slip of paper into a lump and hands it back to John. "The reason it has pictures is because they think we can't read."

Ping San turns to go.

***

That evening when Mummy comes into our room to kiss John and me good night, she looks very sad. She doesn't read us a story. She just sits on the edge of my bed and looks at her hands. "John, Ferfer," she says, "I have some very sad news. Brice, Brian, and Penny's daddy had an accident on his way home from work this evening. His boat was hit by a log that was floating in the river and the boat broke apart. Mr. Gray drowned."

NOTES

1. In the Far East, the word "godown" is commonly used to refer to a warehouse.

2. Craven A was a brand of British cigarettes popular during World War II. They were first sold in 1921, and at that time came in flat red metal boxes of twenty and round metal tins of one hundred; a black cat was pictured on the red cover.

3. Japanese propaganda of the time pitted all Asian peoples against Westerners. The word "Oriental" is used here because although it is now considered offensive when applied to people, it was commonly used by Westerners during the period in which this book is set.

10

Of Beans and Noodles

End of October 1940
Chungking, Sichuan Province, China, to
Guiyang, Guizhou Province, China

Daddy and Mummy don't talk about Mr. Gray, and although John and I were not invited to the funeral, I know that Mr. Gray is buried behind the house where the three doctors live.

Whenever I think about Penny and her brothers not having their daddy anymore, I'm very sad and feel like crying. I'm lucky I'm a girl. Girls are allowed to cry. I cannot even imagine how I would feel if my precious daddy got drowned in the river. Every time I imagine it, I quickly try to think about something else; I run, slamming doors behind me, and do something like ask Cook what's for dessert that evening.

After we've been in Chungking for about a month, Daddy

tells us we're moving to Guiyang,[1] a town about 190 miles (320 kilometers) south. To get there, we'll have to ride with a caravan of Red Cross trucks. I'm happy to leave Chungking, because this is a sad city. Sad not just because of the almost daily Japanese air raids and all the people who get killed and have to go on barges to be buried, but also because I worry about Daddy crossing the river to go to his office every day.

When we start out for Guiyang, it's bright and sunny. A friend from Daddy's office drives us to the edge of the city, where we meet the caravan of six old army trucks. They're full of all sorts of medicines and food. Daddy loads our camp cot and supplies into one of the trucks, the one that Mummy's going to ride in. Daddy and John and I are going to be in the one behind hers, which is being driven by Jack, one of the American aid workers.

"Would you kids like to ride on beans?" Jack asks.

John and I look at each other. "Beans?" we both say, in surprise.

Jack takes us around to the back of the truck. It's full of loose, dry brown beans! The entire truck bed is covered with them. Jack picks up a handful and lets them slide through his fingers.

Daddy says it's all right, so Jack lifts each of us up and puts us on top of the massive heap of beans, where we lie back. What an odd feeling; it's like I'm floating, suspended on an ocean of shiny brown beans. The convoy starts up. We are the last truck in the group. The beans under us slip and slide from side to side. Whenever the truck turns, we slither across the top of the pile. When we hit a bump or hole in the road, the beans slide, jump, and shift under us. Luckily, the truck drives slowly because there's a lot of other traffic along the sides of the road—some donkeys pulling carts, and others loaded with heavy-looking packs tied, one donkey behind the other, into long caravans. John and I watch the interesting sights out of the back of the truck as we pass: goats, a water buffalo with a little boy on his back holding one end of a long stick, and donkey-train after donkey-train, the bells on their harnesses jingling cheerily.

After a while we tire of slipping and sliding. John taps on the window between us and the cab where Daddy sits next to Jack. Daddy asks Jack to stop, and a few minutes later Jack pulls the truck over and Daddy comes to the back to help us out. We stretch our legs and run around for a minute, then move to the cab with Jack and Daddy. Our truck's able to catch back up with the others quickly, since all the trucks must drive slowly. We bump along in silence for a while.

I see a village ahead. "Daddy, I have to go to the bathroom," I say. The odor of urine, mixed with other scents, has been wafting into the open window, reminding me. I've tried not to drink any-thing so I wouldn't have to stop, but sometimes it's hard to wait.

We drive past a few mud cottages. The pungent odor gets stronger as we approach the village—and a giant public tank, a big wooden container on stilts, for every villager to use. Jack pulls the truck up near it, but not next to it. The odor is overpowering.

Daddy gets out and hands me down from the truck. "John, you better go while we're here, too," he says.

I take John's hand and we walk toward the huge ugly tank. Since I'm the one feeling desperate, I approach the ladder that's leaning against the wooden reservoir and start to climb it. The stench gets stronger. I want to run back to the truck and tell Daddy that I'm fine, that I can wait, but a look back down the ladder where John's waiting to follow stops me. Up I climb. As my head is level with the top, I see that a few boards have been thrown across the open space, the open tank top. The idea is to step out onto a board, bend over, and do your business. At this moment, I wish I were a boy. I force myself forward, very careful not to fall in. Then, feeling better, I step across to another board so John can follow me. He's climbed the ladder and stands with his head showing at the top. It's easier for him. He comes to the top of the ladder and pees into the vast expanse—it's at least ten feet across. John finishes and hurries back down the ladder. I follow. We run to the truck. It's a relief to be away from the stinky outhouse on stilts. I rub my nose but it doesn't do much good.

Daddy and Jack are leaning against the truck, smoking and chatting.

"Daddy, why do they keep all that pee?" I ask.

Jack smiles. "The villagers call that liquid gold. They're saving it to spread on their fields. The best fertilizer in the world." He rubs his broad nose. "Besides," he adds matter-of-factly, "if you smell something long enough, you don't notice it anymore."

All I want to do is get back in the cab and away from the horrible stench. By now I'm trying hard not to throw up. I don't want Daddy to think I can't be brave. Jack's look tells me he understands. Although it's only half-smoked, Jack rubs his cigarette out against the fender and hurries around to his side of the truck.

Daddy quickly lifts us in, and we're off. "That's better," he says.

When we catch up with the caravan, we find that one of the other trucks has broken down. So, we didn't hold everyone up as we'd feared. They had to stop and wait anyway.

Mummy comes over to us and suggests that she take John to ride with her in one of the other trucks for a change. I think she's in a hurry to get away from our truck. The awful smell from the village we just left seems to be hanging on to everything around us. Daddy agrees that our cab's a bit crowded and lifts John out so he can go with Mummy.

***

By the time the truck's repaired and we can continue, it's dark. We're now driving through mountains, and the road is narrow and twisty. But one good thing is that there are almost no people or animals along the way to slow us down, just fields and trees and tall rock formations shining white in the moonlight.

We've been driving along for a while when suddenly Jack's hand jerks on the steering wheel. Something's run across the road right in front of us. The truck lurches and slides into the ditch along the side of the road. Luckily, we've been driving slowly so Jack believes nothing is broken, but the wheel is in a deep ditch. Stuck. Whatever startled Jack has run off between the rocks and into the bushes.

Jack rubs his eyes with his fist, then puts the truck into reverse and quickly into forward gear, rocking it, trying to dislodge the truck and get it back onto the road. The maneuver doesn't work. "I'm just getting us deeper into the ditch," Jack says and turns off the engine. He leans on his horn to tell the other trucks in the convoy to stop too. I see them stop and park ahead of us, one by one.

Daddy gets out and lifts me out. Mummy jumps down from her truck and runs back to us. "Oh, it's not serious," Daddy says to her. "We'll have the truck back on the road in a jiffy."

It's a beautiful night. The moon's full, and moonlight spills over the mountains and forests, reflecting off the white rocks. It's so bright I can almost see shadows.

The men collect in a big group, including several coolies who are riding with the Red Cross aid workers. I see the men chatting and smoking. *Perhaps they're enjoying the unexpected break,* I think. Some men go off behind the rocks and reappear a few minutes later.

"What a shame this happened just now," one of the aid workers says. "We're almost to the top of the last hill. From there, we can coast down to the village where we'd planned to spend the night." I've noticed that whenever a road runs downhill, every truck driver without exception turns off his engine and coasts. When I asked Daddy why, he said, simply, "It saves gasoline."

Mummy comes up with John. "Isn't it lovely tonight?" she says. "We're only a few miles away from tonight's stop, so let's walk on ahead. The trucks will catch up to us." She looks as though she wants to tell Daddy but sees that he's very busy talking with the other men.

I glance at the group. It looks like they're trying to figure out a strategy to get the truck out of the ditch.

Waiting for the Red Cross truck to be put back on the road, somewhere in China, 1940. A man bends over the front fender.

As Mummy, John, and I start off, I see Daddy and the other men huddle around the front of the truck. *Are they going to lift it back onto the road?* I wonder. The coolies' voices singsong a chant as they lean into lifting the truck, the chant coordinating the men's efforts. Ping San says something to the coolies, his voice rising above the others.

Mummy, John, and I start off walking down the middle of the road because there're no cars or traffic of any kind—nothing. No one is stirring. Not even a frog or cricket. It's completely still, completely silent. Then a gentle rustle, a breeze, moves through the trees that line the road. The only sound. We walk along.

John picks up a stick and drags it in the soft dirt, scratching a long line in the dust, then drops the stick. I find an interesting pebble on the edge of the road and pick it up to examine it. We walk along silently in the bright moonlight, not wanting to disturb the magic of the night. On and on we trudge. After half an hour we arrive at the top of the hill and now walk faster, downhill. We stop for a few minutes and sit on one of the beautiful white rocks. Mummy smokes a Craven A cigarette.

It seems as though we're walking for a long time, but since the night is so enchanting, it's fun. When we tire of silently walking along, we talk about the books Mummy has read to us—*Ivanhoe* and *Lorna Doone*. In addition to reading to us in the bomb shelter, she reads to us before we go to sleep every night.

I ask Mummy what time it is. She looks at her watch and says it's three o'clock in the morning. *Wow, we are almost never up this early.* We trudge on.

Finally, we see a light off ahead of us. On we walk. We arrive in a tiny village. We glance around. There're just a few little mud buildings. The light we see is shining from the window of a funny little building—a restaurant. How lovely it is that there's a restaurant here. How strange.

"I guess it's an all-night shop," Mummy says as we enter. A few straggly-looking men sit around smoking clay pipes. They look up, astonished. I hear an odd rasping sound, a gasp, six men and a lady gasp, almost in one breath. *We must be a surprising sight,* I think.

I look around and realize that the shop makes noodles. Mummy points to a small table, so we sit on the stools arranged around it. In the middle of the room a huge metal pot's suspended over a wood fire. In the ceiling above the pot there's a hole, and through this hole long, long strands of dough—noodles—fall. Mummy explains: A large lump of dough is placed on a wire grid over a hole in the floor of the room above us. Gravity and the weight of the dough push the dough through the grid and the noodles drop into the big pot of boiling water. John and I stare in amazement.

Mummy orders noodles for us. The lady serves us and gives us chopsticks. Everyone continues to stare. I laugh to myself. I suppose not many white ladies have stopped by here recently, stopping in out of nowhere, in the middle of the night and with two children.

Mummy says she's not worried that Daddy won't find us; there's only one street in this village and only one shop and it has a lit candle in its window.

A half hour passes, when, silently, our truck convoy rolls into the village. One by one, the trucks stop in front of the noodle shop.

Daddy rushes in. He looks worried and angry—very angry. This is a big surprise to me because Daddy is almost never angry. He asks Mummy to go outside with him. From where John and I sit next to the window, I hear Daddy telling Mummy that it was very dangerous of her to leave the protection of the group and to walk off by herself. I hear him say that this is an area famous for bandits and kidnappings. I hear Daddy say "You're very foolish" several times. "There're bandit gangs in these mountains," Daddy says again. "You are lucky your throats weren't cut. You and the children could have been taken hostage." Daddy is shaking. His face is red. I've never seen Daddy so angry.

After a while Mummy and Daddy return to our table. Mummy suggests that he have some noodles but Daddy says he's too upset to eat. After that Mummy is very quiet.

Ping San and the other men come in and eat. When everyone is finished, the men disappear in different directions. We go to a little mud building that's one of Daddy's Salt Administration offices. It's just one room. Daddy puts up his camp cot. I can see how tired he is by the slow way he's moving. Immediately after he's assembled the cot Daddy sits on a wooden chair and rests his head in his hands. Mummy has spread some bedding on the only desk, for John and me to sleep on. Daddy isn't the only one who's exhausted; we all are. John is shuffling his feet.

"What's the matter?" I ask John.

"Why did *your* truck go in the ditch and not mine?" he says indignantly. "You have all the luck."

I smile to myself. *John thinks it's exciting to land in a ditch! Boys have such funny ideas.*

The next day we arrive in Guiyang.

NOTES

1.   Guiyang, the capital of Guizhou Province, is surrounded by
      mountains and forests. It's a city of high elevation with a humid,
      monsoon-influenced subtropical climate. There are two parks in
      the area with caves that are now tourist attractions.

11

The Tiao-Tiao *Coolies*

Mid–November 1940
Guiyang, Guizhou Province, China

When we get to Guiyang, Daddy's office lends us a house on the outskirts of town. To keep John and me occupied and out of trouble, Mummy decides to send us to what she calls a school, but it's really a government-run day care center called Tou Er Saw—"day care center" in Chinese. Every morning we get up early and Mummy walks with us between lovely fields and along a dirt road to get to the school, about a mile away. There we join sixty, seventy, or more Chinese boys and girls, from babies to children up to age six. We're the only Westerners.

Tou Er Saw consists of a simple one-story, rectangular building standing in the middle of a sea of gravel surrounded by a high chain-link fence. The expanse of gravel includes a play area—swings, seesaws, and a large sandbox—and firmly in the middle of all the gravel, there's a tall flagpole flying the Kuomintang (KMT)[1] red-and-navy-blue flag.[2] Right behind the school building there's a big, smelly outhouse with an entrance on one side marked "Boys" and on the other marked "Girls." On the opposite side of the dirt road that runs in front of the school is the city dog pound, full of dirty, mangy, sad-looking yellow mongrels. The Chinese boys entertain themselves on their way to school by running sticks along the chain-link wire fence that surrounds the pound to infuriate the dogs, who bark and jump, attacking the fence.

Every school day begins with all the children standing at attention in a single line facing the flagpole and singing the national anthem while the KMT flag is raised.[3] After this, we're divided into age groups to be sent to play in a room with toys on the floor mats or to do other activities in one of the rooms furnished with low tables and stools. John and I spend our time playing, since the teachers don't expect anything much from us Western children—not even for us to behave!

After lunch and washing up, it's nap time. At one end of the school building is a large room that's been divided into multiple small cubicles, each furnished with four cribs, two per side. Each crib contains a child-size quilt and a Chinese pillow.[4] On our first day of school, John and I were affronted to discover that we were expected to nap in side-by-side cribs—cribs! As soon as the amah left upon lifting us into our cribs, we stood up and started tossing the pillows back and forth between us. This encouraged the two other children, who were Chinese, in our cubicle to join the fun. So, because of this, we naughty Westerners are now put outside each day to play while all the other children must nap.

There's no electricity or running water in the school build-ing. Nonetheless, our hygiene is well attended to. We each have our own pint-sized washbasin, towel, bar of soap, toothbrush, and toothpaste, all housed in a long, narrow room in the mid-dle of the building. Each small, brightly colored washbasin fits into a hole cut at a convenient height into one of the shelves that run down the long sides of the room. While we're eating lunch, a coolie fills each basin with warm water ready for us to wash up afterward. When we've finished washing, we simply tip our basins to let the wastewater flow into a trough that slopes toward the outside wall at the end of the room, where the water escapes through a hole into a barrel. We recognize the basins that're as-signed to us by their location, but mostly by their color. John and I have red and green basins. The teacher let us choose.

***

One day while John and I are swinging on the swings—the ac-tivity we spend most of our time doing—we're surprised to hear an air raid siren. It's the first time we've heard this blast since we left Chungking. The shrill wail is very loud—it must be close by. A moment later another siren starts up, farther away, in another part of the city. Now there are four siren songs, two choruses and two echoes. The sirens echo, back and forth, in the mountains that circle Guiyang. It's as if the mountains call us.

I crunch one foot down onto the gravel. The swing stops. John follows suit. We sit on the stationary swings and watch as three teachers run out of the building and look up at the sky.

"Hurry, hurry," one calls. The teachers are flustered but hastily regain their composure. "Line up. Quickly," another says. "We must go to the cave."

"Remember how we practiced," the third teacher says. "The smallest near me."

Suddenly, children appear from everywhere—from doorways, from around corners, from behind the building. They begin to form a single line, the youngest ones at the front behind the teacher, the older ones at the end of the line. Amahs hurry out of the building carrying babies they've plucked from their cribs. Glancing around, I'm surprised. I hadn't realized there were so many babies here.

John and I jump off the swings and run to join the others. There are toddlers too small to make the two-mile hike to the caves unassisted, so in order to help the toddlers, the amahs pass the smallest babies to the six-year-old children to carry. A pair of chubby little arms reach around my neck. The baby girl I've been handed is surprisingly light—she's like a doll. But I quickly realize she's not a doll, and the responsibility that's been given me is sobering. I hold her tiny body tightly. Most of the children are now standing nervously in a long line on the gravel. The line reaches around the side of the building all the way to and around the outhouse.

The teacher at the head of the line looks over our heads. "Follow me," she calls. She opens the chain-link gate and steps out. Single file, we pass through the narrow opening and turn left. I realize that we are moving in the direction opposite the one we take each morning when Mummy brings us to school. We're going toward the mountains, a direction we've not gone before. It's a bit alarming but exciting, too.

I look past the endless line of little black bobbing heads in front of me as the line disappears into tall grass, grass taller than most of us, along a narrow path between two paddy fields. Amahs and teachers have positioned themselves along the line.

"Hurry, hurry," an amah calls out.

"We don't have much time left to get to the cave," another amah adds.

The littler children trot along, trying their best to keep up, but their strides are short. Occasionally, teachers and amahs stop to help children with their shoes or to retie the bandannas that are tied over their shoulders, bandannas that support the babies they're carrying.

I look back toward the school and now-silent dog pound and see that our coolies, the ones who carry water, have picked up their *tiao-tiaos*—carrying-poles—for another purpose. They rescue the babies from the arms of the children struggling along at the end of the line with them, and place two babies per basket into the baskets tied to the ends of their carrying-poles. Then they lift the poles gently onto their shoulders, and move quickly off—bounce-bounce, bounce-bounce—in a loping trot toward the cave. I marvel at the coolies' speed and nimbleness as they brush past me. In front of me the children squeeze to one side, a ripple of bobbing black heads, to let the coolies pass them as they trudge along the sandy path.

At last, the air raid sirens stop. For a few minutes, the only sound is the shuffle of tiny feet clothed in cotton shoes. The birds are silent, their songs muzzled by the frightening screech. Even the crickets have paused their droning serenade. I sniff the air, fresh and sweet—country air.

We children trudge along, silent and serious, tired but resolute, in a long, long snakelike line leading up into the foothills. I remember the coffins that John and I watched from the window of our house in Chungking and think about how each of these children, here, is doing his part to save his own life and the lives of his friends, although he or she may not realize it. I look at the back of John's head and his tousled brown hair in front of me. I'm glad he's here.

A coolie stops me and lifts the little girl I've been carrying out of my arms. He carefully places her next to another baby in the basket of his tiao-tiao. He lifts the carrying-pole and is gone. I am grateful; my arms ache. The baby girl has become heavy, and it's difficult to walk uphill carrying her. I realize that the coolies have run back and forth many times, each time collecting babies from the back of the line and carrying them to the cave. I look at the back of the last stooped, muscular figure as he hurries up the path.

An hour later, we reach our destination, a large, dark, cool cave. As John and I enter, it's obvious that everyone's feet and legs ache, and no one needs to be told to sit down. We children huddle together along one wall. All the babies are lined up on the other side in the care of an amah.

One of the teachers suggests a song, and we begin to sing. We sing one Chinese song after another, and even though I don't know the words, I pretend to sing anyway. The songs calm us, and we hold each other by the hand. I think about our little cave under our house in Chungking. Here, as there, I hear the whistle of dropping bombs, each followed by a boom. But in this cave the bombs seem far away and unreal. *Where are Daddy and Mummy?* I think.

*****

An hour later the all-clear sounds. We line up to go back down the hill. This time it's easier. No need to hurry. No uphill trudge. No baby to carry.

Mummy's waiting for John and me in front of the school. The other children's mummies and daddies are also there, milling around. They look worried until they see their children coming down the path from the direction of the mountains and that they're safe. Everyone hugs someone.

Daddy comes for us with the car.

NOTES

1. The *Kuomintang* (KMT), Chinese for "People's Party," is also known as the Chinese Nationalist Party (CNP). Formed in 1919, the KMT was the sole ruling party of the Republic of China from 1928 until China lost its civil war (1945–49) to the Communist Party. It then retreated to Taiwan and continued there as the sole governing power until political reforms in the 1990s allowed the creation of a second political party.

2. The *Kuomintang* (KMT) flag consists of a red field with a blue upper-left quadrant containing a twelve-prong white star. A variant consists of just the blue field with the same large twelve-prong white star.

3. The national anthem of the *Kuomintang* (KMT) starts, "*San min chu-i,*" which means "The three principles of the people." I may never have known more than the first line, but certainly that's all I remember now, eighty years later! The anthem was adapted from a 1924 speech by politician, physician, and first leader of the KMT, Sun Yat-sen (1866–1925), and refers to the hopes and aspirations of a new nation.

4. Chinese bed pillows are about six by eight inches in size and are filled with dry rice, not feathers, because the Chinese consider rice to be healthy. These pillows very much resemble large Western beanbags. Ancient pillows were also made of bamboo or ceramics, which could incorporate a small compartment, a place for precious items, thus keeping them safe all night tucked under the sleeper's ear.

12

The Hankie

Early December 1940
Guiyang, Guizhou Province, China

Mummy tells us that in a few weeks we'll be leaving for Kunming,[1] Daddy's next assignment. In the meantime, there's a lot of excitement at school because the head teacher has announced that a special event is coming up—a *gymkhana*.[2]

"What's that?" I ask Daddy.

"It's a day of games and contests," Daddy says, and I'm intrigued. I wonder if there will be a contest to see who can swing the highest on the swings.

When the day of the gymkhana comes, the parents arrive in their best clothes and stand around chatting with each other, obviously proud of the children and their accomplishments, no matter how small the child or the accomplishment. The younger children dance and sing in age groups. The older ones recite poems. There's a tug-of-war and foot races, again by age group, and there's even a prize for the most elaborate sandcastle. There's an activity for everyone to excel in except the babies, who are oohed and aahed over by the grown-ups. It seems to me that the babies' way of participating in the festivities is by looking cute in their little red hats shaped like different animals, all with pointed ears.

The head teacher presents gifts to us all. The girls are given big fuchsia-pink bows for our hair, and the boys receive white cotton handkerchiefs on which a teacher has carefully inked the outline of a cartoon character in one corner. Little square tables are placed around on the gravel between the guests. Then tea is served.

"Oweeeee, I'm bleeding!" John wails, looking down at his knee as he runs from the direction of the swings. Blood trickles down his leg below his khaki shorts.

Mummy takes him in her arms. Tears stream down his face. Mummy pulls the new hankie, the one he's just received as a gift from the school, out of his pocket to dry his tears. Instead, he gets a black eye; black India ink smears across his cheek.

"It's time to say goodbye," Daddy says.[3]

NOTES

1.   Situated at the intersection of major east-west and north-south
      roads, Kunming was already an important trading town when it
      was completely transformed during World War II by the huge
      influx of people escaping from the east coast, many of whom
      were wealthy and were bringing dismantled industrial plants
      and universities with them to be reconstructed in Kunming.
      This newly imported expertise and trade established Kunming
      as Western China's wartime base. In 1938, Lt. Col. Claire Lee
      Chennault trained Chinese pilots there, and Kunming was the
      headquarters of the American Flying Tigers, as well as being the
      eastern end of the Burma Road and the US military ferry route
      over the Himalayas.

2.   *Gymkhana* is an Anglo-Indian word that in the past referred to
      a place where athletic games and contests took place or to the
      athletic meet itself, with an emphasis on children's participation.
      In more modern times, it usually refers to an equestrian activity
      with speed races and timed games.

3.   Besides the trip to the bomb-shelter cave—which has now been
      incorporated into a park—what I remember best about the time
      I spent at *Tou Er Saw* is the "quilt-fluffing man." One day, an itin-
      erant "quilt-fluffer" arrived with what looked like a big fiddle
      bow over his shoulder, and was immediately installed in one of
      the classrooms; all the quilts from the cribs and cots throughout
      the day care center were then brought to him. For the following
      week, all we heard emanating from that room was a whirring
      noise as he dismantled each little quilt and fluffed up the cotton
      stuffing to revitalize its capacity to warm. We children were not
      allowed into the room; thus, the quilt-fluffing man and his ac-
      tivities were a mystery. Nevertheless, I enjoyed the gentle, warm
      whirring sound that he produced.

13

Of Boils and Bandits

Last Week of December 1940
The Road Between Guiyang, Guizhou Province,
China, and Kunming, Yunnan Province, China

Daddy again has arranged for us to travel with a convoy of Red Cross trucks, and Daddy, Mummy, Ping San, John, and I leave for Kunming early one morning. Usually, Daddy and Mummy and Ping San ride in different trucks, wherever there's room, and John and I ride with one of them. In addition to medical supplies, foodstuffs, and whatever else is needed, the old US Army trucks that belong to the Red Cross carry tires, barrels of gasoline, and spare parts, in case of a breakdown. All the trucks are driven by aid workers or their helpers.

It's the first night out, and because there's nowhere to stay in these small towns, the Red Cross workers drop us off at one of Daddy's country offices for the night. Each of Daddy's offices is different. This one consists of a gated two-story building that faces into an enclosed courtyard, the second floor of which is reached by an outside staircase at one corner and along a wall. At right angles to the top of these stairs, a long balcony runs the length of the building and several offices open onto it.

Daddy squeezes past John and me, sitting on the bottom step, as he carries a camp cot up to one of the offices on the second floor. John and I watch Ping San as he prepares to roast a chicken for dinner. He places the metal tray holding the chicken on the hard-packed earth in the middle of the courtyard. Then he places a rectangular ten-gallon tin, one side of which has been cut out, over the chicken and heaps red-hot coals, which he's prepared in a nearby brazier, over the tin. After constructing this impromptu oven, he leaves for the storage room, where he's arranged his cooking utensils and will also spend the night. I look at John. We wait impatiently for the chicken to roast.

Twenty minutes later a heady aroma floats through the court-yard; my mouth waters.

John looks at me and then goes off to find something to play with. He returns with a large red rubber ball that he bounces against the wall beside the stairs. Bounce bounce, bounce bounce. The ball hits the wall and the ground in front of him, back and forth. I decide to swing on the metal gate to distract myself from my hunger, but when I step onto the gate, I find that its hinges are rusty and it doesn't swing freely. I return to my seat on the bottom step.

Bounce bounce, bounce bounce; John continues to play with

the ball when suddenly it bounces over the wall. "Ohhhh, Ferfer," he shrieks. "My ball!"

"Get Daddy," I reply. We're not allowed outside the compound without an adult.

John finds Daddy upstairs. They run down the stairs, out the gate, and around the corner of the compound. They're just in time to see a little white-haired lady hurrying off, a big red ball under her arm.

John and Daddy stop short. "It belongs to another little boy now," Daddy says as he takes John's hand. They turn and return to the compound.

***

After dinner, Daddy gets a large, oval copper tub, one of the many things he's unloaded from the truck, and places it in the courtyard. Ping San fills it with a few inches of warm water, and John and I get baths. In the upstairs office, Daddy assembles the camp cot while Mummy rolls out a quilt on one of the desks, adding some sheets and a blanket for John and me to sleep under.

Moonlight streams over the little compound, and all is silent. Exhausted, we quickly fall asleep. The last thing I see before I close my eyes is Generalissimo Chiang Kai-shek's icy gaze from his picture on the wall behind the desk. *Does every office in China have a Generalissimo in it?* I ask myself.

***

Ping San's asleep on his bedroll in the storeroom and we're in the office on the second floor when we're awakened by a loud pop, then another.

Daddy leaps off the cot next to the desk where he and Mummy were snuggled together, almost knocking Mummy off the bed. "What's that?" he whispers. "It sounds like gunshots." Daddy slides up to the side of the window and looks down into the courtyard.

I'm wide awake and see that Mummy and John are too.

"Perhaps bandits," Daddy says. "Stay calm." Then he looks through the window again. "I don't see anything," he says. "But bandits are common in this area."

Bang.

Daddy puts his hand on the doorknob. "It sounds close—from the courtyard," Daddy whispers.

We wait to see what will happen next. All is quiet. We wait some more. "That's strange," Daddy says. He peers out of the window. Finally, when nothing more happens, he gets back on the cot next to Mummy. "It sounded so close. But I didn't see any movement," he mutters. "Tomorrow . . . ," he whispers and gets back under his covers.

The next morning, I hear Ping San tell Daddy that the corks in the bottles of yeast that he always carries with him to make bread had popped out during the night. Daddy doesn't reply, just shakes his head and smiles.

What also popped out during the night is a big red puffy wet spot on my left calf. My leg hurts. "Ouch, Mummy," I say, "I can't walk."

Mummy looks at it and says it's a boil. I hop around the room on my right foot as I get dressed. Then I hop out onto the balcony and down the stairs, slowly, holding on to the railing with both hands. I am sitting on the bottom step, feeling sorry for myself, when Ping San comes to look at my boil.

"It's bad." Ping San frowns. "Ping San can fix," he adds and turns to go back to his room. After a few minutes, he returns carrying half of a ripe tomato that he's heated in a frying pan. He tells me not to move while he carefully places the cut side of the tomato over the boil. It feels hot and smells bad but feels good. "Don't move. I'll get a piece of ginger dipped in honey for you." Ping San smiles and pats my shoulder.

***

The next morning is Christmas. John and I wake to discover one of our own stockings safety-pinned to the sheets next to our pillows. Each is stuffed with exciting little things. We quickly unpack them. In my stocking I find two oranges, some walnuts, a little doll, a yo-yo, a whistle, two barrettes, and my favorite toffees from England. Like me, John has a yo-yo, a whistle, and fruit, but he also has a blue rubber ball, a penknife that's not very sharp, and two little cars, one red and one green. We play with our new toys as quietly as we can so we don't wake Mummy and Daddy. I'm glad that Father Christmas can find us wherever we are, even when we're not at home in Shanghai.

14

Tungsten

*Last Week of December 1940
The Road Between Guiyang, Guizhou Province,
China, to Kunming, Yunnan Province, China*

The morning after Christmas, I feel fine. The boil's almost gone and I skip around in a circle in the courtyard.

The trucks come to pick us up for the day's journey. We are on our way to Kunming, where Daddy plans to rent a car and driver to take us to Lashio, Burma, where we'll stay while he goes to Rangoon. Mummy doesn't tell us why Daddy's going to Rangoon. I wonder if his trip is to see the English officers I saw him talking to in Shanghai. Mummy says driving down the Burma Road will be an interesting trip; this part of China is wild, and many different ethnic people live here.[1]

While standing around waiting for Daddy to tell me which of

the trucks to ride in, I look into the back of one. It looks empty except for two fifty-five-gallon drums that I know are full of gasoline. As Daddy loads the bundled camp cot and bedding into a different truck, I examine this one more closely and see that the entire truck bed is covered in a layer of what looks like individually cloth-wrapped bricks. I don't understand what's so precious about bricks that they need to be wrapped in cloth. You can get them everywhere. I often see men making them from mud and setting them out in the sun to dry on the side of the road. I want to ask Daddy about this, but I see that he's busy.

All loaded, we start off driving west. For once Mummy, Daddy, John, and I can all ride together in the first truck with the driver; Ping San's in another one. Soon we're slowly bumping along the main road, dodging water buffalo, carts, goats, donkeys, and pedestrians trudging along on each side.

"How far is Kunming?" I ask Daddy.

"It's about three hundred twenty miles," Daddy says. "It'll take us a few days to get there because the way is very mountainous."

"Look, Daddy." John points excitedly to what looks like a group of people walking along ahead of us in the distance.

We move slowly along the road and finally reach a dozen or so men, their clothes torn, stained, and grimy but still recognizable as Nationalist Army uniforms. Most wear bandages in a haphazard manner. Many limp, and one is hobbling along using a tree branch under one arm as support. At the back of the group two men carry a soldier on a stretcher.

"Why are these men here?" the driver asks Daddy. "There're no Japs in this area."

Daddy looks at the driver's eyes in the rearview mirror and

slowly says, "My guess is that they've been fighting Communists, not Japanese."

Mummy looks alarmed. "Fighting! We need to find out where there's fighting around here."

Suddenly, as we approach the last stragglers, a short, stout soldier steps out in front of the truck, turns to face us, and raises his arm—a pistol in his hand.

Mummy gasps.

"Stop," Daddy says softly to the driver. He stops the truck.

Mummy grabs my arm and I look sideways at her, not knowing whether I should be terrified or not. John opens his mouth to say something, but Mummy shakes her head slightly, and he silently closes it. She glances at the driver. He's sitting stiffly and staring straight ahead.

Daddy, who's been sitting by the door, opens it slowly and slides out of the cab. He circles the front of the truck and bows his head, politely. "Good morning, Officer," he says.

"Take my men in your truck," the officer barks.

"I regret, sir, that's not possible," Daddy says. The officer stands resolutely, staring at Daddy. There's a long pause. Daddy gestures an invitation to the officer to follow him around to the back of the vehicle. Mummy, John, and I slowly turn to watch what's happening through the cab's back window.

Now both men are behind the truck. The officer pushes the canvas aside with one hand and grunts, as he again brandishes the pistol. "You take the men. The truck is empty," he spits out the demand. His voice is low and gruff.

Slowly, Daddy lifts the canvas that hangs across the back a

little further. I see both men look in. "The truck's not empty," Daddy says in a calm voice, "it carries metal bricks."

"The truck's empty," the officer repeats, firearm still aimed at Daddy.

Daddy points toward the truck bed. "These bricks are very heavy," he says, calmly. "Please allow me, sir, to invite you to lift one of them." Again, Daddy bows politely.

The officer places the pistol back on his hip. Gripping the side of the truck, he pulls himself up onto the back bumper, leans over, and casually grasps a brick with one hand. It doesn't budge; it remains glued to the truck bed. Surprised, the officer tries again, this time using two hands. Still the brick does not budge. The officer glares at the neat rows of bricks, a puzzled look on his sweat-streaked face. Then, angrily, the officer jumps down from the bumper. Waving his arm over the space above the bricks he again demands that Daddy allow his injured soldiers to board. "Take my soldiers to the next town," he demands loudly. "You must take my men to the next town." Although he sounds fierce, I see that he's not removed his pistol from its holster again. That's a relief.

Daddy and the Chinese officer look at each other silently. Then, taking a step toward the truck, Daddy calmly says, "I can take one soldier. I can take the soldier on the stretcher."

The officer's shoulders slump slightly, then he straightens up and looks at Daddy. "You must also take the men that carry the soldier," he says.

Daddy nods and offers his hand to the officer. The officer shakes Daddy's hand.

At this gesture, Mummy, John, and I take a deep breath and relax just a little.

The officer then orders the two stretcher bearers to load the wounded soldier into the back of the truck; they slide the stretcher with some difficulty over the wrapped bricks, then climb in and squat beside the injured man.

After Daddy assures the officer that we'll take the wounded man to someone in the next town who can care for him, he climbs back into the cab. There're drops of sweat on Daddy's neck although it's not hot outside. Daddy waves at the officer and his men as we slowly pull away from the side of the road and gain speed.

Later, Daddy tells me that the bricks are made of tungsten,[2] which is why they're so heavy.

We have not driven very far when—tap, tap, tap—one of the stretcher bearers has crawled up to the window at the back of the cab and is knocking on it.

Startled, the driver slams on the brakes. Then he pulls slowly to the roadside. Daddy jumps out of the cab and runs around to the back.

"Water, water," the soldier on the stretcher whispers in a pleading tone, pointing at a metal barrel.

"Oh," Daddy says, "that's not water." Then, "It's not water," he repeats. "I'm very sorry, but it's gasoline."

When Daddy returns to the cab, he tells us that the wounded soldier must have malaria because he's very thirsty, begging for water. Daddy thinks that when we started up, the poor man heard the gas sloshing back and forth in the metal drums and thought it was water.

"I have water in this thermos," Mummy says, passing the flask to Daddy.

"Please, stop again," Daddy says to the driver. And we stop.

NOTES

1. There are fifty-six ethnic minorities in China, twenty-six of which are represented in Yunnan Province (but are not necessarily unique to Yunnan). The people in each minority group, many of which have subgroups, speak their own language or dialect and have their own costumes, customs, artwork, music, dances, festivals, and traditions.

2. Tungsten carbonite is the second-hardest substance (diamonds being the hardest) and is two and a half times denser than iron. During World War II, it was an integral part of the production of more than fifteen thousand military wares and thus was vital to the war effort. At the beginning of the twentieth century, China was the biggest producer of tungsten, followed by Burma and the United States. When the Japanese captured Shanghai, the export of tungsten through this east coast port was disrupted, requiring a westerly exit route. Tungsten was therefore transported by train to Rangoon and then by ship or plane to the United States over the air ferry route.

   An interesting sidebar on this subject is that throughout World War II, China traded with Germany—tungsten for firearms.

15

Miss Morgan

First Week of January 1941
Kunming, Yunnan Province, China, and
Chuxiong, Yunnan Province, China

We arrive in Kunming and settle in at a guesthouse on Shulingkai Road. It has stone steps in front where we sit in the evening because the weather's warm, even though it's January. While Daddy gets the things we need for our trip on the Burma Road,[1] Mummy takes John and me to see the city.

First we go to Green Lake Park, a large park with lovely lakes and humpback bridges. We rent a rowboat, but Mummy can't row very well and the boat goes around in circles; John and I are no better. Then we walk around and watch as people throw bread up in the air for big white birds with black tails to catch.

"Mummy, please buy some bread for the birds," John asks, pointing to a vendor on the edge of the path.

"I don't think you can throw it high enough," Mummy says. "Look how the men are doing it. Let's just watch."

Whoops! Mummy tries to dodge, but a large bird dropping hits her shoulder—*squish*. "Run!" she says, so we race out of Green Lake Park. Then we walk a few blocks to the bird market. Here we stroll up and down two narrow streets and paths between the streets and look at all the different kinds of birds hopping around in little bamboo cages.

We see a man carrying a cage with a beautiful yellow bird in it. He lifts the cage up with a hook on the end of a long pole and hangs it on a bar next to a row of other cages. Some of the birds twitter and one even sings, but most just continue to hop around silently pecking at the little cups of food in their cages.

After we get back to the guesthouse and have lunch with Daddy, Mummy tells us to take a nap because we are starting off in the early evening. Daddy has rented a car and driver, and we'll join a convoy of trucks that are also going on the only road that goes to Lashio, Burma.

"Why are we leaving so late?" I ask, as we usually leave in the early mornings.

"We have to travel at night because of the war, Ferfer," Daddy says, "and we don't want the Japanese to see us. The drivers will darken the cars' headlights by painting the upper half of each light black. And we'll be crossing rivers on temporary bridges, pontoon bridges, that are made to disappear during the day."

John puts down his toy truck and looks attentively at Daddy. "Disappear?"

"The bridges are actually a row of little flat-bottom boats that are linked together side by side. Boards are then laid across the boats to form a roadbed," Daddy continues. "To hide the bridge from the Japanese, men unfasten one end of its moorings and let the river current carry the bridge downstream until all the little boats lie against the opposite bank, where shrubs and branches are pulled over them. They do this every day just before dawn." Daddy takes a deep breath. "Then, after dusk each evening, a man swims across the river with one end of the rope tied around his waist and the other tied onto the first pontoon boat. In this way he pulls the bridge back into place."

John rubs his eyes. I see that he's very sleepy. Daddy's story about the pontoon bridge and how it's made every day is interesting, and I'm looking forward to seeing the floating roadbed. I turn to ask John something about the bridge but he interrupts me.

"Daddy," he says as Daddy tucks him into bed.

"Yes, small son."

"Please get me another red ball."

I know John's interested in the bridge, but he misses his big red ball. It was his constant companion when there were no children for him to play with, so his lost ball is on his mind. And because we don't have Daddy's attention all that often, he takes every opportunity to remind Daddy about it when we do.

***

When Mummy wakes John and me at five o'clock, I see that Ping San has organized near the front door the camp bed, the bedding, the portable box with a bucket in it Daddy had made for

Mummy, and a pile of suitcases. He's also packed canned food and cooking utensils. I know he gets fresh vegetables and chickens along the way.

Someone knocks. The driver has arrived with the car, a black Buick. The driver is a wiry little man with a wispy black beard and watery eyes. He smiles, and I'm surprised to see that his teeth are red. Behind him stands a boy of about ten or twelve. The driver introduces himself as Mr. Chou and the boy as his assistant, Xiao, which means "small" in Chinese. Daddy goes out to look over the Buick as Mr. Chou and Xiao load our baggage into it.

We leave to meet the convoy, with Ping San squeezed into the front with the driver and Xiao. Half an hour later, Ping San gets out of the car and into the last truck as we join the end of the convoy. After Daddy returns from talking to the men in the truck, we're off.

***

The road is bumpy. Thankfully, Mummy has remembered, as she always does, to bring something in case I feel sick. Silently, she produces a red plastic basin about a foot in diameter and passes it to me. Luckily I don't need it. Not yet, at least.

We leave the city. The buildings begin to thin out. We drive between mud cottages and then between green fields and rice paddies.

"Stop," Daddy says, "please stop the car." Mr. Chou stops. Then to my surprise, Xiao jumps out from beside him and runs

behind the car and quickly jams a triangular block of wood behind each tire. After this is repeated each time we stop, I realize
that in addition to passing shelled betel nuts to Mr. Chou,[2] this is
Xiao's primary responsibility.

Daddy walks behind some bushes to go to the bathroom.
I'm glad Daddy told the driver to stop. I needed to go behind the
bushes as well, but hadn't realized it.

Back in the car, I'm lulled by the growing twilight and the
bumpy road, and fall asleep cuddled against Mummy, who is also
sleeping. When I awake, it's inky dark. We are crawling along
even more slowly than before. The car stops with a jerk, and Xiao
jumps out with his wooden blocks. Daddy and Mr. Chou get out
and I see in the moonlight that we're stopped at the end of a very
long line of trucks. The drivers have turned off their engines
and are standing around in the grass along the edge of the road,
stretching, chatting, sharing cigarettes. Some trucks have their
hoods raised. I suppose it's to cool the engines that always seem
to get very hot.

"Why are all the trucks stopping?" I ask Daddy.

Daddy turns his head into the breeze. "It feels like we've come
to a river," Daddy says, "and so the cars must wait their turn to
cross." He has spread out a map on the front of the car and is
looking at it with a flashlight. "I think it must be the Tanglang
River. We've gone about fifty-six miles since we left Kunming."
Daddy rubs his eyes. "Mr. Chou, do you know the name of the
village we just passed?"

"Anning," Mr. Chou says.

After about twenty minutes, we hear the trucks ahead of us

start their motors one by one. When there's movement immediately in front of us, Daddy quickly folds the map and we all jump back into the car as Xiao grabs his wooden blocks.

Slowly we creep along behind the truck in front of us. When we reach the water's edge, a man on the side of the road waves to us to wait. We stop and the engine is turned off, then it's restarted a few minutes later when we're waved on. Thump, thump. Slowly we inch ahead. The car dips and moves forward. Looking out the open window, I see water rushing by under the car. We are on a very narrow pontoon bridge. Thump, thump. We pick up a little speed as we edge across the river. Thump, thump. Thump, thump. Our dimmed headlights flash onto each successive pontoon boat as we pass over it. Thump, thump. Thump, thump. Finally, we're crossing the last little boat and the road climbs away from the river. I look back through the rear window. I can just see the shadow of the man whose job it is to control the vehicles as they drive onto the bridge, waving to the next truck. Its lights shine onto the first pontoon boat.

Mummy breathes a sigh next to me. "How far are we from Chuxiong?" she asks. "I'm looking forward to seeing Miss Morgan."[3] I know that Miss Morgan has offered us a place to stay overnight on our first day on the Burma Road.

"Not far, now, darling," Daddy says. "But it's taking a while because we have to drive slowly."

We pick up speed, although we're still only driving ten to twelve miles an hour. The road is steep, narrow, winding, and rough, and the dim light and the slow speed of the trucks in front of us are limiting our progress.

"Mummy, I'm hungry," John says.

"And I'm cold," I add.

"Let's have a sandwich while we're all still awake," Mummy says. "And I'll get sweaters out for both of you."

"I'm sure you realize that we've been driving uphill since we crossed the pontoon bridge," Daddy says.

"Yes, Daddy," I say sleepily. I did realize that, and I also realize that the car has made many, many, many sharp turns in which it had to stop and back up. I'm glad Mummy remembered the red basin.

***

Sometime after dawn, we arrive at the courtyard at Miss Morgan's. Miss Morgan is a tiny lady wearing wire-rimmed glasses, her brown hair twisted into a small bun on the back of her neck. She wears a Chinese padded jacket and trousers.

"Please, please, come in," she says. "You are most welcome to the Lord's house." Miss Morgan bows as she extends her arm in a welcoming gesture. "May I introduce my assistant, Marjorie," she says. "And these are my daughters."

Two young women bow shyly. Mummy and Daddy have told us Miss Morgan has three adopted Chinese children.

"My son, Michael, is away at one of my other stations at the moment," she says. "Would you like some tea? You must be cold and tired."

I notice that Miss Morgan is speaking to us in English. She appears to enjoy the chance to use her native language, although she does so hesitantly, as if it's a rare opportunity.

"We were driving all night," Mummy says, "so we're a bit confused."

Daddy tells the driver to come back for us the following morning. He tells me that the men will sleep in the trucks. They like to make sure their cargoes are safe from thieves, he says. "Mr. Chou will want to protect his Buick, too," Daddy adds with a wink.

⁂

Miss Morgan takes a sip of tea, then says she'd like to tell us how she found her children. "One day I'm riding my horse on my way to another of my stations," she begins, "and as I pass the city dump, I happen to glance over and I think I see something move. So I dismount and go to investigate, and what do I find but a little baby, a baby girl! She couldn't have been more than a few weeks old.

"I was delighted. I always wanted a child of my own, and here she was. Truly, a gift from God. So I immediately take her up and clasp her to my chest, the dear little thing. I then ride as fast as I can to find a new mother who will share her breast milk with my baby, which I do, and here is the result of that blessed day." Miss Morgan smiles broadly.

"What a lovely story," Mummy says.

"And my second daughter was given to me by her father," Miss Morgan continues. "One day, a man came to me and said, 'Please take my little girl. Her mother died and I cannot care for her when I go to work in the fields. You have one daughter, and it's just as easy to raise two daughters together.' So I did. I was thankful to accept this second gift from God."

After we have our tea, Daddy and Mummy go off to discuss the war. Miss Morgan's busy too. John and I ask if we can go into the courtyard where Miss Morgan's daughters are playing.

NOTES

1. The Burma Road is 1,154 kilometers (717 miles) long and runs through Yunnan Province from Kunming, China, to Lashio, Burma, through the highest mountains in the world, the Himalayas. It was built between 1938 and 1939 by two hundred thousand Chinese laborers, men and women who were brought from all over Yunnan Province because there were not enough local people to do the work. These laborers camped on the land while they worked with very few tools beyond their bare hands.

   The Burma Road was built to transport military supplies into Western China after the Japanese captured China's eastern coast. It is only wide enough for two cars to pass, and in many places it's carved into the side of the mountain, thus having a precipice on one side and a sheer wall of earth on the other. In order to ascend and descend the elevations that are as high as 1,830 meters (six thousand feet), the road has a great many hairpin bends, up to sixty-eight in one 6.5-kilometer (four-mile) stretch and fifty-three in another; these bends are so sharp that a vehicle is forced to stop and back up to make the turn. To conserve gasoline, it was customary during World War II for drivers to turn off their motors and coast when going downhill, and since there were no service stations along the way, trucks carried their own gasoline in fifty-five-gallon drums, as well as spare parts and tires. Because the drivers came from many different cultures and were often illiterate, road signs consisted of pictures, such as a skull and crossbones to indicate danger and a bulb horn to advise drivers when to sound their horn.

2. Betel nuts, the seeds of a type of palm tree, are chewed by millions of people in the Far East. The practice has been passed down through generations. Betel nuts are thought to produce an energy boost; they have a mildly stimulating effect that is comparable to that produced by caffeine and nicotine, and they are considered just as addictive. Some studies indicate that betel nuts may cause cancer, while other studies suggest that they fight it. Chewing betel nuts over a long period stains the teeth reddish black.

3.　　As a child, Arkansas-born Cornelia Ada Morgan met the Chinese ambassador to the United States while visiting her grandfather, a US senator whose home was next door to the Chinese ambassador in Washington, DC. The Chinese ambassador so enchanted Miss Morgan with stories of Yunnan Province that years later, when she learned that the China Inland Mission (CIM)—an international, interdenominational Protestant Christian organization—was seeking missionaries for China, she resolved to go. It was 1907. Some years later, when her request to her superiors at the Mission to be posted to Yunnan was refused (they felt the province was too remote a posting for a lady), she left the CIM and worked for many years independently in Yunnan, often working under harsh circumstances, walking countless miles per day with little food. The Communist takeover in 1949 forced Miss Morgan to leave China. She died in the United States with her son, Michael, who has become a US citizen and minister, by her side.

16

The Black Cow
Salt Mine

Two Days Later in January 1941
Near Chuxiong, Yunnan Province, China

The next morning, Daddy announces we're going to visit a nearby salt mine called the Black Cow Mine.[1] It's not a mine that people go down into, he tells us; it's a deep hole in the ground.

"Why does it have that funny name?" John asks.

"Oh, I suppose that the man who first discovered it saw a black cow nearby," Daddy laughs. "Anyway, it's interesting to see how they get the salt out of the ground. Would you like to see that, little son?"

"Oh yes, Daddy," John says.

"Oh yes please, Daddy," I echo.

Mr. Chou stops the car on the side of the road, and we get out. We walk along a path for about half an hour. While we're walking, Daddy tells us about salt, how valuable it is, why it's mined, and how many governments use it to tax people, because everyone needs salt. Daddy's explaining about taxes when, abruptly, we come over the top of a small hill and see the mine—swarms of people running in all directions and steam, steam, steam rising into the air. What a surprise! It reminds me of an anthill. Daddy tells John and me to stand on a grassy spot so we're not in anyone's way, and he'll explain how the mine works.

"This is a brine mine," Daddy says. "First, a very deep hole, about four inches in diameter, is bored into the ground. Then a tube made of bamboo is pushed down the hole." Daddy looks around. "Do you see the three mules walking around in a circle there?" He points. "The wheel that the mules are harnessed to is attached to a bamboo tube, and as they walk around and around, this tube is forced sometimes as much as a half mile down into the ground and into a huge underground pool of salt water. When that happens, the salt water gushes up the tube, and the men that you see over there catch this water in buckets and carry it into the shed where all that steam is billowing out of."

John and I follow Daddy's finger as he points to a low structure. We take a few steps to the left so we can see into the shed more clearly. The men are pouring the water into huge round pans that stand, steaming, over fires. "Wood or charcoal is used for the fires," Daddy continues, "which make the water slowly evaporate, leaving salt." Daddy points further up the slope, beyond the shed, to men carrying big round dirty-white slabs of something on their backs. "That's the dry salt as it was left in a pan," Daddy says. At this distance I can just make out that each man has a strap tied around the circle of salt and around his forehead. Farther along the path I see mules loaded with these slabs, being readied to leave. "That's how it's done," Daddy says.

We stand and watch. There's a gust of wind. Steam billows out from under the shed.

I watch as raggedy children scrape the path where we saw the bucket carriers pass. "Daddy, what are those children doing?" I ask. "They look so poor and skinny."

"They're scraping up bits of salt. It's what's left from the water that was spilled by the water carriers on their way to the pans," Daddy says. "There's no tax on that salt."

Silently, we walk back to the car. I think about the children scraping at the dirt in their dirty, torn clothes. I hope the war doesn't come to them; their lives are hard enough already.

Mummy and Daddy don't talk about the Japanese and the war when John and I can hear, but I know that they're thinking about them all the same. The war seems to be creeping closer every day. I don't know if we are moving toward it or away from it. Or maybe it's everywhere, and we won't be able to get away from it at all.

We walk back to the car and learn that we must hurry to join the caravan of Red Cross trucks we're traveling with. They're waiting for us along the main road.

***

As we drive along, Mummy points out some unusual fields. The plants have very big leaves. "Tobacco," she says.

Here the road is flat and runs beside a river for a few miles. Daddy pulls his map out. "I can't find the name of this river," he says. "On the map its name changes several times!" Daddy tries to flatten the map on his lap, but it's hard to do in the jostling car and the cramped space. The next time the convoy stops, Daddy decides to ride in the truck with Ping San.

We drive slowly along, trying not to get too close to the truck in front of us, to avoid mud from its tires splashing up on our windshield. Occasionally, Mr. Chou stops and Xiao jumps out and wipes the window with a very muddy rag. We pass a recent landslide; the earth's been shoveled aside just enough for trucks to pass. Once, trying to get past an area of deep mud, the car gets stuck. "It's not long since the rainy season," Daddy says as he and Xiao get out to push.

John and I watch all day as we slowly climb and then descend mountains, endlessly crawling along, watching the line of trucks and an occasional car in front of us, stopping, backing up, and starting again to make the sharp turns, and then doing it over and over again. Driving uphill we hear motors struggling along. Going downhill there's silence, the motors turned off. Every once in a while, a metallic screech punctuates the quiet. The first time this happens, John asks what's making that sound, and Daddy tells us that it's a truck's brakes.

Long sections of the road have been cut into the side of the mountain, so when you're sitting on one side of the car all you can see is the tall mudbank, and on the other you can see forever—deep into the valley. Often there's a river at the bottom of the mountain. John and I take turns sitting on the side of the car that faces away from the wall of earth. Often when I look into the valley below, I see the remains of a truck that left the road and rolled over and over down the hill. All that now remains of these trucks are bare, rusting skeletons. Daddy says that the villagers pull off everything they can use or sell.

John and I get tired of looking at the countryside, so we play a game called "animal, vegetable, or mineral" until the trucks stop. The men get out to pee, smoke, and stretch.

We get out too. I overhear Daddy and Mummy. "How far do the aid workers plan to drive today?" Mummy asks.

"They're ambitious," Daddy replies. "They hope to reach Dali. It's an important local market town. We should get there shortly after dark if we don't run into any problems."

✻✻✻

Several hours later we've ascended and descended two mountain ranges. On the last descent we see a river glistening far below. We continue slowly. Then all the trucks stop, and we stop behind the last one. Xiao jumps out with his blocks and Daddy comes back to tell us to look closely at the approach to the bridge below. When we look, we see that all the drivers have gotten out of their trucks and are congregated on the bank at our end of the bridge.

Now that the roar of the motors has been silenced, I can hear the rush of water over rocks in the deep gorge below; the river gurgles and rushes over massive boulders, hurls itself against the stone piers, and sends sprays of water into the air below the bridge. I sniff. How fresh the air is!

John points. "Look," he says excitedly, "the bridge is made entirely of bamboo."[2] We stare intently, and I see that the entire suspension bridge is indeed made of bamboo; strand after strand of split bamboo has been wound, woven, and tied together to form every section of it, even the suspension ropes and poles. Daddy takes out his Leica and snaps pictures.

As John and I sit on a bank and watch, we see the men unload the first truck and pile spare tires, gasoline drums, boxes, bundles, and barrels on the grass beside the men. Then we see a man walk onto the bridge, hold the bamboo railing, and, after he looks down at the surging water hundreds of feet below, walk to the middle of the bridge and then wave to the driver of the first truck. Gingerly the driver inches the truck onto the creaking, groaning, swaying bridge. I hold my breath. He drives a few more inches; slowly, slowly the truck moves forward. The guide walks a little farther across the bridge and turns to motion to the driver again. I watch as this scene is repeated over and over until the truck reaches the opposite bank.

The crossing a success, the driver jumps out of his cab and, running to the man who guided him, gives him a huge hug. When they see that the first truck is safely across, a cheer erupts from the men lounging on the grass on our side of the river. The men jump up to move the truck's contents; they roll the gasoline drums and spare tires and carry the boxes and bundles over the bridge to the other side. Then, returning to their own vehicles, they unload everything—spare tires, barrels, bundles, and drums, and stack the baggage beside their trucks.

In this way, each truck is unloaded and carefully driven across the bamboo bridge, to be followed by its contents, which the men then reload. Finally it's our turn. Mummy tells us to get back in the car.

"But the other men walked!" John says indignantly.

"Our car with everything in it is not as heavy as one truck." Mummy's tone is serious.

Daddy smiles. "Get in," he says as he opens the door to Xiao and his wooden blocks.

***

Hours later we roll into Xiangyun village and find Daddy's office in one of the back streets. Here we wearily make up our beds on desktops and Daddy sets up the camp cot. After a little cold food, we're ready to turn in for the night.

"Tomorrow we'll go to Dali. It's about five miles north," Daddy says.

"And tomorrow, Monday, is market day in Dali, so that should be fun," Mummy adds.

NOTES

1. Salt has been mined in China for two thousand years and used as the basis for taxing its citizens for almost as long. Salt is not only mined as brine and as crystals, but also evaporated from seawater. The salt towns in Yunnan Province include Chuxiong village and three smaller villages—Heijing, Nuodeng, and Shiyang. These made up the ancient Chinese salt route.

2. Although I cannot find a bamboo bridge in Yunnan, or anywhere else in China, on the internet, both my brother John and I vividly remember this bridge and how vehicles very carefully drove across it. Perhaps the bamboo bridge was destroyed in World War II.

17

Market Day in Dali

Mid-January 1941
Dali, Yunnan Province, China

The sun's just risen when Mummy gets us up the next morning.

"Market day starts early," she says as she bundles us into sweaters and our winter snowsuits.

We drive through narrow streets and the west gate of Dali's old city wall until we burst upon a colorful scene.[1] Crowds of people bustle between huge baskets of vegetables and makeshift tables piled high with all manner of other goods. Everyone is chatting or maybe haggling, discussing prices, and no doubt gossiping, too, passing along what's new since last Monday's market day. I hold Mummy's hand. She bends down to whisper in my ear, discreetly pointing out a lady in an interesting blue outfit with a blue headdress that looks like a donut; she calls it a Bai ethnic costume.[2] Another lady in a Bai headdress is wearing a red vest and a little black apron. We pass a row of baskets and tables. Mummy admires various green, leafy vegetables, nodding to the lady behind the basket, although we don't know exactly what the vegetables are. They're new to us.

Mummy speaks to another lady, who's wearing a multicolored round headdress, about the blue print fabric she displays; it's a tie-dyed print with countless tiny butterflies all over it. The lady unrolls the bale a bit more and tells us that the men in her family grow the plants to make the blue dye, the ladies tie the pattern into the fabric, and everyone dips the fabric in the indigo liquid. She also tells Mummy that this is a special craft of the Yi people and that each family in the clan has its own unique design;[3] her family's design is butterflies. She points to the many tiny butterflies scattered over the tie-dyed fabric. It's very hard for me not to laugh because the lady calls the butterflies "butterfleas" in English. And I see she is very proud that she knows some English words. Mummy buys several yards and tells me she'll make a tablecloth with it. I see Daddy nearby in the crowd, trying to keep up with John.

John and Daddy stop to watch two men chatting, one who has a wooden crossbow slung across his back and the other who is wearing a sword that trails in the dust. I notice John staring at the sword. Daddy holds him back. The men pause in their conversation. Daddy speaks to the man with the crossbow.

"Yes, I hunt for rabbits as well as other small animals," the man replies. "There're plenty of wild animals in these mountains, even if I must climb over the rocks to find them," he laughs.

Daddy asks the man if he made the bow himself and tells him how much he admires it.

John continues to eye the sword dangling from the second man's belt. Finally, noticing John's unrelenting glances, the man ceremoniously draws the sword from its scabbard and offers it to John. John looks at Daddy, who nods. John touches it. Daddy and the men smile and laugh together.

Mummy and I resume our stroll, looking at the ladies in colorful costumes and unique headdresses. There're several noodle sellers, including an old lady in a Bai headdress who scrapes noodles off a block of dough and serves them to a second elderly lady. I look at Mummy, who with a slight shake of her head indicates that, no, I can't have any noodles.

A girl walks by wearing a wide silver necklace and so many bracelets that they cover both arms up to her elbows. Mummy tells me that she's of the Miao people and that unmarried Miao ladies wear their dowry as bracelets and necklaces and even ornate silver headdresses;[4] the headdresses are saved for special occasions like festivals and feast days, so we're unlikely to see any today, she says. I watch as Mummy asks the young lady if she would be willing to sell her some of her bracelets. The lady slips a few off her arm and offers them to Mummy.

"Why did the lady sell you her dowry?" I ask after we have strolled away from the silver-clad teenager.

"Oh, she was happy to sell them to me. She'll buy twice as many with the money I paid for them," Mummy says, smiling, as she slips the intricately worked bamboo and silver circles on her left arm.

I see one of the Red Cross men come to talk to Daddy. "We have to get on our way," Daddy calls to us. "The aid worker told me earlier that it's about sixty kilometers to the next village, and another thirty-two to the Mekong River.[5] We've a very high mountain range ahead of us."

We go to meet Mr. Chou and Xiao. As we drive away from Dali, I look back and see the outline of three tall, narrow pagodas and another building on the top of the mountain. "What's that place?" I ask.

"It's a monastery," Mummy says. "And there's no road up to it. Everything has to be carried there. I read that it takes a couple of days to reach it on foot."

***

Days pass. We follow the truck in front of us. Again, we drive, stop, back up, and drive again to negotiate hairpin bends up the hills, then repeat the process until we reach the top of the mountain. Going downhill we turn the motor off and roll, braking so that we don't run into the army truck ahead of us.

At night we usually sleep on a desktop in one of Daddy's offices, although once we stayed at a little Chinese inn. After we ate, Mummy carefully rolled out our sleeping bags on the hard wooden beds. I was so tired I didn't have much time to worry about things that might bite us. I knew that John and I were safe from bugs, because when we lived in Shanghai, I'd seen Amah sew flat little cotton pouches and slip a tablespoon of white powder into each one, and now every time Mummy changes our undershirts, she carefully removes the pouches from the dirty undershirts and safety-pins them into the fresh shirts. But as I fell asleep at the inn, I wondered, *Would the little bags protect us from rats? And from snakes?*

***

I see a group of goats far off on the mountainside, jumping from one rocky outcropping to the next—little white spots against gray rocks off in the distance. By now the beautiful snowy peaks on the horizon have become so familiar that they hardly draw a comment. John and I pass the time playing animal, vegetable, or mineral when we're not snoozing.

Suddenly there's a steady roar. We hear the Mekong River long before we see it.

"The river's high this late because the monsoon season was extra heavy this year," Mummy says. We approach the bridge and inch our way over, following the truck in front of us closely. John and I put our heads out of the window. The thundering water rushing over the rocks under the bridge is so loud it's impossible to speak, or even think. I enjoy the damp mist that billows up from below and swirls around my face. I watch as a hazy cloud engulfs the truck in front of us, swoops down behind it, and evaporates. A moment later the truck is swallowed by another foggy cloud.

Mr. Chou coughs and I see him rub his eyes. In fact, I realize that he has been rubbing his eyes a lot recently. I wonder why he does this and whether Mummy has noticed it. He frequently clears his throat, too. Is that a sign that he's sleepy? I hear Xiao remind him of things he has to do, like check the gas tank, from time to time. I decide to watch him more closely.

After crossing the Mekong, the trucks stop along the side of the road for a pee-and-smoke session. This also gives any faster vehicles that have piled up behind us a chance to pass. Daddy tells us that the men have decided to press on to the next town, Baoshan,[6] before stopping for the night.

John asks if he can climb one of the massive banyan trees that are growing by the road; the many-branched roots growing down from the tree's thick branches provide excellent footholds. "Yes," Mummy says, and John scrambles up. Twenty minutes later, the men in front of us get back into their trucks and start the motors.

"John, John, come quickly, we're ready to go," Mummy calls. John jumps down out of a tree and into the Buick with Daddy and me, and we start off again. For a change, Daddy's riding with us and Mummy's riding in the last truck.

We've been driving up the mountain on the west bank of the Mekong for about ten minutes when John wails, "Ohhhh, Daddy, my belt; I forgot my belt in the tree." John tells us he took the belt off—a new belt Daddy had bought for him on Dali's market day— and hung it by its buckle on the stub of a broken branch. *That's because he wanted to admire his pretty new belt,* I think. "Daddy, can we go back and get my belt? Please?" John wails.

There's a long pause.

"I'm very sorry, little son, we can't drive back. I'm sorry."

I see that John is heartbroken by the loss of his shiny new leather belt, the first real grown-up belt he's ever had. I try to console him, but he refuses to be consoled. He leans against

Daddy and stares out the window beside him, silently pressing his hands on his knees.

***

John and I spend the night on yet another desktop in yet another one of Daddy's offices. This time we're in Baoshan.

NOTES

1. Dali, also known as Tali, sits on a plain between Erhai Lake to the east and the Cang Mountain Range (Cangshan) to the west. This range has many waterfalls and nineteen peaks, all of which are more than thirty-five hundred meters (11,483 feet) high; the highest is 4,122 meters (13,523 feet). Dali is the seat of the Bai ethnic minority.

2. Eighty percent of the two million members of the Bai ethnic minority live in Yunnan towns and villages. The word *bai* means "white," which is the color favored by both men and women in their dress. Generally, women wear a bright-red, blue, or black vest over a white blouse; frequently a camellia flower is embroidered on the vest or the blouse sleeves. Men often wear white jackets and dark loose shorts. It is traditional for unmarried women to wear an embroidered apron. All women wear a red headdress embellished with bright embroidery.

3. The Yi ethnic minority is the seventh-largest ethnic minority group in China. The Yi live primarily in rural, mountainous areas in Yunnan and three other provinces in China and north Vietnam. The group has a number of subgroups. Another ethnic group, the Kachin, who live mainly in Burma but also in Yunnan, were hired by the US Army during World War II because of their well-organized and ferocious jungle-fighters.

4. The Miao ethnic minority is a large group with many subgroups differentiated by the predominant color of the women's clothing: Red Miao, Black Miao, and Green/Blue Miao, as well as Big Flowery Miao and Small Flowery Miao. The Miao peoples have spread over many areas in Southeast Asia (as well as in Australia and the United States) and are also known by other names. The Miao peoples in Yunnan primarily belong to the Big and Small Flowery Miao subgroups. The unmarried women in some Miao groups customarily wear their dowry on their person in the form of silver bracelets and necklaces. On festivals and special occasions, they also may wear silver headdresses.

5. The mighty Mekong River, the twelfth-longest river in the world,

is notoriously powerful. The flow and volume of its waters vary widely depending upon the time of year, swelling exponentially during the monsoon season, July through October. There are no major Chinese cities along its banks. Portions of the Mekong are unnavigable due to its many rapids and waterfalls. Nevertheless, the Mekong has served as an important trade route throughout history. It flows through Cambodia, Laos, Vietnam, Burma (Myanmar), and Thailand, in addition to Yunnan Province in China.

6.   The city of Baoshan once served as the beginning of the southern Silk Road to India. The eighty hot springs that surround Baoshan cover an area of nine kilometers (5.6 miles). During World War II, the US Army Air Force maintained an airfield there.

18

Destination Ruili

*A Few Days Later in January 1941
Dali, Yunnan Province, China, to Ruili,
Yunnan Province, China*

The next morning, John isn't worried about the loss of his grown-up's belt, probably because there are so many interesting things to see on our drive. We watch the countryside slip by, looking for animals, and wave at little boys riding on the backs of giant water buffalo. They only stare back at us. I tell myself they don't expect to see children along this road.

As we come around the last hairpin bend and roll silently down the mountainside, the widest river I've ever seen, even wider than the Mekong, sparkles into view. Daddy says it's the Salween River.[1] *How amazing it is!* I think. *How beautiful!*

The line of trucks stops, then moves forward slowly across the bridge over the river.[2] Carefully we cross, staying behind our Red Cross truck. I look up and admire the cables holding the bridge. I think how lovely they are, how symmetrical. Then I look down at the water rushing and roaring over the rocks far below us.

After creeping across the bridge, the trucks stop again. Again the men get out and congregate along the side of the road, smoking and chatting. I suppose they have to catch their breath after concentrating so hard on getting across safely. I look over at John, but I can't figure out what he's thinking. When Mummy says we can get out and stretch our legs too, John and I go behind some trees to pee, and I finally realize that I was scared, scared although we were driving slowly over the long, long Salween River bridge. Scared of the rushing, gurgling water. It's hard for me to admit to myself when I'm scared.

Mummy calls us to get back into the car, and Daddy decides to ride with us while Mummy goes to the last truck. Xiao retrieves his blocks of wood, and we're off again.

Daddy squeezes John's hand and brushes hair off his forehead, out of his eyes. Daddy doesn't say anything, but I know he'll surprise John with another belt to replace the one from Dali. I settle back for another day of riding.

We pass a group of people, some in colorful outfits, leading donkeys laden with baskets strapped on their backs. The ladies wear bright scarves tied over their heads. "That's an ethnic costume we've not seen," Daddy says as he reaches for his notebook. "Your mother will want to know more about them."

We descend a mountain and the land flattens out—Daddy calls it a plateau—and we're able to drive faster. We ride past fields of crops and rice paddies, but mostly forests. Sometimes the trees are planted in neat rows. I ask Daddy about them and he says they're walnut trees, which are plentiful in this area.

We stop to eat, and Mummy and Ping San join us. Ping San passes a sandwich each to Mr. Chou and Xiao, who looks at it as if it's strange before he takes a little nibble. Ping San says something to him in Chinese that I don't catch. Daddy and Mummy look at each other and smile.

Back in the car after lunch, I notice that Mr. Chou is rubbing his eyes again. His color is peculiar. He doesn't look well. He speaks to Daddy, Daddy says something to him, and Mr. Chou stops the car. Daddy takes the wheel and drives for the rest of the day.

Finally we reach the town, Ruili,[3] where we'll stop for the night. The atmosphere in Ruili seems different from the other villages we've visited along this road. Huge piles of logs line both sides of the street. Daddy says this is because there's logging in the area. He says this is the last town we'll pass through in China before we reach Burma.

***

As John and I snuggle down in our bed on the office desktop, I hear Daddy and Mummy talking. Daddy tells Mummy that Mr. Chou wasn't well, and that's why he drove all afternoon. Then he tells her that Mr. Chou tries to hide being ill, insisting he's fine when he looks terrible. Mummy says she'll check on him in the morning. Daddy goes on to talk about the people on the road with the donkey caravan. He says he's learned about this ethnic group from a man who works in the office where we're camped out. The group's called the Wa ethnic minority.[4] The Wa live primarily in this part of China.

NOTES

1. The swift and powerful Salween River is 2,816 kilometers (1,750 miles) long and flows from Tibet through China, Burma, and Thailand. Only the first ninety kilometers (fifty-six miles) from its mouth are navigable due to the steep canyon walls on both sides of the river.

2. The bridge over the Salween River, formerly known as the Burma Road Bridge, is now the Huitong Bridge. It is 103 meters in length and rises 3.4 meters above the water when the river is at its highest point, swollen with melted snow and summer rains. Its eastern bridgehead was blown up by retreating Chinese soldiers in May 1942, preventing the Japanese Army, advancing eastward up the Burma Road, from crossing the Salween. The bridge has been reconstructed for limited use to commemorate this battle, but the bulk of its former traffic is now borne by a new bridge built upstream from it.

3. As a major border crossing, Ruili is an important trade route between China and Burma in both goods and services, legal and illegal. Sixty-five percent of its population is composed of five highland and lowland ethnic minorities.

4. The people of the Wa ethnic minority live in the rugged mountainous area between the Salween and Mekong Rivers in Yunnan, as well as in Burma along its borders with China. The Wa live on subsistence farming of poppies, beans, rice, and walnuts. Many are animists and at one time practiced headhunting.

19

The Dak Bungalow

End of January 1941
Lashio, North Shan State, Burma

Two soldiers step out of a little wooden shed. Mr. Chou stops the car and Daddy gets out, takes a sheaf of papers out of his leather briefcase, and hands it to one of the soldiers. We're at the China-Burma border. I look out the car window. A bamboo fence runs from the road through the fields in both directions. This must be the edge of China, I think. The soldier glances quickly at Daddy, takes a longer look at Mummy seated next to me, and then stares, back and forth, at John and me.

Mr. Chou, who rarely speaks, says simply, "They rarely see white women and never white children."

Daddy asks Mr. Chou for his and Xiao's identification papers

and gives them to the soldier, who looks over all the paperwork
and passes it back to Daddy with a nod.

We cross into Burma and begin what will be a long drive
to Lashio.[1] The road runs downhill. Daddy says we are in the
Gaoligong Mountains,[2] a submountain range of the Meili Snow
Mountains that straddle the China-Burma border.[3] He says
the road will flatten out before we reach Lashio. It is a pleasant
change from the dizzying mountain roads we've been on for the
past week.

After ten hours, we finally reach Lashio just before dark.
We drive along a dusty street lined on each side by one-story
wooden buildings until we arrive at a building Daddy calls "the
dak bungalow."[4] It's easy to find our way because the town has
only four parallel streets. The dak sits in the center of a well-
tended garden, which, in turn, is surrounded by a three-foot
wooden fence.

As we get out of the car, a servant in a startlingly white
starched costume appears from the house, steps forward, opens
the gate, and steps back to join two other similarly dressed men
to stand in a line. They bow in unison as we walk up the path to
the front door.

John looks around the garden. "I don't see any ducks."

"It's not a duck bungalow," I say. "It's a dark bungalow." I look
around the garden too. "But it's not dark either, Mummy. Why is
it called that?"

Mummy and Daddy laugh. Daddy tells us that it's a dak bungalow, which is a guest house for government officials. The house
is very nice, with lots of spacious rooms. John and I even have
bedrooms to ourselves. There is a lovely bathroom with a big tub,

but I look for spigots and there are none. No running water! After exploring the house and looking into every room and even every closet, John and I go to see what the servants are doing. We've heard some scuffling coming from the dining room, so we head in that direction.

At first, we watch from the doorway as two servants carefully lift the large mahogany dining table and move it to one side. I'm mystified as the men roll up the oriental carpet that was under the table and carry it outside, where they unroll it on the grass in front of the house. Then they proceed to carry the dining table out the front door and place it in the middle of the carpet. John and I follow them and sit on the grass to watch. A lovely white lace tablecloth is spread on the table, and the table is laid with silver tableware and two silver candelabra. The last things the men bring out are two oil floor lamps in the shape of torches, which they place on each end of the carpet.

Mummy and Daddy find us outside. Mummy tells us the cook has made a special dinner for our first evening, and Daddy suggests we stroll around Lashio until dinner is ready. We hear banging and hammering sounds, so we start out in that direction and find, to our surprise, two elephants helping build a house. The elephants raise the entire side of a building as several men guide the large panel with ropes. The elephants seem to know just what to do to help the men get the panel into place. Then the workmen hammer the wooden wall to secure it. We watch in amazement as the elephants lift and position another heavy panel. The foreman comes over to chat with Daddy and invites us to look at the house.

"What's that square ball?" John asks admiringly, pointing to a ten-sided cube sitting on top of a pile of wooden planks nearby. "May I see it?"

"It's the newel post for the staircase," the foreman says. He picks it up and passes it to John, who turns it around and around in his hands.

"You may keep it," the foreman says as he turns back to chat with Daddy.

Awestruck by his good fortune, John thanks the foreman.

**

It's nine o'clock. Dinner is announced—in the garden.

As I step through the front doorway, I catch my breath; the night is enchanting. The stars above look close enough to touch. And they're huge. Bright. Sparkling. Beautiful. A gentle breeze makes the candles flicker and blows the smoke rising from the gas lamps toward the west. The crickets sing noisily. They sound like fiddlers hiding in the tall grass that grows in the fields stretching off into the darkness beyond the fence.

Looking around I see four huge bright spots off in the distance. Fires in the form of the letter x jump and dance on the far-off hillside. I shudder but then realize the fires are far away, too far to be dangerous like the burning houses in Chungking. Nor do they look like the aftermath of a bombing raid. I point. "Daddy, what are those fires?"

Daddy turns to look. "They're bonfires lit by the Burmese soldiers along the border with China," he says. "They mark Burma's boundary. And they're to keep the Japanese pilots from bombing Burma by accident. This is a neutral country."

"Neutral?" John asks.

"A neutral country is a country that doesn't want to fight in a war."

"Oh" is all I can say as I stare at the fires and admire the glow they create against the inky sky.

"And during the day, giant white *X*'s are painted on the ground in place of the fires," Daddy adds.

After dinner Mummy asks a servant to bring warm water to the large tub. "Bath time, John," she calls.

John's been playing with his square ball since he brought it home. Now he takes it with him to his bath.

He drops it in the water and is very surprised when the wooden ball sinks. "Daddy, why did it sink?" he calls from the tub, a note of distress in his voice. But everyone is busy and John doesn't get an answer.

That's how he discovers that the square ball is made of teak.

***

The next morning Daddy puts on a suit and tie and his rust-colored suede overcoat. I think he looks very handsome. We all walk to the railway station.[5] There we meet Ping San, who will accompany Daddy on his trip and carry his leather briefcase and two small suitcases.

"Where are you going?" John asks.

"To Rangoon,[6] but just for a few days. He'll be back soon," Mummy says.

"Why's Ping San going too?" I ask.

"Daddy said the English officers always take a valet with them when they travel, to care for their uniforms and carry notes and things like that. So, Daddy thought he'd take Ping San."

"Oh," I say. I feel like I've been saying that a lot.

We say goodbye to Daddy and get home in time for lunch in the splendid dining room at the dak bungalow. After the meal, Mummy suggests we walk around the town and see what we can find.

We've not walked far before a boy about my age approaches us and asks if we would like to see his zoo.

"What a good idea," Mummy says, and we follow him a short distance to a field beside a small wooden house.

First the boy shows us a white goat in a pen. She looks rather scrawny, but Mummy compliments the boy on his goat. Then he waves a hand toward a water buffalo lying in the shade close by. Mummy compliments the water buffalo and says he looks like a good worker. Finally the boy whistles, and a thin yellow mongrel crawls out from under the house and slinks over to him. Mummy asks his name, but it's hard to understand the boy's reply. I think the boy says he doesn't have a name.

It looks as though we've seen everything, but the boy leads us behind his cottage to a large wire cage. He runs a stick across the bars to rouse the cage's inhabitant, a furry wildcat.[7] I feel quite sorry for the animal and reach for the boy's stick to silence it, thinking the cat would be happier back in the forest where he belongs. As we turn to start back to the guesthouse, the boy indicates he has another animal to show us and walks over to a large, long wooden box, the size and shape that a grandfather clock might be packed in. He lifts the lid. Inside a massive Burmese python presses its scales against every side,[8] completely filling the box. Mummy gasps and steps back. John's mouth flies open, and so does mine. I stare at the snake and quickly notice a large bulge in its middle. Questioningly, I point to the massive lump. The boy turns and points to a wooden pen nearby. In the dust lounges a mother pig surrounded by a pile of piglets.

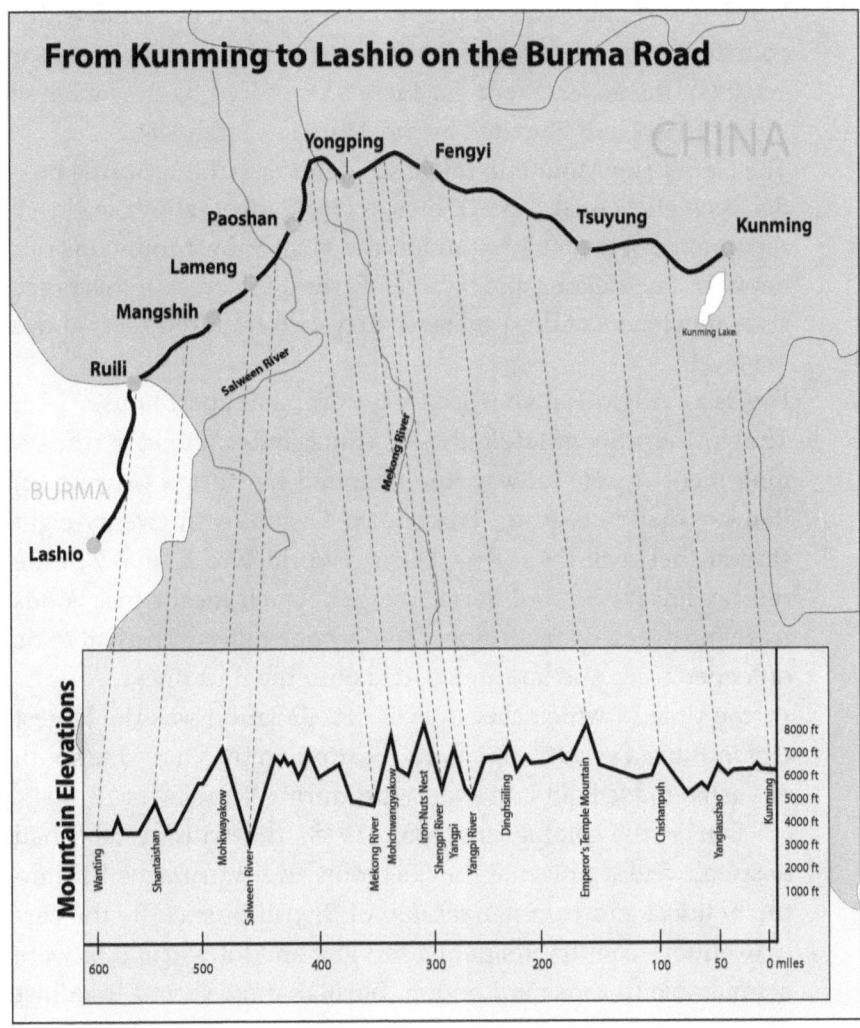

NOTES

1. Lashio, a town in northern Shan State, Burma (Myanmar), is home to the end of the railway to Rangoon (Yangon) and was important during World War II as the Burmese terminus of the Burma Road. During the British colonial period in India (1887–1947), there was a European-style station in Lashio with a courthouse, quarters for civil officers, and, no doubt, housing for guests of the government. Lashio was captured by the Japanese in April 1942 and liberated by the Allies in March 1945.

2. The Gaoligong Mountain range straddles the China-Burma border. Its highest peak is 5,128 meters (16,824 feet) above sea level.

3. A subrange of the Nu Mountains, the Meili Snow Mountains rise between the Mekong and Salween Rivers. The crest of this range rises nineteen hundred meters (sixty-two hundred feet) above sea level.

4. *Dak* is an Anglo-Indian word for government guest house.

5. The Northern Shan State Railway is a thousand-millimeter- (thirty-nine-inch-) gauge railway line operated by Burma (Myanmar) Railway that runs from Rangoon to Lashio, with twenty-eight stations between the towns. During World War II, many of the railway lines were of differing gauges, which meant that goods traveling over a distance not served by one railway line had to be offloaded from one line and loaded onto the next one.

6. At the time in which this story is set, Rangoon was the largest city in Burma and its capital. Its location on the coast due south of Lashio made it an important port during World War II.

    During the colonial era (1852–1948), the British established hospitals and a university in Rangoon and transformed it into the political and commercial hub of British Burma. By the early twentieth century, its public services and infrastructure were comparable to those in London. Burma's most sacred Buddhist pagoda, as well as another pagoda reputed to be two thousand years old, is located in Rangoon.

7. There are eight species of wildcats in Burma (Myanmar), including tigers and leopards. This was probably an ocelot or one of the

several species known as wildcats, with various Latin names.

8. The female Burmese python, the larger of the sexes in both length and girth, can reach from five to six meters (seventeen to twenty feet) or even seven meters (twenty-three feet) in length depending upon the availability of prey.

20

Back to Kunming

Early February 1941
Kunming, Yunnan Province, China

Daddy returns from Rangoon. He tells us interesting stories about how in the hotel in Rangoon, the Indian valets who accompanied British officers sat cross-legged on the floor in the hall outside their officers' rooms. Daddy says Ping San thought this was very silly and placed a chair for himself near the door on the inside of Daddy's room, where he sat reading a newspaper when not otherwise occupied.

Daddy doesn't say much else about his trip. When I ask him what he did in Rangoon, he just looks at Mummy across the table and says he looked for a new leather belt for John.

Early the next morning we start back up the Burma Road to Kunming.

The first afternoon, at about two o'clock, Mr. Chou gets very sleepy. He wants Xiao to drive but Daddy insists on driving himself. We arrive in Ruili very late.

The following day the same thing occurs, and, although Daddy's not happy about it, we have to continue on our return trip riding in Mr. Chou's car. We need Mr. Chou, Daddy says, because he's a clever mechanic. Whenever the car breaks down, which happens fairly often, he's able to fix it. I saw him fix the car with a bit of wire he'd pulled from under the hood and, once, a hairpin he dug out of his pocket.

On the third day, Daddy says that he's finally realized why Mr. Chou falls asleep every afternoon. Mr. Chou's an addict. He's addicted to opium. Daddy then says that we'll have to work our way back to Kunming by sharing the driving between Mr. Chou, Daddy, and even Xiao if need be. Mummy looks on during this conversation. She doesn't know how to drive.

On the fourth day, the car breaks down again. Daddy tries without success to find the part we need by asking the Red Cross workers and the other Westerners we run into in town. But Mr. Chou solves the problem. He tells Xiao to sit on the front bumper, dripping gasoline into the carburetor from a teacup, while he drives.

We arrive back in Kunming a day later than planned.[1]

That night as Daddy tucks us into bed, he asks John if he put water in his bottle of whiskey.

"Yes, Daddy, but it was *drinking* water."[2]

✳✳✳

A few days later Mummy says she has a surprise for me; she's enrolled me in school. The school is run by French nuns especially for French girls. I don't understand a word of what the teacher says, but I follow along and copy what the other little girls are doing. Everyone wears a school uniform, so Mummy suggests I wear my uniform from the Girls' Cathedral School in Shanghai that she's brought along. It's a school uniform, after all, and the teacher just looks at me, smiles, and nods her head when I enter the big classroom in my freshly pressed white blouse and navy jumper. I don't think she expects very much of me, but she's pretty; her hair is in lots of little waves and she smiles a lot. I know Mummy put me here to keep me out of trouble.

NOTES

1. On my trip to China in 1998, I wasn't successful in finding the guesthouse in Kunming where we stayed, although the street remains residential. The wide boulevard—reminiscent of a French city, via Vietnam—that goes to the railway station has not changed. Green Lake Park and the bird market remain much the same as they were in the 1940s.

    I also ventured onto the Burma Road. Much of it has been replaced by a new, more streamlined highway, but you can still see portions of the original road. A girlfriend and I rented a car and driver and, accompanied by a Chinese friend, went to Ruili. The trip was reminiscent of the 1940s trip; the car even managed to get stuck in the mud, because it had rained and there'd been a landslide. When we got stuck, one of the men told my girlfriend and me to get out and push while they (the two men) remained seated in the front seat, even though the trucks ahead of us were being pulled out of the mud by other trucks with chains. We didn't free the car but got covered in mud! In time a truck came along and pulled us out with a chain, and we went on our way.

    In Ruili, huge piles of logs lined the roadsides. My Chinese friend said there was a lot of valuable timber being logged, probably smuggled, from Burma across the border. The atmosphere was very frontier-like, very Wild West. The men wanted to stay overnight, but since it looked like more rain was expected and I assumed any accommodation would be equally frontier-like, we opted instead to visit the wreckage of a China National Aviation Corporation (CNAC) C-47 downed during the war, which had recently been found and brought out from the jungle, and then start back.

2. In wartime China, all drinking water—used also for face washing and tooth brushing—had to be boiled, cooled, and stored in bottles that were carefully distinguished from the water used for other purposes. This was critically important given the variety of serious diseases that could be, and were, contracted from

water that had not been boiled. In China to this day, one does not consume tap water, ice cubes, or beverages served from open containers.

21

The Rubber Band

"I wish Mummy and Daddy were here," John says.

Many months have passed since our return from the Burma Road trip, and Mummy and Daddy have gone to Hong Kong. They left last evening. When I'd asked why they had to leave so late, when we were on our way to bed, Daddy told me that to get to Hong Kong, the plane has to fly over Japanese territory, so to avoid being seen by the Japanese, planes fly at night. That scared me. To me the word *Japanese* means bombs, fire, danger.

"They're going Christmas shopping," I say, trying to cheer John up. "They'll be back soon. Ping San is here to take care of us." Mummy had also told me she needed to go to see a dentist, but I don't think that information will interest John, so I don't mention it. Mummy also says that Daddy has business to attend to, but I only listen carefully when Mummy talks about Christmas.

We dress and eat boiled eggs for breakfast. Just when we're trying to decide what to do today without our parents—*Ping San will have an idea*, I think—an air raid siren wails.

Ping San's thin frame appears in the doorway. HooooOOOO-oooo, the siren continues. "John, Ferfer," Ping San says. "I don't know this town, so Amah will take you to a safe place." The amah is new; Ping San found her in Kunming. She's plump as a cherry and smells good.

The siren continues screeching. *It's very loud, so it must be close by.* I put my hands over my ears, but that doesn't help. It's the first time we've heard an air raid siren in Kunming, but its message is the same as the one in Chungking: *Run.* But where should we go? There's no cave under this house, no Mummy to read to us. Mummy hadn't told me this might happen. I feel frozen. I don't know what to do.

HoooOOOOoooo, hoooOOOOoooo, hoooOOOOoooo. The siren sounds as if it's right outside the house. I want to hide under my bed but look at John and know that I can't.

"Ferfer, John, come, quick. Amah knows a good place. I've called Master's office to send a car to take you," Ping San says.

We go out the front door and find Amah already standing next to a very shiny Ford. I don't recognize the driver because Daddy hasn't taken us anywhere in an office car here in Kunming. I ask myself what Daddy would do. We get into the car.

As the driver pulls away from the curb and turns into a street, people swarm around the car. There're people everywhere, crowds of people. The street is choked with masses and masses of people—men, women with babies tied onto their backs, and children hanging on to their parents' trouser legs. Men and boys jump onto the running boards and bumpers and cling on to the black metal. There're so many people choking the street that the driver must creep forward very slowly. We rock and bump along at the pace of the throng. Everyone is moving in the same direction—out of the city. I look through the back window. Other cars follow far behind, creeping along as we are.

John turns the window handle a half-turn. The glass slides down an inch. Grimy fingers instantly slip in to get a firmer grip. The stench of garlicky perspiration pressed against metal seeps through the open space.

"Close the window," the driver says curtly. But John can't. There're too many fingers in the way.

After a while, the street narrows, and the large stone houses, like the one we're staying in, become smaller and change to brick, then to wood. We turn left and continue to crawl forward, slipping into narrow spaces as they open in the throng, a big fish engulfed in a school of smaller fish. Boys who are clinging to the car jump or are pushed off; others jump on.

Amah scowls and raises her little knotted fist. She shakes it at the boys hanging on to the car but the leeches ignore her. John seizes a moment when no fingers are in the opening and quickly winds the window up. I know he feels as sorry for these boys as I do.

The car's stuffy. The driver's face is stern. The unrelenting air raid siren continues to howl. No one speaks.

We creep forward. The street narrows to a road, then a lane, then to hard-packed earth. Houses give way to huts, then to single-room huts surrounded by tiny gardens of winter stubble.

Finally, we reach the country. The surging throng dissolves, people slipping one by one into the fields on either side of the lane. We continue a little farther. Over the sound of the fluctuating air raid signal, I hear a hum, a far-off drone. I'm not sure what it is.

"Is this good?" the driver asks, and pulls over.

We leap out. Amah follows. Taking each of us by the hand, she lurches over a ditch. The unmistakable stench of raw sewage rises to meet my nose. We surge into a field. *"Didi, Jie Jie"*—Little Brother, Big Sister—"come," Amah says.

The field is ridged with half-frozen tufts of sharp rice stubble, plowed and hard to run across. I stumble and catch myself. John's stumbling too, but manages to pace his steps between the earthen ridges so that he doesn't fall. I let go of Amah's chubby hand. It's hard to hang on. John and I continue across the soggy field, struggling to keep up with Amah, who is surprisingly fast.

The sound of the air raid siren dips. I hear a second hum clearly—a deep drone, unmistakable, off in the distance. Is it an echo of the air raid siren?

"Look," Amah says, and points to a tussock of tall grass ahead of us. "That's a good place to sit."

I trip on a root and slide in a muddy puddle. I fall on one knee but quickly manage to get up, mud splattered but unhurt. Amah glances back and grabs my slippery hand. The huge clump of grass looms closer.

I try to look at the sky to see what's causing the second hum but can only look to the side. I can hear people stumbling across the field behind us.

We approach the tussock.

"Stop! Stop, go away!" A teenage boy in a baggy Chinese army uniform stands among the tall grasses and waves his arms over his head vigorously. "Go away. People, go away," he repeats.

Another teenage soldier, shaggy hair falling around his ears, appears motionless next to the first. I see the gleam of an anti-aircraft gun between the two teenagers. At the same moment I realize the steady drone is the sound of planes.

The drone in the distance grows louder and louder still. The airplanes are flying over the city, they're flying lower, one's flying over the field, flying over us. The plane swoops down. The noise is deafening. Crack, crack, crack. Fire spurts from the front of the plane. *Fire!* I think. *The plane's on fire!* Then, *No, the plane's firing at us!*[1]

Amah collapses in the mud and pulls John and me down with her. The chilly water oozes through my skirt. I turn and look at John. He's all right. We lie still. The drone of the airplane recedes.

"Don't look," Amah says. She gets up warily. I get up on one knee, then stand and try to brush the mud off my skirt, but it's too sticky. For some reason, I'd put on my old Shanghai Girls' Cathedral School winter uniform when I got up this morning, although today's not a school day. Probably because it reminds me of our happy days in Shanghai. My legs are shaking.

"Pao, pao!" Amah says—run, run! She grabs John's hand and my wrist, yanks us out of the mud, and pulls us forward.

"Ouch, Amah, don't squeeze so tight," I say. My wrist hurts;

it's red. For the first time I look at my legs and see that they're scratched and bleeding. I stretch to look at John's legs; he's wearing shorts. Bloody scratches rise as welts through the caked mud, which is now beginning to dry.

"I'm tired, Amah," I say. "Can we sit down?"

"No, don't sit." Amah looks around.

There's a huge cement culvert off to one side. We step as fast as we can over the plowed ridges and reach the culvert. I look into the dark circle.

An old lady is crouching with a boy about John's age under one arm, like a mother hen. The lady is silent but I see her inch aside. We crawl into the space beside her.

"*Xie xie*—thank you" I whisper as I try to make myself as small as possible.

Amah is breathing loudly. I feel sorry for her. The cement of the culvert is cold and scratchy, so I tuck my skirt under my legs. Amah takes a hankie out of her pocket, wets it with spit, and applies it to the dried mud on my knee, which only turns it into mud again. I close my eyes. The air raid siren has stopped. The field's silent—eerily silent. After a few minutes, Amah's breathing calms.

Squatting next to the little Chinese boy, John smiles and draws a red rubber band from his pocket. Slowly he flexes it, stretching it almost to the breaking point and releasing it. I hold my breath. John repeats the exercise several times. The little boy watches intently, fascinated. John holds the rubber band out to him and then places it in the boy's open hand.

NOTES

1. It wasn't until years later, when I thought about this incident,
    that I realized the reason the plane was strafing this particular
    field was because of the antiaircraft emplacement positioned
    there.

22

Foolishly Optimistic

Mid–December 1941
My Imagination[1]

Alice gasps. "Oh my!" She's looking out the window of the DC-2 as it makes its final approach to Kai Tak Airport in Hong Kong.[2] The China National Aviation Corporation—CNAC[3]—plane has just flown over Victoria Harbour and now makes a low-altitude right turn to descend past a row of apartment building windows as it approaches the runway. "I'd forgotten how close this flight comes to those buildings. I have the feeling the people in those apartments can look right into our window!" she exclaims.

"Don't worry about the tricky landing," Ted says as he squeezes Alice's hand. "The pilot's done it a thousand times."

Alice looks at the sun rising above the skyline and yawns

behind her hand. It's been more than eight hours since they left Kunming. She wiggles and stretches in the narrow seat.

"We're almost there. And then we're going to have a lovely holiday away from the Burma Road, its problems, and the children."

"Yes," Alice says.

"You'll want to shop—Lane Crawford,[4] I presume. And I've a great many calls to make, some long overdue, including seeing Major Boxer[5]... but first things first. Let's have breakfast once we get to the hotel."

Following a pleasant drive through the city and then along a hilly, winding road, the taxi reaches the hotel. As they pull up in front of the Repulse Bay Hotel,[6] Alice glances at the wide entryway and then the crescent of sand stretching below them. "The beach looks lovely. It's a shame it's too chilly to swim, but we certainly can take a stroll," she says. "Remember when we were here in '37? When you took John down to the beach and all he wanted to do was put sand in his mouth? He was just one, after all."

Ted smiles and nods; he's busy with the bellhops, two young Chinese boys in impeccable uniforms and pillbox hats who've run down the steps to take their suitcases from the taxi. After admiring the miniature Italian garden with its fountain, Alice and Ted turn to mount the stone steps, cross the balcony, and enter the lobby.

Alice glances at the breakfasting guests in the dining room and out on the veranda. She looks admiringly at the row of potted palms swaying gently between the large windows. "I'm famished," she says. "Let's eat on the veranda."

As they're shown to a table, Alice looks around. The guests

wear colorful outfits native to their various homelands. She smiles to herself. She's going to enjoy this holiday.

**

In their attractively decorated room at the hotel, Alice examines the somewhat travel-worn outfits she's packed. Deciding that she should correct the sorry state of her wardrobe immediately, she grabs her handbag and heads out to Lane Crawford. As she enters the store, she admires the pretty dress displays and thinks about the evening wear she was obliged to pack away and leave in the godown with all their household goods in Shanghai. She and Ted have no use for his top hat or her white fur evening cape, or any of her pretty evening clothes, in war-torn Chungking or Kunming. *I did so enjoy dancing on the deck of the American ship that came up the Yangtze to Chungking,* she thinks, *but I suppose that sort of thing is over for the duration. And if anyone is even interested in dinner parties, in Kunming there's little sign of it.* When the war's over and they return to Shanghai or head to another jolly posting, she'll retrieve all of their belongings. She's looking forward to resuming their carefree life, the social invitations, dances, bowling, horse races, concerts, plays, and dinner parties.

At Lane Crawford, Alice picks out a dress suitable for her current life in Free China and two pairs of slacks. Then she takes a rickshaw to Wing On Department Store on Des Voeux Road to choose Christmas gifts for the children[7]—games, a small doll, and a metal truck, things that will fit into her suitcase and current unsettled lifestyle.

Alice and Ted are very busy during the next few weeks. Ted, fulfilling long-overdue business and social obligations, calls on colleagues and friends. Alice knows that visiting Major Boxer is at the top of Ted's list. The trip to Major Boxer's office on Stonecutters Island means taking a ferry, which is a pleasant diversion.[8]

She and Ted spend one evening dancing in the Des Voeux Road hotel's beautiful ballroom; Ted loves to dance almost as much as she does. The band's wonderful, and they so enjoy dancing to the latest tunes from America. But the most fun they have in Hong Kong is meeting old friends for cocktails and conversation, friends they knew in Shanghai who'd moved to Hong Kong, or Hong Kong friends who happen to live in gorgeous homes on Victoria Peak.[9]

On December 6, Alice watches as Ted leaves for the Hong Kong police station to pick up the exit permits required for their return to Kunming. The permits are valid for two weeks. "I'll be glad to get back. I miss the children," he says as he closes the door behind him.

***

On December 8 at 8:00 a.m., four hours after they attack Pearl Harbor, the Japanese bomb Kai Tak Airport.[10]

Alice and Ted are having breakfast on the hotel veranda. At first, they and the other guests and staff don't realize what's happening; they think the planes they hear are part of a training maneuver. After breakfast, though, when they return to their room and turn on the radio, they learn that seven CNAC and a number of Royal Air Force planes have been destroyed at the airport. Now thousands of Japanese soldiers are swarming over the mountains between China and Hong Kong's New Territories and heading toward Kowloon and Victoria.

On hearing the news, Ted drops heavily onto the edge of the bed. "The Japanese are attacking. It's unimaginable." He looks out of the window, clearly considering his course of action. Finally, he takes a deep breath. Without looking at Alice, he says, "I must go and do my part, Alice. I'm going to join the Hong Kong Volunteer Defence Corps."[11] He looks at her then. "I'll return as soon as I'm able."

Stunned, Alice is speechless for a moment. Then she says, "Take your warmest things. I'm glad we brought your heavy overcoat. And don't forget your hat and gloves."

They kiss. And Ted is gone.

Alice sits on the bed where Ted had just been sitting. Everything is happening so fast. *Of course, he's going to the Volunteers. Of course he's going to join the fight*, she thinks. *He's British, after all; British before all. Sitting out the battle would be unthinkable.* Alice looks at the door and then at Ted's suitcase standing in the open closet. He'd taken his clothes out and put them in the bureau drawers when they first arrived for their relaxing holiday.

Alice hears the boom of distant artillery. She gets up, crosses the room to the windows, and closes the curtains. She curses the war and the beastly Japanese and prays for Ted to return quickly and safely.

Ted returns that evening, intact but a bit grubby. He quickly heads to take a bath. When he emerges a little later, rubbing his hair with a towel, he says, "My job with the Volunteers is quite safe. I'm not trained as a soldier, so they've assigned me to work in a warehouse. I'll be managing foodstuffs and food distribution."

Alice is flooded with a feeling of relief. "Oh, that's good. You'll be useful there."

He frowns. "But I worry about you, Alice. Please be very careful. Stay away from the windows, darling."

"I'm fine, really, Ted, fine. Don't think about me. There're lots of other ladies here. We play bridge and there's a lovely library downstairs. And at any rate, the Japanese won't come this far."

They hear the unmistakable sound of gunfire in the distance.

"The Japs are over in the New Territories, aren't they?" Alice says. "I don't think they'll be able to cross the bay to Victoria."

"Look," Ted says. "I admit that at first, we were caught completely off guard. But after a bit of confusion, we're now organized. We've absolutely marvelous chaps in our military. Our command staff's top-notch. Absolutely top-notch! This war will be over very soon. Yes, before we know it."

***

The following evening, Ted returns late. He tells Alice he had trouble finding a taxi.

On the third day, Ted doesn't manage to get back to the hotel at all. But he telephones.

"I really can't tell you just where I am," he says in reply to her query. Alice hears the sound of heavy arms in the background. "I'm sorry, darling. Security and all."

Now Alice is worried. More than worried—frightened. But

she doesn't want Ted to detect her fear in the tone of her voice, so she remains silent.

"Alice?" he says. "I promise. I'll be back tomorrow."

Alice keeps busy. She introduces herself to some of the other hotel guests; one of the ladies was recently married in Shanghai. Alice discovers that her mother, Katie, had designed the lady's wedding gown and bridesmaids' dresses in her shop in the French Concession, so they chat about current bridal fashions and ladies' fashions in general. Alice tries to ignore the sound of gunfire as they sit together. Alice makes every attempt to look calm and behave as if everything is under control, even though it clearly is not. She tells herself that Ted is a clever man, he'll be all right, but she's terrified at not knowing where he is and what is happening around him. She wishes they hadn't made so many social calls and had spent more time alone together. She wishes they had left Hong Kong earlier, right after his business calls were completed. She wishes they had postponed their trip to Hong Kong altogether, then realizes that Ted wouldn't have been able to put off an important interview, in any event.

That night, just after midnight, seven young Canadian soldiers slip into the hotel's back entrance. Three are wounded. They tell Alice and the few other guests still in the dining room that Japanese soldiers are in the mountains behind the hotel. The muffled sound of gunshots supports their account. One of the elderly ladies, Mrs. Mosey, a retired nurse, quickly takes charge of the wounded men and turns a small anteroom off the lobby into an infirmary. She'd accepted a nursing position at the hotel thinking there would be only minor mishaps to contend with.

Days pass. By December 16, Ted has neither returned to the hotel nor called, and Alice is frantic with fear. All but four of the male guests have gone to join the Volunteers, leaving only elderly retirees, including one gentleman in a wheelchair, remaining at the hotel. When the water supply is suddenly cut off—no water to cook with, no water to wash in, no water to flush the toilets, no *water*—a quiet gentleman with a thin mustache that resembles a pencil line, a retired military officer, steps forward and directs the hotel's sommelier to take a couple of bellhops with him into the wine cellar and bring up every bottle they find, no matter how precious. When the bottles of Chablis, merlot, Riesling, and champagne are standing in rows on one table and the brandies, rums, cognacs, scotches, gins, and vermouths on another, the officer instructs several bellhops to open them and fill all the toilet tanks, which have not been flushed for days. "This is a far better use for the liquor, no matter how fine, than to have it fall into the enemy's hands," he says. Alice shudders, picturing drunk Japanese soldiers.

A few days later, a British soldier manages to get to the hotel, bringing news. "On December thirteenth, the Japanese high command sent a surrender petition to Major Boxer," he says. "British high command refused. 'Who do they think we are?' they'd replied. 'Surrender? Never!'" The solider goes on to say that the same proposal was made again on the seventeenth, and again the British refused.

Finally, on December 20, Ted manages to call. Alice is elated to hear from him and asks whether there is something she can do to help the war effort. He tells Alice he just wanted to hear her voice to reassure himself that she's fine, as well as to tell her that he's safe. Ted hurries off the phone; he can only tie up the line for a few minutes. "I'll call you tomorrow, I love you," Ted says.

And Ted does. On December 21, he gets through for two minutes, just long enough to reassure Alice again that he's fine. Then, on the twenty-second, when there's no call, Alice doesn't worry, at least not more than usual.

***

On the twenty-third, a call comes in from Ted's commanding officer. He tells Alice that the building where Ted and several other men were working on food distribution had been shelled the night before, a direct hit, causing its boiler to explode.

Alice's voice catches in her throat, her legs feel weak, then crumple. Still holding the phone to her ear, she collapses into a wicker chair that's standing near the phone. *Oh my God, no! Please God. No!*

The officer says that the men working with Ted, who escaped out the front of the building, believed that Ted had run out the back, but Ted hasn't yet returned to the post. There's a long pause. "I'm very sorry, Mrs. Dobbs," the commanding officer says. "I'll call you with any further news."

Two days later, in the morning, the officer calls to say Ted has officially been listed as missing. It's Christmas Day.

Alice puts her hands over her closed eyes. She tells herself that her husband cannot possibly be dead; it's just not possible. The officer said he was missing—that's not dead. *If he's missing,* she thinks, trying to stay calm, *where could he be? I'll look for him. And I'll find him.* Her eyes snap open. *I can find him.*

Alice approaches the hotel's concierge, a distinguished-looking gentleman with a friendly smile and bushy white mustache and short beard. "Perhaps you could try the hospitals," he says in a sympathetic tone, opening a drawer in his desk and handing Alice a sheet of paper—a list. "Perhaps he's unable to talk, unable to tell the staff where to contact you. But don't go out just yet, Mrs. Dobbs—please. The fighting . . . it's far too dangerous."

"Listen, the shelling seems to have stopped," Alice says. "Do you think the Japanese have silenced their guns to commemorate the holiday?"

"I don't know," the concierge says. "Maybe it's on the radio." He approaches an ornate wooden case and turns the tall radio on. And in this way the hotel guests, and Alice, learn that Hong Kong has surrendered.

The same afternoon, Alice takes the list of hospitals and heads through the lobby.

"Missy." A bellhop approaches. "Please don't go out. I hear that gangs are roaming the streets, looting."

"Thank you, I must look for my husband," Alice replies softly.

Alice walks out to the street, where she finds a Chinese workman with a truck who agrees to take her to the various hospitals—for a price. The man drives carefully, steering around the bomb craters, large and small, in the road.

At Precious Blood Hospital on Castle Peak Road, the sisters are gracious but say that although they're caring for many wounded soldiers, they haven't seen anyone meeting Ted's description. Alice then visits St. Paul's Hospital in Causeway Bay and then St. Teresa's on Prince Edward Road, but Ted is not in either of them.

Again Alice consults her list. She thinks she should check at the British Military Hospital; it sounds more promising. She asks the driver to take her to the hospital on Borrett Road.

At the military hospital Alice introduces herself to the first person she meets, a man in uniform. "You're welcome to walk through the wards, Mrs. Dobbs," the officer tells her.

Alice walks up and down between the beds, greeting the men who're not asleep or bandaged to the point of invisibility. But Ted's not there either.

Looking around the large ward and at the haggard faces, Alice realizes how terribly busy, how overworked, the staff is. She has an idea. If she volunteers here, she'll know right away if Ted is brought in. Alice speaks to a woman in a nurse's uniform who introduces her to the head nurse. Alice says she'd like to volunteer to help in the wards, and the head nurse says they can use an extra set of hands. The matron tells Alice she's welcome to stay in the brick mansion across the road, where the nurses are housed.

The next day, Alice brings her suitcase to the mansion and is assigned a bed. She crosses the road to the hospital.

"What's your training?" the supervisor asks, eyeing Alice up and down.

"I'm sorry," Alice says. "I'm not a nurse."

"No training?"

"No, but I do have three children."

"Probably with amahs," the supervisor says under her breath. She turns and rummages around in a closet behind her and comes out with an aide's uniform. "Please go down to the basement. Someone there will show you how we wash the bodies to prepare them for burial."

***

A few days later, one of the doctors comes to find Alice in the morgue to tell her that the Japanese military have laid out the bodies of the unidentified dead at the racecourse in Happy Valley. "May I leave right away, sir?" Alice asks. As she rushes out of the building, a friendly voice calls from behind her, "Here, take this." An orderly hands Alice a large handkerchief, saying, "You'll need it."

Alice manages to find a taxi. The driver agrees to take her to the racecourse but insists on stopping to let her off a block away from the entrance. "Be careful, Missy, there're many bad spirits in this area," the driver says. Alice pays him and steps out of the taxi, giving him something extra to help him face the possibility of encountering an evil spirit. "I don't like to drive in this area," he says, shaking his head. "It's bad luck."

Alice hurries away from the taxi and walks resolutely, as fast as possible, toward the racecourse. She's not sure whether she wants to find Ted's body there or not. If he's dead, what will happen to her? Her mind goes blank. Then, resignedly, she tells herself, *I will look. I will look, no matter how hard it is. At least in that way I will know he's not here. I must look. What's going to happen without Ted?* She forces herself to continue toward the racecourse. What will happen to John and Ferfer? Her throat closes up at the thought of John and Ferfer being in danger. *No,* she tells herself, *no. They're safe. They're with Ping San. There's no war, no fighting, no bombing in Kunming.*

As Alice reaches the entrance to the racetrack, a ghastly stench engulfs her as if rising from the pavement. She claps the big handkerchief over her nose, but it does little to mask the penetrating odor. Every nerve in her body begs her to turn around, to return to the hospital, but she grits her teeth and forces herself forward. *I've come this far,* she thinks, *and I'm not turning back now. Ted is here. I can feel it in my bones. I just have to find him.*

Alice pushes through the double doors and past other searchers, single men and women, couples leaning on each other, and small groups—families—even a few children. Just ahead of her walks an elderly and elegantly dressed lady leaning on her amah. She forces her eyes to stay in focus, to look ahead. She can hardly believe the ghastly sight laid out in front of her. She demands each foot to take one more step forward, holding the square of cloth over her face, trying not to gag at the stench. Stretched out before her are hundreds, perhaps thousands, of mangled human bodies and body parts, placed side by side around the grassy embankment of the entire racecourse, a distance of almost a mile.[12] Some of the forms are recognizable as men, others so disfigured that it's almost impossible to believe that the mass of blackened flesh was once a living, breathing human being. All are stained with blood and smeared with dirt, earth, or oil—whatever they happened to have fallen onto when they were killed. Alice forces herself to keep looking.

Walking slowly, Alice fights her body's reactions. She struggles to keep standing, to keep moving forward. A sob grows in her throat; she feels sick. Trying not to vomit, she reaches for a post to steady herself. As she glances at the ground, she realizes again that she's now alone and on her own. She forces herself to put one foot in front of the other, makes herself examine the soldiers' faces—white, Indian, Chinese . . . but mostly white—and she's barely able to hold her head up, barely able to look at them, these poor men. Each of them someone's love. Each of them someone's husband, brother, father, son. Many young, barely out of school. She looks at the mangled uniforms and tells herself Ted was not in uniform. He could not be one of these horrifying cadavers. But there're many bodies not in the uniform of any country.

On and on she plods around the oval, feeling the racetrack under her feet, her legs getting heavier with every step. *Ted, my love,* she thinks in despair, *where are you? I have to find you. I need to find you.* Now only stubborn determination guides Alice around the track. She arrives back at the entrance; she's completed the circle.

Ted's not here.

NOTES

1.   This chapter is partially based on the one short letter, written to her mother, that Alice was permitted to write while interned in Stanley Civilian Internment Camp, Hong Kong.

2.   Opened in 1925 and closed in 1988, Kai Tak Airport was considered the sixth most dangerous airport in the world because of its location: mountains topping 610 meters (two thousand feet) to the northeast of the runways, water on three sides, and tall residential buildings close by. Landing at Kai Tak was technically demanding because all approaches had to be made visually, not by instruments.

3.   China National Aviation Corporation (CNAC) was established in 1929 by China's Nationalist government. Within two weeks, the airline entered into a contract with Curtiss-Wright and several other American firms to service a number of airmail routes in China. Subsequently, after a series of events—including threats of bankruptcy, scandal, and heavy competition—45 percent of the airline was sold to Pan American Airways.

4.   Lane Crawford department store opened in Hong Kong in 1850 and continues to be a premier department store there.

5.   Maj. Charles Boxer (1904–2000) attended England's Royal Military College and served in the British army for twenty-four years. After language and intelligence training, he spent three years in the Japanese Army as part of an exchange program. Following work in London, he was sent to Hong Kong and became a key member of the British intelligence organization that stretched from Shanghai to Singapore. Severely wounded in action during the Japanese attack, Maj. Boxer was taken prisoner and remained a captive until 1945. After the war, Maj. Boxer had an illustrious career as an academic historian.

6.   When the Repulse Bay Hotel opened in 1920, guests could arrive only by sedan chair or seaplane. Very shortly thereafter, however, a road was built to accommodate the owner's Rolls-Royce, the first such car in Hong Kong. A favorite among artists, movie stars, and royalty, the hotel was considered the premier hotel

in the East, with 190 staff catering to just thirty-two rooms. Its massive flower and herb gardens kept the lobbies and rooms decorated, as well as the kitchens stocked with herbs. The hotel was demolished in 1982.

Although it's possible that Alice and Ted stayed at the Repulse Bay Hotel in 1941, they probably stayed at the Hongkong Hotel, where Alice and Ted's Shanghai friends stayed at the time. Standing at the corner of Queen's Road Central and Pedder Street, the Hongkong Hotel opened in 1868 and was Hong Kong's first luxury hotel, having been modeled after large London establishments. It had a large restaurant, the Gripps, that was popular with the public. The hotel was expanded along the waterfront of Victoria City in 1893 and closed in 1952.

7. Established in 1907, Wing On Department Store on Des Voeux Road is the largest and best-known department store in Hong Kong.

8. Once an island in Hong Kong's Victoria Harbour, Stonecutters Island is now attached to the Kowloon Peninsula following land reclamation. The island was initially used by the British for quarrying, hence the name. In 1935, a Royal Navy radio-interception and direction-finding station was installed on Stonecutters Island, and it became the primary Far East location for radio interception.

9. With an elevation of 549 meters (eighteen hundred feet), Victoria Peak is the highest of three hills in the area on Hong Kong Island. "The Peak" is prime residential property because it boasts a magnificent panoramic view of the town, harbor, and surrounding island, as well as a temperate climate. There are also public parks and trails on the hill, all of which can be reached by the Peak Tram funicular built in 1888 and still functioning.

10. The British authorities were unprepared for the Japanese attack on Hong Kong in many ways. Because they believed that any attack on the colony would come from the sea—not the land or air—all artillery was aimed in that direction and difficult if not impossible to turn.

During the Battle of Hong Kong, the colony was defended by British, Indian, and Canadian troops. The latter had arrived only a few weeks before the battle began. These forces were supported by the Hong Kong Volunteer Defence Corps (HKVDC), made up of local citizens from all professions. Hong Kong's defenders were outnumbered by well over three to one: Japan had fifty-two thousand troops, whereas they had only fourteen thousand. In addition, the Japanese Army was supported by collaborators placed throughout the city, who, for example, signaled the location of Allied gun emplacements to the enemy. Hong Kong lacked not only airpower, but also military vehicles; the military were forced to commandeer cars, trucks, and vans from the citizenry. Military casualties included 2,113 killed or missing; twenty-three hundred wounded; and ten thousand captured. Civilian—mostly Chinese—casualties included four thousand killed and three thousand severely wounded. Japanese casualties included 675 killed and 2,079 wounded. The battle lasted just seventeen days.

11. The Hong Kong Volunteer Defence Corps (HKVDC), first formed in 1854 when Hong Kong's military defense left to fight in the Crimean War, was made up of civilians from all walks of life. When the Battle of Hong Kong began, it had twenty-two hundred members. When it ended, 289 were listed as killed or missing, and although some managed to escape to Free China (i.e., Chungking), most became prisoners of war.

12. Happy Valley Racecourse was built in 1845 to provide entertainment for the British residents of Hong Kong, but over the years, it was opened up to the Chinese citizens as well. The racecourse is .85 miles (1.37 kilometers) long.

23

The Firecracker

Last Week of December 1941
Chengdu, Sichuan Province, China

It's December 25, and we're in our kitchen in Kunming with Ping San, listening to the radio. John sits at the table watching Cook chop vegetables. I look out the window, wondering when Father Christmas will come, and since I'm just beginning to make the connection between my parents and Father Christmas, wondering *whether* Father Christmas will come at all if Mummy and Daddy aren't here. An announcer says that Hong Kong has surrendered to the Japanese, and Ping San snaps the radio off. He looks worried.

A few days later at breakfast, he tells John and me that our parents have been delayed on their way back to Kunming and that they want us to go and stay with some friends.

This is how we learn that John and I are going to Chengdu.[1] Ping San tells us that an American couple with children in Chengdu have offered to take care of us until Daddy and Mummy come and get us. We also learn that our wash coolie, Shou Fung, has agreed to accompany us there. Ping San tells us that the new wash coolie's home village is north of Chengdu and he wants to return there. He's afraid that he might get picked up and forced to go into the army if he stays in Kunming. He can hide at home.

Before we leave, I hear Ping San tell Cook and Amah that the money Master gave him to manage the household while they were gone is running low, but I don't understand what that means. Then I see Ping San selling Mummy's and Daddy's things, even their clothes, and I get very upset. Why is Ping San selling these things? Won't Mummy and Daddy need them when they come back? It seems very odd, but I don't say anything to Ping San, something tells me not to ask him about it. I can't ask John, either; he wouldn't know. I decide to ask Daddy when he and Mummy get back.

Ping San packs a small brown suitcase for each of us with our toothbrushes, toothpaste, and a change of clothing and lots of the little bags of flea powder that Amah in Shanghai made. The next morning Shou Fung straps our cases on his back and leads us by the hand up the broad, tree-lined boulevard to Kunming's railway station. There we must push through a large crowd of soldiers, young men, who are milling around on the platform as we try to reach the ticket-seller's office. When we finally get near the window, Shou Fung motions to two men on a bench to move over and tells us to sit there, placing our cases between us.

I watch as Shou Fung elbows his way up to the ticket window.

The teller ignores him until Shou Fung rattles the bars between them.

"Go away," the teller says. "The train's full. It only takes soldiers. The soldiers go to fight."

"We want to go to Chengdu," Shou Fung says.

"I don't care where you want to go. There's no space on the trains."

"We're going to Chengdu," Shou Fung repeats.

"That's fine," the railroad agent says, "but there's no space on any train."

Shou Fung turns around to collect us and the cases, and we squeeze our way back out of the waiting room and the platform. Now hanging on to Shou Fung's jacket, we trudge back to the house.

"There's no places on the train," Shou Fung says as we come through the front door. Ping San's very surprised to see us.

Shou Fung drinks a glass of water, then heads over to the bus station to see if we can take a bus, telling us he'll be back shortly. When he returns, he tells Ping San and us that the bus is also full of soldiers.

The next morning, Shou Fung takes us to a main road several blocks from the house and bundles us into the cab of an old army truck with a Chinese driver. He climbs in behind. "Ping San arranged this ride last night," he says. I think how clever Ping San is to find a truck going in the direction we need to go.

I look back through the cab's muddy little oval window and see that we're carrying a load of fifty-five-gallon barrels.

"Is that gasoline?" I ask, pointing toward the window. There's no reply. The driver's and Shou Fung's eyes are pasted onto the road ahead. I realize that there are more people on foot than I'd remembered seeing in the past, so the driver has to be very careful. I look at John. He doesn't look happy. "It's all right, John," I say. "Ping San arranged for us to ride with the Chinese truck driver." Then I ask the men, "How far away is Chengdu?"

"It's eight, nine hundred kilometers," Shou Fung says. "It'll take us three days, maybe more. This driver's not going all the way there, we'll have to find another ride."

I'm lulled to sleep by the sloshing back and forth of the gasoline in the large metal drums. Two hours later the truck stops with a sudden jerk, shaking me awake. I see trees and farmland. The men get out and go to the side of the road, turning their backs. John joins them, so I look for a tree to hide behind while I have the chance.

***

It's dark now. The truck bumps to a stop outside a low building curled around a walled courtyard, a typical Chinese house. A great number of mules are clustered in the courtyard, being fed and watered. Some mules still have packs on their backs, while some have had the packs lifted off and placed on the ground next to the wall. John and I watch with interest as the mules shake, stomp their feet impatiently, and breathe out great streams of mist as they wait to be fed. A young boy runs around the yard with a shovel and bag, picking up droppings as quickly as they fall.

Daddy once told us that strings of mules are used to carry loads such as tea and silk for long distances on the famous Silk

Road;[2] are these the mules? Then I realize they're probably not, because although the Silk Road starts in Kunming, it goes to the west, and Shou Fung said we have to go north to get to Chengdu.

"Come," Shou Fung says.

We follow him into a big, dim room and stand silently behind him while he talks to a man who must be the owner of the inn. Stretching to look around Shou Fung's sturdy body, I see several *kang* heaped with quilts.[3] People are huddled on top of them, so I assume they've been claimed for the night.

Shou Fung turns to John and me and points to a narrow wooden ladder I hadn't noticed against the wall. "We'll sleep up-stairs," he says.

We return to the cab of the truck, which is parked in the street outside the courtyard, to eat the last of the sandwiches that Ping San made for us. Then, wearily, we go back into the inn. Shou Fung goes up the steep ladder first, followed by John and then me.

At the top of the ladder, a big room, the attic, opens up under the inn's sloping roof. Adjusting my eyes to the dim light, I see that the floor's covered by a thick layer of straw, and then—before I realize just what the lumps scattered about in the straw are—coughing, wheezing, hawking, and spitting reveal coolies. When my eyes finally adjust, I see that there's an attic full of coolies, rolled in cloaks or blankets. They're lying or half sitting up in the straw.

Why do they make so much noise? I wonder. *Are they sick?*

John's hand is covering his nose. The stench of garlic and hot peppers makes me want to turn and climb back down the ladder, but I wait to see what will happen next as we squeeze together at the top of the ladder. Shou Fung doesn't seem fazed. He looks around and then points to an unoccupied spot near where the wall meets the roof. "There," he says. "That's a good place." We quickly crawl over to the spot Shou Fung has chosen and snuggle down in the straw. The straw's comfortable. It's not bad at all.

I take John's hand. He's already fallen asleep. I'm exhausted and want to close my eyes too, but I notice in the dim light seeping in from the few paper-covered windows that two men are glancing in our direction, so I force myself to stay awake. Sure enough, when the chorus of spits and snores subsides, telling me that some of the coolies have fallen asleep, I can hear the two men whispering. I understand a few of the words, clear even in dialect: *English children, money.* I look at Shou Fung, who is between us and the mule-team drivers. He's still sitting up, chewing on betel nuts and spitting the shells into the straw. He won't sleep, I think; he'll guard us. I close my eyes. But I'm restless all night and wake up almost as tired as I was the night before.

The following day I see Shou Fung go out and talk to the drivers who've parked and slept in their cabs outside the inn. When he returns to us, he says he's found a truck going north—the direction we need to go. I know in Shanghai the servants talked to the servants of the other Western people, so they knew everything about everyone in the city. Mummy told me once that when she and Daddy went to England on home leave, Ping San knew when they were returning without her even writing a letter to him, and he was waiting for them on the dock when they got back. I usually ask Ping San if I want to know something.

The new driver is a friendly young man with thin eyebrows and a big smile. He seems to like children, because he tries to talk to us, especially John, but it's hard to understand his dialect. We ride all day with him. The weather is nice, and although we must drive slowly because of all the carts, donkeys, mules, goats, and people that we share the road with, the ride's fun. The only thing that's not fun is we've finished the food that Ping San gave us for the trip.

In the evening we stop at a truck driver place. A field where drivers going in all directions stop for the night. They especially love John, probably because he's a boy—and because he's little. They talk to him, tickle him, and tell him jokes and stories. They are very good at telling funny stories. It's hard to understand their stories that are told in dialect, but when all the drivers laugh heartily, we laugh too. We sit around a big cauldron built over a fire, waiting for the rice to cook. When all the water has boiled away and the rice is ready, the drivers pull chopsticks out of the folds of their blue padded jackets as the steaming bowls are passed to them.

The man serving the rice puts the crusty scorched bits in John's bowl. The portion scraped from around the edge of the pot is considered the tastiest rice, and a treat. I'm happy that the men are nice to my brother. I try to hide how I feel from him. I don't like being passed from person to person, to people who I think don't know Mummy and Daddy. John's happy with everyone. Unlike me, he's good at showing the men that he enjoys their attentions. He smiles and laughs with them.

That night when we go back to the truck to sleep, I notice that John keeps pulling at his shorts; he's been doing that off and on all day. Shou Fung takes John's hand and tells us we'll arrive in Chengdu tomorrow.

***

While driving the next day, we make one last stop so the men can pee while we're still in the countryside away from houses. I'm glad we are almost there. Traveling without Mummy and Daddy is worrying. I think of stories I've heard about bandits, thieves, and pirates—but of course, that's only when you're on water. It's easy to get carried away when you don't know where your parents are.

"Do you have the address where the children are going?" the driver asks Shou Fung when we finally arrive in the city. Shou Fung pulls a scrap of paper out of his jacket and hands it to the driver, who glances sideways at it. "I can't read," he says.

Shou Fung reads from the scrap, but the driver shakes his head and pulls the truck over to ask for directions from a shopkeeper. The man's standing outside a small butcher shop; slabs of raw meat hang above his head, and live chickens cluck, crammed into bamboo cages around his feet. The butcher says the house is near the university, and the driver gets back in the truck.

We drive past stores, tall hotels, office buildings, and finally a university campus, then onto a dirt road. The driver stops in front of a handsome Western-style brick house surrounded by a low brick wall and a gatehouse.

A man, a woman, and two little girls come out onto the front steps. The girls look to be about the same age as John and me. The sight of this family reminds me of our own family. I do hope that Mummy and Daddy come to get us soon. Ping San said they would.

The woman waves us into the big house. The front door opens

directly into a wide hallway. Through archways on each side of the hall, I see a pretty living room with a piano on the right and a dining room with a big oval table on the left. There's a staircase that leads to the second floor.

"I'm Dr. Fenn,"[4] the man says, "and this is Mrs. Fenn. And these are our daughters, Mary Frances and Sarah Alice." I wonder if their parents always address the girls by their two names. They're beautiful girls, with lovely long pigtails, long enough for them to sit on. And they're wearing clean, pretty dresses. I look down at my dirty shorts.

"Amah," Mrs. Fenn calls, and an amah comes into the hall from the dining room. "Draw a bath for the new children, please. And be sure to wash their hair," she adds, looking back and forth between us.

Then Mrs. Fenn turns to look at John again. He's tugging at his shorts. The expression on John's face worries me.

"Girls, please go into the dining room," Mrs. Fenn says. "And John, please go to the kitchen." She looks at her husband. "We need to see if there's a problem." Mrs. Fenn waves toward Mary Frances, Sarah Alice, and me. We hurry toward the dining room.

Dr. Fenn takes John's hand and, followed by his wife, pushes through a swinging door. I slip as close as possible to it and overhear Dr. Fenn say, "John, please take down your shorts." There's a pause and a noise I think is the sound of my brother's shorts landing on the floor. Then I hear a gasp and what sounds like someone loudly drawing in a breath. Then a sob.

"Poor little boy. It's red as a firecracker." It's Mrs. Fenn's voice. "Cook, give the child a cup of warm water that he can soak it in."

NOTES

1. Chengdu is the capital and, at the time of this story, was the third-largest city of the Western Chinese province of Sichuan. During World War II it also served briefly as the capital of China before Chiang Kai-shek moved on to Chungking. Universities and businesses, as well as their academics and employees, migrated there to escape the invading Japanese. Chengdu managed to remain beyond the enemy's reach throughout the war. It is now the largest city in the province.

2. The Silk Road was a series of trails through Central Asia, about sixty-four hundred kilometers (four thousand miles) in length. Camel and mule caravans traveled back and forth along the Silk Road carrying goods such as silk, sugar, salt, gold, jade, tea, and spices to trade.

3. A *kang* is a Chinese sleeping platform built of brick under which a fire can be lit. Often the entire family, or a group of people, lie on it together. *Kang* are popular mainly in the North China countryside.

4. Although the Rev. Dr. William P. Fenn was born in the United States, he grew up in China, where his father was a highly respected Presbyterian missionary. Dr. Fenn was the head of foreign languages at Nanking University in 1932 and moved to Chengdu with the school ahead of the Japanese advance. His wife, Frances Fenn, was also an educational missionary. During my 1998 trip to China, I went to Chengdu, but even equipped with a photo of the Fenns' house, I was unable to find it.

24

Imprisoned

Early January 1942
My Imagination: Hong Kong, British Crown Colony

Alice presses her eyes tightly shut as she leans against the railing of the rusty old Star Ferry heading to Stanley Civilian Internment Camp in Hong Kong.[1] Only women and children are on the deck; the men have been sent below. She listens to the constant slapping of the bay against the sides of the ship as it moves through the harbor. She's squeezed into a narrow space along the railing and grateful to be able to fill her lungs with the fresh sea air. She thinks about the poor men who are forced to inhale what must be fetid air belowdecks.

Alice tries to blot out the memory of everything that's happened since January 4, when the Japanese posted signs ordering all British, American, Dutch, and other foreign nationals to assemble at the Murray parade ground. She tries to forget the past three weeks locked in a filthy, dilapidated narrow building, the Mee Chow Hotel—hotel by name, brothel by vocation—where four or five people, regardless of age or sex, were squeezed into each tiny cubicle with little food, practically no water, and one bed and one chair per room. She doesn't know what would have happened to her if her Chinese friends and other friends' loyal servants, as well as those who just wanted to make some cash, hadn't passed food through the windows to the detainees.

The ferry begins to roll, the water is rough. Someone behind her vomits. Alice opens her eyes. *Oh my God,* she thinks. *What now?*

***

Two hours later the group disembarks. The men, women, and children slowly cross a narrow gangplank and an old wooden somewhat-dilapidated jetty that wobbles as the crowd walks over it, then climb a rocky path. The Americans are directed toward three white rectangular concrete buildings. The British, Dutch, Russian, and other civilian nationals are sent in the opposite direction to other similar buildings. Someone tells Alice that the apartment blocks were originally constructed to house the wardens of a nearby prison and their families, but she hardly hears.

Alice goes with the Americans. Although she's had a British passport since she and Ted were married, when Hong Kong surrendered to Japan, a friend of theirs from Shanghai, Norwood Allman,[2] told her to throw it away and to say she's an American and that she'd lost her passport. He said this was the logical thing to do, since America was farther away from the war. Alice had torn up her British passport without emotion. She thought that as an American, she might also be in a better position to find her children.

Alice finds a place to sleep, albeit on the floor, in a tiny room with two families, one with two young children. The Japanese have made no provisions for the arrival of the internees, have provided no furniture, no cooking or eating utensils, no beds or bedding, no stoves, nothing. There are bathrooms, mostly Chinese-style holes in the floor, but there's no water.

In spite of everything, Alice gets accustomed to the grueling life in the camp. The internees, determined to survive, find, make, or make do with what they can find, organize and run their small community. Desperate smokers roll cigarettes out of pine needles, leaves, grass, or discarded tea leaves. Handles are soldered onto tin cans to make mugs; clothes are created from sacks and old curtains; shoes fashioned from cloth, with hinged wooden soles. But the biggest worry is food. The little food provided by the Japanese is practically inedible. The rice requires picking over to remove little brown weevils, grubs, dirt, and rat and roach droppings. The turnips, pumpkins, and Chinese cabbage make only a thin, watery soup. Occasionally there's a sweet potato—a huge treat. And very occasionally, packages arrive from family, friends, and the Red Cross. Alice's weight falls to eighty-five pounds.

The Americans and British internees keep busy, each in their own group, with innumerable chores and committee assignments: cooking, hygiene, medical care, schooling, entertainment, religious services, and sports—although no one has much energy for sports. Alice contributes by helping the sewing committee stitch shorts and tops for the ever-thinner ladies and by taking her turn in the kitchen, peeling, chopping, and picking debris out of the foodstuff before it's cooked.

Alice moves from the room she shares with the two families to a tiny room and porch with just one other woman. When this woman comes down with beriberi and is moved to the infirmary,[3] Gwen Dew,[4] the only lady journalist in Hong Kong at the time, moves in with Alice. They had first met, although briefly, at the Repulse Bay Hotel.

With each passing day, Alice gets more and more worried about John and Ferfer. Where are they? Are they being looked after? When will she see them again? She hopes that Ping San is keeping them safe. *I trust him, I have to trust him,* she thinks. *I have no choice. When I lost Ted, I lost a part of myself, but I'll get through this however I can and I'll find the children. I must survive. I will survive.*

In the spring of '42, Alice hears a rumor that's flying around the camp, the topic foremost in everyone's mind, second only to food: repatriation.

✳✳✳

Unlike most, this rumor proves to be true when on June 29, 1942, the Japanese ship the *Asama Maru* is seen steaming into Hong Kong's Victoria Harbour.[5] A few days earlier, the ship had picked up American diplomats and members of the Spanish consulate in Yokohama, Japan, and tomorrow it's leaving for New York. There's to be a prisoner exchange: Americans for Japanese.

The approximately three hundred American internees in the Stanley
Civilian Internment Camp in Stanley, Hong Kong, gather before repatriation, 1942. There were also about 2,500 British internees in this Japanese
camp. The British citizens were not repatriated until the war ended in 1945.

In camp, Alice hadn't thought much about repatriation and
what it would mean to her. She'd stumbled around the barbed-
wire enclosure living from minute to minute, day to day, week to
week, numb and half-paralyzed by grief, yet determined to survive. She knows she couldn't have done it without the encour-
agement and support of her friends—Gwen, and Norwood, and
Bill Taylor,[6] friends from Shanghai days. Of their many Shanghai
friends, these happened to be Americans. Their voices constantly
rattled around in her head. *Alice, it's time to get in the chow line,
and don't forget to bring your plate. Alice, what's your identification number? You must say it in Japanese. Remember it, memo-
rize it, you'll need it for roll call.* Alice had thought, *Yes, my tin
plate. Yes, roll call every morning. Yes, yes . . .*

Alice. Alice. Alice.

And then they said, *Alice. Come with us to America.*

***

Alice joins the line and gets vaccinated against cholera and smallpox. With Gwen's help, she manages to complete the required paperwork. Norwood has vouched for her American citizenship and tells her to join the line with the other Americans and Canadians from the camp who will board the boat that will carry them out to the *Asama Maru.*

Everyone is chattering excitedly about going to America, but all Alice can think of is not where she's going but what she's leaving behind. Leaving Hong Kong means abandoning everyone she holds most dear. Ted. The children. Where *are* the children? Where is Ted? The last she knew, Teddy was at Chefoo School and John and Ferfer were in Kunming with Ping San. How will she be able to find them after all this time? She is confused but then remembers that Teddy's probably safe; Katie's written that the progress of the war news had bothered her, that Teddy was too far away. She'd asked permission to take him out of school. The letter had caught up with them in Kunming, forwarded by Ted's office. There hadn't been time to reply to it. How could she have forgotten?

Alice considers leaving the line. Perhaps she could join the Brits and wait to be released here in Hong Kong after the war, then look for the children, go back to Kunming. But how? She has very little money, no resources, and she doesn't even know if

CNAC Airlines is still operating. *Where is my beloved Ted?* she thinks. *He would know what to do.* A hundred times a day, she silently asks Ted what she should do, but he never answers.

Alice draws in a long breath. She's going to have to make this decision by herself. Perhaps the best thing to do after all is to go to America and ask the government for help in finding her children. There's no more time to decide. The Americans and Canadians begin walking single file down the path to the rickety pier and somberly climb aboard the tug that will carry them out to the *Asama Maru*. Other American citizens who had not been interned in Stanley but were allowed to stay in town join the group.[7] Alice glances back and sees a crowd of British internees standing near the barbed-wire fence, waving goodbye.

On board the *Asama Maru* Alice is asked her name and given a slip of paper with her cabin and bunk assignment. She stumbles down stairways and along passages to find her cabin. Even the little she has to carry feels heavy. As she enters the cabin, she glances around and notes that she'll be sharing it with five other women. *At least this cabin's above the waterline,* she thinks as she looks through the one grimy porthole. She puts her suitcase under her bunk and decides to go up to the ship's deck to clear her head. And maybe she can find her friends.

On her third lap around the deck, Alice sees Norwood.

"Alice!" Norwood says, extending his hand. "Sorry I've not had a chance to look you up since coming aboard. How are you?"

"I'm all right. In fact, I was looking for you," Alice says. "Have you heard anything of your wife and son?"

"I just learned their whereabouts; Louise and John are on the

Conte Verde. They set sail from Shanghai and will meet us when we dock in Singapore," Norwood says, smiling. "It's been almost a year since I've seen them."

Alice is thrilled to hear his news. Still, she can't help wishing that she were in his place, soon to be reunited with his family.

And when the ship steams out of the harbor the next morning, all the thoughts and feelings Alice suffered when she first arrived at the POW camp resurface. Now, she tells herself, she's leaving Hong Kong. She's leaving China. She's leaving the children. She's leaving Ted. For a second time she must face—and this time it's harder, yet she must accept—that the life she knew in the East is gone, past, lost forever. Her husband, her marriage, her home—all now only a mirage. She catches herself. There're still the children. Only the children are real. She must find them.

***

When the *Asama Maru* stops in Saigon on July 3, 114 additional repatriates are taken aboard, and three days later, in Singapore, another group of Americans board, including Norwood's Louise and John. At each port, natives row out to the ship in canoes or small boats to sell fruit, souvenirs, and other trinkets. Alice looks on as melons, pineapples, and gaudy cotton shirts are hoisted aboard in baskets tied onto ropes provided by the ship's stewards. Although Alice sold everything she possibly could before she left the camp, she's now afraid to spend the little cash in her pocket.

After the American and Canadian passengers from the *Conte Verde* are transferred to the *Asama Maru*, the two ships depart Singapore and sail in tandem across the Indian Ocean. When the *Asama Maru* reaches Lourenço Marques, Mozambique, on July 23, Alice learns that a total of 789 American and Canadian civilians will be exchanged for fifteen hundred Japanese citizens and a few Siamese diplomats who are currently on board the MS *Gripsholm.*[8] Lourenço Marques was chosen for the prisoner exchange because it lies roughly halfway between New York and Yokohama, she also hears.

The ships spend six days in port. There's a lot of paperwork to be done, and the two ships must also take on additional supplies. Finally, the exchange is ready. Alice is told that in order to avoid the possibility of a confrontation between the American and Japanese repatriates, train cars have been positioned on the pier so that the two groups are unable to see each other as they file by.[9]

Before taking her place in line, Alice makes herself as presentable as possible, but she still feels shabby in her best outfit, a peach-colored shorts-and-shirt set she'd stitched from an old curtain found in the room she'd shared with Gwen. Gwen had handed the fabric to her, saying, "Alice, I know you can make something nice out of this. I saved it for you."

Well, Alice thinks, *gone are the days of chiffon dresses and T-strap sandals, but at least I'm tidy.*

Once aboard the *Gripsholm,* Alice's circumstances take a turn for the better. On the *Asama Maru,* there was only cold water in the washrooms, and, in addition, the water was only turned on for short periods of time, so she had to hurry to wash. And on the *Asama Maru,* stewards and crew were rude and surly. In contrast, on the *Gripsholm* the stewards do everything they can to make everyone comfortable. And the food! On the

Asama Maru, it wasn't much better than the food in the internment camp, while on the *Gripsholm* there is almost endless meat,
fresh fruit, fresh vegetables. There are oranges. There are pineapples. Alice cannot believe her eyes.

"Be careful, don't eat too heartily," Alice hears a tablemate say
to the man assigned to the seat beside her, as everyone eyes the
roast turkey on a large platter in front of them.

"I know, I know," he says, "my cabinmate made himself ill. I'll
be more careful."

But the aroma wafting from the platter is mouthwatering. It's
hard to get used to having enough food again.

On August 10, the *Gripsholm* arrives in Rio de Janeiro, Brazil.
The layover is short; she's set to depart the next morning. This
is the last leg of her trip to the United States. Alice's long trip is
almost over. Along the route, she's been forced to think about the
future. She's been discussing her misgivings with her friends, like
Norwood and Louise. Slowly she's resigned herself to her new
fate, whatever that might be. *There's no other choice,* she tells herself over and over.

✻✻✻

On August 25, 1942, the MS *Gripsholm* slips into the dock at Pier
F in Jersey City, New Jersey. Alice squeezes between the throngs
congregated at the rail; many have tears running down their
faces, happy to see America, some for the first time. Standing on
tiptoe, she scans the crowd. She's searching for her mother, Katie
Gibb,[10] and perhaps her son Teddy. Not seeing either of them, she

goes back to her cabin and collects her suitcase. Finally, it's her turn to disembark.

On the dock, there's still no word from Katie. Alice is a bit bewildered. As she's trying to decide what to do, a young man approaches. His uniform announces that he's a customs officer.

"Excuse me, ma'am, are you Mrs. Dobbs?" he asks.

"Yes, yes, I am." Alice is startled. How does he know her name? *Is there a problem?* she thinks.

The officer hands Alice a slip of paper and a ten-dollar bill. "A lady asked me to give you this," he says and nods his head. After a pause he adds, "Can I call a taxi for you? There's a line of 'em outside."

Alice looks at the note. *Wonderful, an address.* "Oh, yes, please, a taxi," she replies. Now that she's found her mother, all she needs is to find the children.

***

Alice bounces along for almost an hour, from Jersey City to the Upper West Side of Manhattan, until she arrives at the address on the note. Thoughts and emotions are whirling in her head. Maybe her mother will know where John and Ferfer are. Possibly they're even with her! That would be a wonderful surprise.

At her gentle knock, the apartment door flies open, as though Katie's been waiting impatiently behind it. Katie pulls Alice into a warm hug, then holds her at arm's length.

"Oh, Alice, thank goodness you're here. It's wonderful to have you here at last. But"—Katie holds Alice at arm's length—"look at you!" she exclaims. "You're so thin. We'll go shopping tomorrow to get some clothes that fit." She squeezes Alice's shoulders, gingerly, as though she's afraid to bruise her thin frame, and hugs her again. "But let's not worry about that right now. The important thing is, the nightmare is over. Thank God."

Tears flood Alice's eyes. *My lost Ted* is all she can think of. *The children.* She cannot speak.

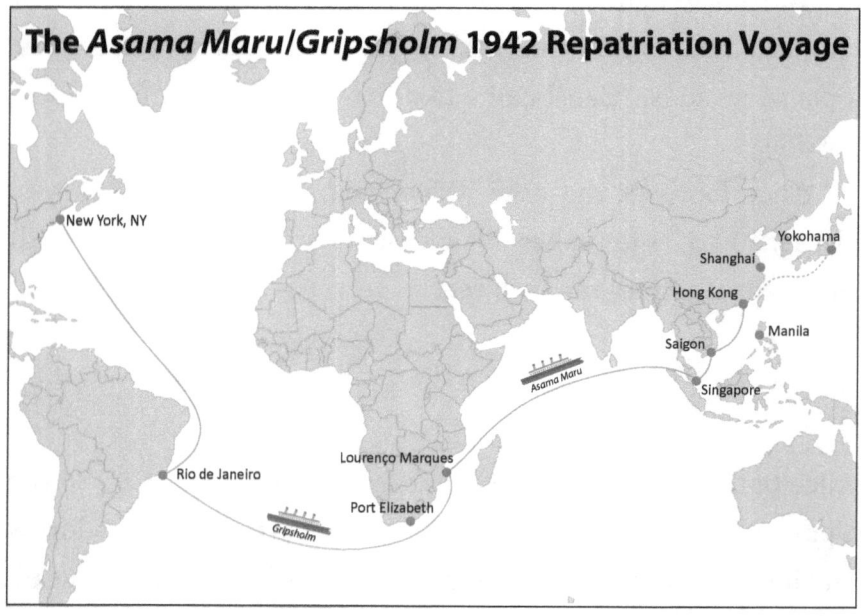

NOTES

1. The Japanese civilian internment camp near the village of Stanley was located on a peninsula at the southern end of Hong Kong Island. In the aftermath of the Battle of Hong Kong, the Japanese hadn't anticipated the presence of captured civilians, so when the approximately twenty-five hundred British and three hundred American prisoners of war, as well as about five hundred other foreign nationals, arrived at the camp, the Japanese were completely unprepared to accommodate them. There were buildings but no running water, kitchens, or adequate toilet facilities.

   The Americans and Canadians in the camp were repatriated in 1942 in two separate sailings. The British didn't go home until the war ended in 1945.

2. Norwood F. Allman (1893–1987) was a lawyer, consular officer, member of the Shanghai Municipal Council, and newspaperman in Shanghai. He was caught on a business trip in Hong Kong when the Japanese attacked, and like my mother, he was interned in Stanley and repatriated on the MS *Gripsholm*. His incredibly detailed memoir, *Shanghai Lawyer*, was published in 1943.

3. Beriberi is a disease caused by a vitamin B1 deficiency. Symptoms can include shortness of breath, mental confusion, vomiting, decreased muscle function with swollen lower limbs, and difficulty speaking.

4. Gwen Dew (1903–93) was an American journalist, photographer, and writer. Gwen had initially evaded internment when the Japanese allowed her to stay in a hotel where she was caring for an elderly gentleman, but she was ultimately transferred to Stanley. She was one of the repatriated Americans in the 1942 prisoner exchange, and after she returned to the United States, she toured as a war bonds rally speaker. Her book *Prisoner of the Japs*, which detailed her experience in the Stanley internment camp, was published in 1943. She wrote two additional books.

5. The Japanese ocean liner *Asama Maru* led a long and checkered life, first as a high-speed trans-Pacific liner between America's West Coast and the Far East, and then as a troop transport and

diplomatic exchange ship. She met her end when she was torpedoed and sunk toward the end of World War II.

6.   William Henry Taylor (1906–65) worked for the US Treasury Department. When the Japanese attacked Hong Kong, he was in China to advise the Chinese Currency Stabilization Fund. Like my mother, he was interned in Stanley and repatriated on the MS *Gripsholm*.

7.   A total of 376 repatriates sailed from Hong Kong on the *Asama Maru*.

8.   The MS *Gripsholm*, built in England for the Swedish American Line, was chartered from 1942 to 1946 by the US Department of State as an exchange and repatriation ship and sailed under the auspices of the International Red Cross. As such, she transported more than twenty-seven thousand men, women, and children.

9.   The contrast between the prisoners who sailed on the *Asama Maru* and the *Gripsholm* was striking. The American repatriates were drawn and gaunt, bowing under the weight of shabby cases and bundles. The Japanese repatriates, on the other hand, looked well fed, were snappily dressed—the women were wearing hats—and carried new leather cases.

10. Kate Candlin Gibb (1885–1968) was born one of six children in Tientsin, China, to Rev. G. T. and Mary Candlin, who had emigrated from England in 1878. Katie married John McGregor Gibb (1882–1939), a chemistry professor at Yenching University in Peking, in 1905. At the outbreak of World War II, Katie took her grandson Teddy out of boarding school and boarded the last ship out of Shanghai—the SS *President Taft*—before the Japanese captured the International Settlement. Katie subsequently made a home for Alice and the children in Wayne and Haverford, Pennsylvania, outside Philadelphia.

25

Count After Me

Mid-January 1942
Chengdu, Sichuan Province, China

Standing on the front steps of the Fenns' house, I watch as John is lifted and placed, facing backward, into a big square metal basket above the back wheel of the gatehouse keeper's bicycle; the basket that the gatehouse keeper uses to carry vegetables home from the market.

Since we arrived two days ago, I've been overhearing anxious telephone conversations in which John's name is frequently mentioned. It seems that Dr. Fenn wants John to go to a hospital right away[1]—I hear the word *emergency* several times—so that must be where John's headed. I should go with him; I don't like to be separated from him, but no one has asked me anything or even told me anything. It's as if he's not my brother. Why doesn't Dr. Fenn realize that I am responsible for him?

Mrs. Fenn did tell me that a piano teacher is going to come and teach me how to play the piano. That's nice, but I'd rather learn how to ride a bicycle. Sarah Alice has a red one that she said I could borrow. I watch as John squirms in the bicycle basket. Someone should at least have put a pillow under him.

The gatehouse keeper turns the bicycle around and pushes it through the gate and onto the dirt road in front of the house. It rained recently, maybe last night, and puddles and tiny rivers still stand or flow in the soft earth on the roadsides.

Since no one's going to tell me anything, I guess I'll just have to wait and watch for John to come back. I hope it's soon.

***

John returns a few days later with a very sore weenie and a very, very sore throat. He says that riding on the back of the bicycle was mostly fun, but not when they rode over bumps. When they got to the hospital, there were a lot of ladies in white dresses. They were nice and told him not to be afraid.

"Afraid of what?" I ask.

John shrugs. "I liked the lady named Helga best. She helped me put on some funny pajamas and get into the high bed. And she helped me count."

"Count! Why did you have to count?" I ask.

"I don't know. The lady, Helga, put a silvery basket over my nose and said to count. Then, when I told her that I don't know how to count, she said, 'That's all right, sweetie. I'll help you. Just count after me. One . . . two . . . three . . .'" John frowns. "I don't remember the rest. Then, when I woke up, Helga was there and she gave me ice cream. Some of the other children in our room talked to me and some didn't. I didn't care because I didn't want to talk anyway. My throat hurt too much. Then the gatehouse keeper came and brought me back."

Sarah Alice (age nine) and Mary Frances Fenn (age six) and me. I'm wearing my favorite borrowed dress, borrowed from Sarah Alice, Chengdu, 1942.

I hug him. It's nice to have John back with me. I'd missed him while he was at the hospital. John and I share a bedroom, so I was especially lonely at night.

Our bedroom is on the second floor. It's the first room along the hall that passes the bathroom as it goes to the door to the outside stairway—the one the coolie uses to bring water up to the bathroom *kong* (a huge ceramic pot). I've never seen a bathroom like the one at the Fenns' house before. It's very clever. The bathtub has a big copper lid that Amah closes and stands us on to dry us after our baths. There's hot water, which is heated by a pipe that comes right from the kitchen below, and cold water that you ladle out of a big ceramic kong. The toilet is not even in the bathroom; it has a little room of its own next door. There's a kong there too, which you ladle water out of when you're finished doing your business. Every day a coolie brings more water to fill the two kongs.

A big steamer trunk stands in the hall just to the right of the doorway into our room. On top of the trunk are some blankets in case we get cold at night. Sarah Alice and Mary Frances's schoolroom is farther down the hall. Their school desks are there by the window. After that is the girls' bedroom and Dr. and Mrs. Fenn's room. The last thing on the second floor is a big screened porch. Sarah Alice tells me that in the summer everyone sleeps on the porch because it's cooler. Of course, they sleep under mosquito nets too, she says.

Some nights, when I'm supposed to be asleep, I lie awake in the darkness wondering where Mummy and Daddy are. When I ask Mrs. Fenn or Dr. Fenn, they tell me they'll be coming to get us soon. I don't think Mrs. Fenn likes me asking. I also don't think she likes me very much. She doesn't believe me when I tell her things.

One night, I see a man standing in our room, behind the door.

I am very scared. *Who could that be?* I watch him very carefully to see when he moves, and I think he moves, just a little. After that, I can't sleep for a long time. The next morning when I tell Mrs. Fenn about the man, she tells me it was my imagination and not to tell fibs. I hear her telling Dr. Fenn that I fib. That night before I go to bed, I look behind the door and see a dark bathrobe hanging there. Maybe what I saw *was* my imagination.

A few nights later I'm awake again. As I lie in the dark, I see a skinny arm reach across the open doorway. I say, "What are you doing?" in Chinese, because I think he's one of the water coolies. The arm quickly snatches a blanket from the trunk and disappears.

The next morning, I hurry to tell Mrs. Fenn; again she tells me not to fib.

That morning, while we're at breakfast, Amah comes to tell Mrs. Fenn that some clothes that were in the laundry basket in the back hall have disappeared. Mrs. Fenn just nods. And then a few minutes later still, Amah runs in and asks us to look out the front window. There, strewn across the lawn from the bottom of the outside stairs to the garden wall, are the missing clothes.

NOTES

1.   West China Medical Center was located at 37 Guoxue Alley
     in Chengdu. It originated in 1914 out of West China Union
     University, which was formed in 1910 by five missionary groups
     from Canada, Britain, and the United States. The public institu-
     tion became the first medical school in China to teach dentistry
     and in 1924 accepted women into the student body. It now has
     forty-three hundred beds, employs ten thousand people, and is
     considered the second-best hospital in China. Although I have
     no proof that this hospital is the one that my brother was taken
     to, it seems the likely choice.

26

Naughty Silkworms

Mary Frances and Sarah Alice go to school at home. Mrs. Fenn is their teacher. She says for now, we can join the girls in their studies. The girls have their own school desks where they study everything—history, geography, science, mathematics, reading, spelling, writing—but the most fun thing they study is silkworms.

They have hundreds of silkworms that live in a large aquarium and climb around on the dry branches that have been placed in it. Sarah Alice tells me the branches are there for the silkworms to use to exercise and to build their cocoons on. Every day we pick fresh leaves from a mulberry tree in the garden—they're the only thing the silkworms like to eat.

I peer into the aquarium and see that the worms are many

different sizes. Sarah Alice says it's because the worms are different ages. The big ones weave a cocoon around themselves, she says, and when they're finished, they change into a chrysalis inside it. The thread a silkworm makes to weave a cocoon is the silk we use for dresses and lots of other things.

Sarah Alice then says that to get the silk, she and her sister put the cocoons in boiling water, which kills the chrysalis. Then the cocoons are placed on a towel to dry. Sarah Alice gets a tiny spinning wheel from a drawer and shows me how to stick the dry cocoon on a pin, pick one thread loose, and unwind the entire silk thread from the cocoon. After what seems like a long time of turning the little handle on the spinning wheel, we have a tiny skein of silk.

Most of the cocoons are white, but there are pink, yellow, and blue ones too. I ask what makes the cocoons different colors, but Mrs. Fenn doesn't know. "It's probably what they eat," she says. But since they all eat the same leaves, this doesn't make much sense to John and me.

One morning we come into the classroom with our fresh supply of breakfast leaves for the silkworms and find that they've all escaped. We look around the room and discover them crawling around in the clothes closet, climbing all over the girls' coats and dresses. We spend the rest of the day laughing, picking silkworms off the clothes and putting them back into the aquarium. We have a lot of fun until Mrs. Fenn says we have to make up the time we lost on our other studies and stay at our desks a little longer that day.

Today turns out to be a sad day for me, and not just because Mrs. Fenn had told me I'd fibbed earlier. John gets into trouble—again—and is sent to stay with Dr. Greene,[1] who lives at the university.

The first time Dr. Fenn got angry with John was when John saw something interesting in the ditch that runs along just inside the garden wall and went to examine it—after he'd been told never to go into the ditch. Then today John took apart the manual meat grinder to see how it works, which wouldn't have been so bad except that when he tried to put it back together, he found that one of the parts was missing. Cook had given the grinder to John when John had asked if he could see it. John had taken the grinder into the garden to study it. Dr. Fenn got really angry when he learned about the missing part.

I don't think Dr. Fenn knows about boys. Boys like to figure things out—to see how they work.

I was sad before, but now I'm really sad. John is the last of my family. No Mummy, no Daddy, and now no little brother.

I try to cheer myself up. It's May 1, May Day, and the girls tell me that on May Day they make little baskets, put flowers in them, and hang them on the doorknobs of their friends' houses and run away. So we get out some colored paper, cut it, fold or roll it, and make little baskets. Some baskets are round with flat bottoms, some cone shaped, and some are like little boxes. We glue them with paste that Cook makes out of flour and attach long handles to them; handles long enough to fit over doorknobs. We pick pansies and marigolds in the garden and fill the paper baskets, then Mrs. Fenn takes us to the houses of Mary Frances and Sarah Alice's friends and to Dr. Greene's apartment, where we hang them.

Just before bedtime I sit on the edge of my bed and look at

John's empty bed across the room. I'm still sad. I listen to Dr. and Mrs. Fenn downstairs playing bridge with friends, laughing and talking, and think about John at Dr. Greene's. I wonder what he's doing. I wish I could talk to him. Maybe I can call him on the phone. But I don't ask.

NOTES

1. I have not been able to find any information about Dr. Ted Greene, who was a dental or medical doctor in Chengdu in 1942. Although I have found a number of Dr. Greenes, even Ted Greenes, none are identified as having been in Chengdu, China, in 1942.

27

Is She Alive or Dead?

It's autumn, and Dr. and Mrs. Fenn decide to send John and me to a boarding school established in Western China for the children of Canadian missionaries.[1] The school is about forty-two miles (67 kilometers) south of Chengdu, in a small village called Renshou.[2]

I don't think Dr. and Mrs. Fenn like us staying at their house very much. They think we are naughty. They're not fun like our mummy and daddy, and they don't even read to us at night. It's hard when people aren't your real parents.

I also don't think Mary Frances and Sarah Alice like to share their pretty dresses or other things like barrettes and ribbons with me. I especially love Sarah Alice's dress with chickens all over it, even on the collar. I ask to wear it whenever I know it's been washed and I see it hanging in the closet. Perhaps it's a favorite of Sarah Alice's too. I have pretty dresses, but they were left in Shanghai when we moved to Chungking. I guess I wouldn't like it either if another girl wanted to wear my clothes all the time.

Early in the morning on the day we leave for our new school, Amah packs our few belongings, and John and I join a group of other Western children and their parents at the university gates. All the children climb into the back of an old army truck and sit on benches that are lined up in rows on the truck bed. It's very jolly and I am especially happy because I'm with my brother again. But seeing all the parents in the crowd makes me think about our mummy and daddy and wonder where they are and why they don't come to get us.

During the trip to Renshou, John tells me the things that happened when he stayed at Dr. Greene's apartment on the university campus. He says that Dr. Greene was very nice and showed him how the weight on the screen door works to keep the door closed and how pendulums and pulleys work. At night, Dr. Greene would take him up on the roof of his building to look at the stars through a little brass telescope and talk about the constellations. Dr. Greene taught my brother the names of the stars.

John also tells me that one day, when no one was home, he was bored so he decided to go and look at the university's swimming pool, which was close by the apartment house. And while he was looking down into the green water in the pool, he accidentally fell in. And because he doesn't know how to swim, he sank to the bottom—all the way down to the very bottom. And it was the deep end. "I was very, very scared because I thought I wouldn't come back up," John said. "I thought this was the end of me. But then, all of a sudden, a lady, maybe a teacher or someone's mummy, reached into the water, grabbed me, and pulled me out.

"The lady didn't say anything. She didn't hug me or tell me I was all right or that everything would be all right or anything. She just dropped me at the edge of the pool. I wanted her to hug me—to go and get Dr. Greene or take me back to Dr. Greene's house. But she just left. So I got up and went back to Dr. Greene's by myself."[3]

I hug my brother. It's nice to have him sitting next to me. And I think, *Why haven't Mummy and Daddy come to get John and me? Where are they? Why are they taking so long?*

***

The day is sunny and we bump along the dirt road. At noon, a teacher who is riding with us gives us sandwiches and something to drink, and we arrive at the school in Renshou a little while later. The school is made up of several buildings grouped together in a hilly area, surrounded by a tall brick wall. Where the wall runs along the street there's a gate, next to which is a little hut—it's a gatehouse but not like those in Chungking and at the Fenns', because this gatehouse is a small hut built a short distance from the gate. Everyone jumps off the truck and goes through the gate and up a brick path. Most of the other children have been here before, so they know where to go; we follow.

Brick paths run between all the buildings. One of the girls shows me the way to the girls' dormitory while an older boy takes charge of John, showing him to the boys' dorm, a large brick building just beyond a thick bamboo grove. When I get to my dorm, I'm told to go upstairs to a large room, which I share with three other girls. Luckily, I get to sleep on the top bunk of one of the two bunk beds. Next to our room there's a long, narrow screened porch where all the girls play in our spare time. In the middle of the dormitory's second floor, there's a large room that's the bathroom. There's no electricity or running water.

Every evening at seven o'clock, we line up, single file, in our bathrobes in front of this tub, each of us holding her own soap and towel. When it's my turn, I follow the example of the other girls and place my hand straight down into the middle of the tub, with the tips of my fingers touching the bottom. This shows the water coolie, waiting with warm water in a bucket, just how much water I'm allowed. He pours enough water into the tub to just cover the palm of my hand. In this way tall girls get more water than little ones, which seems very fair. Then after a quick wash I stand up, the teacher gives me a rub with my towel, and I slip back into my robe, ready to return to the bedroom. By this time it's dark outside, so as we girls leave the bathroom, we each pick up a small oil lamp from a table next to the doorway. The lamps are tiny ceramic teapots with the wick threaded up the spout—like the one Mummy had when she read to us in the cave in Chungking.

When it gets dark, we go to bed. Miss Becker, the teacher, comes to say good night. "Have you said your prayers?" she asks every night as she blows out the little lamps we've placed together on our study table.

We all reply, "Yes, Miss Becker," whether we've really said our prayers or not.

***

Each weekday morning, we get up early, just after dawn, wash up, and run down a brick walk to breakfast and then another brick walk to the classroom building.

I'm in third grade and John's in first, but we're in the same classroom. I think it's lovely that the school's plan is for me to be with my brother. In our class, two children, including John, sit in the front row—first grade; two children sit right behind them— second grade; and four children, including me, sit in the last two rows—third grade. Our teacher teaches all three grades.

I'm happy at this school. I like the teacher, I like the school-work, I like playtime, and I especially like being there with John. Although other than in the classroom, we don't see each other very much. He's in the boys' dormitory, so he plays with the boys. But it's very nice to know that he's close by even when we don't talk. We don't have to talk to be happy and feel that we're together.

One Saturday afternoon while I'm playing with two girls on our screened porch, I look out and see the boys playing in the thick bamboo grove that's between the girls' and boys' dormitories. The boys chase each other around with peashooters, hollow bamboo sticks through which they blow dry peas. I listen as the boys shout, tease, and have fun.

I'm busy fashioning a woolen tube from a ball of red yarn; I use a wooden spool, a spool that once held sewing thread but now has four discarded gramophone needles nailed around one end of the hole that goes through it. I pull the yarn around the base of the metal needles. Then, using a knitting needle, I carefully lift the wool over each needle, all the while pulling the woolen tube that's slowly emerging through the other hole in the spool. I repeat this process again and again, around and around the spool. It's fun.

***

One night while I'm sleeping snugly in my upper bunk, I'm awakened by loud voices outside.

We all jump out of bed and run to the windows. It's hard to see what's happening. "Let's go down and find out what's going on," one of the girls, the most adventurous one, says. We grab our robes; one of the older girls lights a lamp. We run down the stairs as fast as we can without tripping in the dim light and go outside. Leaving the dormitory after "lights out" is forbidden, so I've never been out here at night. It's a bit scary, with all the shadows and the trees, and the wind making a scratchy noise as it blows through the bamboo. We join the group that has gathered near the gate—teachers and other students. I look around for John but don't see him.

"What happened?" one of the girls from my room asks a teacher who's standing by a tree.

"I don't know," the teacher says. "But I heard that the doctor's coming."

Everyone stands silently in the moonlight, waiting, expectant. Soft crying and moaning is heard from the direction of the gatehouse and I wonder, *Could it be a child?* Then the school's doctor runs up, pulling on his jacket over a long nightshirt. Someone behind him, an amah, is carrying his black doctor's bag and hands it to him. I squeeze past two girls and look around another one. The doctor goes into the gatehouse hut. After a few tense minutes, the people nearest the hut start to whisper. Slowly the whispers seep back to our teachers and the other students and me.

"Something happened to the gatehouse keeper's daughter," someone says.

"Is she all right? Is she sick?" another person asks.

"She's just a little girl. Very sweet," I hear from another side.

"I think she was bitten by something," someone else whispers. I hear the scuffle of feet.

"Oh my God, was it a scorpion?" comes another voice.

"Oh, I hope not. They are very dangerous," another student adds.

"Scorpions worry me a lot," I hear from just in front of me.

"Me too. Every time I get into bed I look under the sheet and make sure there aren't any there," the girl standing beside me, a girl I recognize from my dormitory, says in a low tone.

Whispers are swirling around me dizzyingly. I wait, silent, for whatever will happen next.

After a few minutes the doctor comes out of the hut. I see him talking to one of the teachers, their bowed heads close together. They both look solemn. Then the teacher says something quietly to a small group of staff near him. The whisper rushes through the group, getting louder as it travels to the back rows, toward me.

"The gatehouse keeper's daughter was sleeping with her arm hanging over the edge of the bed. A snake came into the hut and bit her."

"The gatehouse keeper's daughter was bitten by a snake," I hear someone say.

"The gatehouse keeper's daughter was bitten by a snake" is repeated by a shrill voice.

"Oh, how awful," a teacher whose voice I recognize, Miss Becker, says.

"What kind of snake was it?" someone else asks.

"Please, girls, boys—go back to your rooms and back to bed," the headmaster says. Then, more loudly: "Please go back to bed right away. The little girl's being cared for."

Only a few of the students seem to pay any attention to the headmaster. The chatter continues.

"I wonder what kind of snake it was."

"Was it poisonous? My dad told me there're poisonous snakes in this part of China."

"You mean venomous, don't you?" an older boy chimes in.

"Yes, yes, of course," another student replies.

"What kinds of snakes live here in Sichuan?" yet another student asks.

"Yes, there are pit vipers here."

"Pit viper is a generic name; there're lots of pit vipers like rattlesnakes and copperheads," an older boy confidently says.

Just then the gatehouse keeper comes out of the hut holding a stick in front of him. A long snake is draped over it.

Everyone gasps when they see it, even me. I try to make out the pattern or color of the snake, but it's too dark to see more than its outline dangling over the stick as it's paraded in front of the upper-class students.

"I'd like to skin that one," one of the boys jokes.

"Please, students, go back to bed." The headmaster's voice sounds firm.

My roommates and I look at each other, then turn and start back to our dormitory.

Someone whispers, "I wonder, is she alive or dead?"

NOTES

1. The Canadian School in Renshou was organized by the Canadian Methodist Church West China Missionary Council to serve the children of the missionaries in Sichuan. It first opened in 1909 and had three consecutive locations: Chengdu (1909–38); Chungking (1922–35); and Renshou (1939–43). It closed when it became obvious that the Communists would replace the Nationalist government. The school's last location in the small village of Renshou, sixty-four kilometers (forty miles) south of Chengdu, was selected because an unoccupied hospital building and former school property were available there. Every effort was made to give the students a Western educational experience. The school conformed to the Toronto public school requirements and curriculum, and adjustable school desks and chairs, dinnerware, and bedding were brought from Canada.

2. During my 1998 trip to China, my girlfriend and I went to Renshou to see the Canadian School. To get to Renshou I'd asked for help from Chengdu University, and we were provided a car and driver. The young lady driver arrived at our hotel in very short pink shorts and a matching baseball cap.

    The school's gatehouse was gone, but the wall that encircled the campus and the brick paths that we ran up and down were still there. The bamboo grove between the dormitories where the boys played had been turned into hard earth—a basketball court. We were unable to enter the girls' dormitory because the campus was now a training site for young soldiers, and the girls' dorm was where the staff lived. We were able to enter the boys' dorm. Although I'd never been inside before, I imagined that the faded, grubby pale-blue walls had not been updated since the 1940s.

    I don't know what the university officer who arranged the trip told his counterpart in Renshou about my girlfriend and me or who we were, but we were treated like royalty—invited to a banquet with, I assumed, the village elders. One of the courses at the banquet included a huge bowl of turtle soup. In the middle of the tureen floated, or sat, what appeared to be a box turtle. I had to kick my friend under the table to keep her from sliding off her chair. She said the turtle shell looked just like a pet she had at home.

3.   When I visited Chengdu during my 1998 China trip, I looked for but was unable to find Dr. Greene's apartment house or the swimming pool in which John almost drowned.

28

Animal, Vegetable, or Mineral

First Week of November 1942
Renshou, Sichuan Province, China, to
Chengdu, Sichuan Province, China

The air feels damp. Everyone is talking about monsoon season. My roommates, who were here last year, tell me that in monsoon season it never stops raining. Now I understand why all the buildings are connected by brick pathways.

We girls run up and down these hilly paths and stairs to get from our dormitory to the dining room and then from the dining room to our classroom, then back to the dining room and, at the end of the day, back to our dormitory, each of them in a separate building. The air is soggy when we play or read, color, or cut out paper dolls on our large, long porch. We don't go outside as much as we used to because the air feels too heavy, depressing. We go to bed early and get up early, almost with the sun. I'm happy. I see my little brother when I'm in class every day sitting in the front row, and I have lots of nice girls to play with. I don't think about Mummy and Daddy very much, or at least I try not to. It's been a long time since I've seen them. I hope I can remember what they look like when they come to get us.

One afternoon, after I've been at the Canadian School for about two months, my teacher comes to tell me that Dr. and Mrs. Fenn have arranged for a friend to come and take us back to Chengdu. And from there we're going to go to Rhodesia to stay with our aunt Elizabeth Dobbs-Higginson, our father's sister. I know that I've got an auntie Betty who lives in Rhodesia on a ranch, but I've never met her. I remember that she has two sons about the same age as John and me.

"Will our mummy and daddy be there?" I ask.

My teacher says she doesn't know. "Perhaps," she says and tips her head to one side as she looks at me over her glasses.

The following day John and I meet Bill, who has ridden from Chengdu on his bicycle. Bill says he's a high school student and his father is Dr. Greene's cousin, and anyway, he's happy to come to get us.

"How long did it take you to ride here?" my teacher asks.

"The road's rough," Bill says. "It took two days."

The following morning, I say goodbye to my roommates and teachers, and Bill, John, and I set off for Chengdu; John and I ride in a rickshaw and Bill pushes his bicycle beside us. The day is clear but cloudy.

We've just left Renshou when it begins to rain—heavy monsoon rain. The rickshaw coolie quickly stops and pulls something that looks like a bundle of palm leaves out from under the rickshaw and drapes it around himself; it's his raincoat. I look at the rickshaw coolie's feet; all he has on are straw sandals, while Bill, John, and I are wearing rubber boots. The coolie smiles when he sees my concern and says he's fine. Then he suggests that Bill tie his bike onto the back of the rickshaw rather than push it. Bill thanks the coolie as he scrapes mud off the bike's tires.

As we now start off for a second time, the monsoon rain falls in earnest. It washes down in torrents, soaking the countryside, Bill, the coolie, and everything else—except John and me. We're snuggled down under the rickshaw's oilcloth hood, wrapped in a blanket and covered by an additional sheet of oilcloth.

The rickshaw coolie trots along stoically in front of us, dodging the occasional mule or buffalo. Bill walks beside him, trying his best to keep up, now and then wiping water out of his eyes. When the rickshaw gets stuck in mud, as it does several times a day, Bill helps the coolie push it free.

The rain beats a thunderous rat-a-tat-tat on the rickshaw's oilcloth hood. The rain's loud, so loud that it drowns out our efforts to talk to Bill. I peer out from under the hood. Bill's head is bowed as he trudges along, and the coolie, a bundle of palm leaves, jogs along tirelessly—each wrapped in his own tiny world as they concentrate on getting us back to Chengdu. I get drowsy. John stirs beside me and points to the soggy countryside from under the rickshaw's hood. "I spy something that's vegetable," he says with a grin. And so we begin a game of animal, vegetable, or mineral that lasts for most of the trip. When we get hungry, Bill digs around in his bicycle basket and produces sandwiches for all of us that he'd been given before we left the school.

At night we stop at a little inn. We're shown to a room that has one big bed and paper in the windows. Bill asks for the sheets to be changed, for us to have fresh, clean sheets, and we go to look for something to eat. We're down the hall but hear the hustle and bustle as sheets are pulled off and replaced on our one bed. Returning to the room, Bill inspects the bed and shakes his head. "When I asked for the sheets to be changed, they were changed, but with the sheets from the next room!" he says. "And the next room probably has ours."

The next day and the day after we travel on . . . and on . . . and on. We have long since run out of sandwiches. We play animal, vegetable, or mineral every day. No one expected the road to be so dreadfully muddy. No one expected the going to be so very slow. After a week, we arrive in Chengdu.

＊

The next several days are busy. Mrs. Fenn finds our passports, and it's discovered that because of a change in the law between 1934 and 1936, our birth years, John can no longer share a British passport with me and has to get a passport all his own—an American one! Now, instead of following Daddy's nationality, he has to follow Mummy's. We sit on the Fenns' side porch to have new passport pictures taken; we're wearing borrowed clothes and seated in front of a bedsheet suspended from the ceiling. John has on a little boy's outfit that buttons around the waist. He hates it.

John hated this Buster Brown suit that he was put into for his new American passport photo. I watch for the "birdie," as instructed by the photographer. Chengdu, November 1942.

It's the weekend before John and I are to leave for Rhodesia. Mary Frances and Sarah Alice's friends are invited to our good-bye party. We wish our new friends from school in Renshou could also come, but they're too far away to join us. Nonetheless, everything's very exciting: the passports, the packing, the party. Most exciting of all is that we're finally off and will soon see Mummy and Daddy. Everyone has said we'll see them soon. We hope they'll be at Auntie Betty's in Rhodesia when we get there.

Then we have a big surprise. At the very last minute, we're told that we're not going to Auntie Betty in Rhodesia but to

America instead. And that a pilot named Hal Sweet will meet us in Chungking to take us there.[1]

America!

Mummy and Daddy at last.

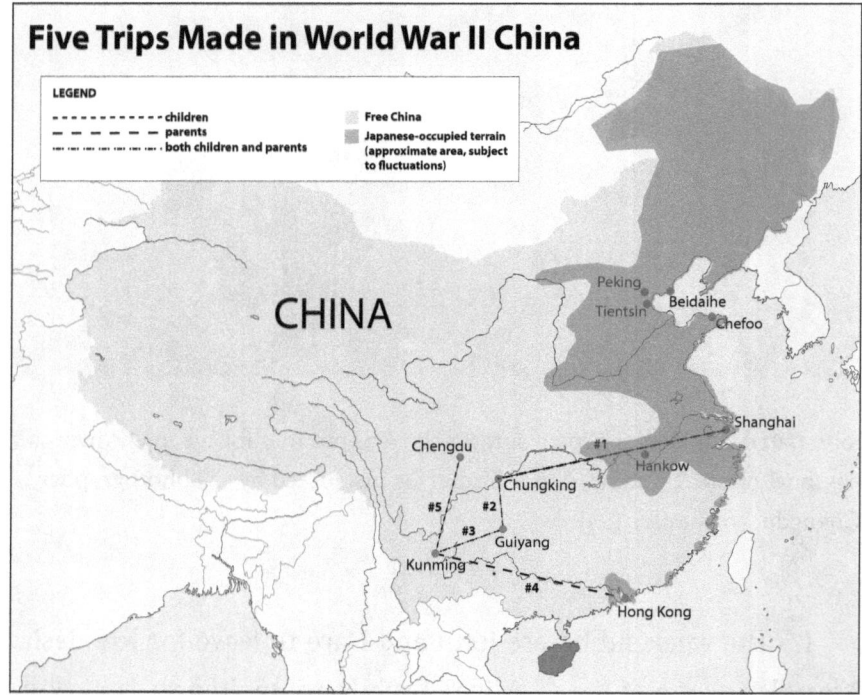

NOTES

1. Capt. Harold A. Sweet (1904–48) was one of the pilots who flew sixteen round trips between Hong Kong and Chungking to rescue civilians when Hong Kong was attacked by the Japanese. When I met Hal's wife, Mabel, in 1998, I asked her why he'd agreed to fly two young children (most likely brats) out of China. She replied simply that he loved children; they'd had six of their own.

    Mabel told me that she and Hal met in the Philippines, where she lived with her aunt after emigrating as a young girl from Spain following the death of her parents. Hal died at age forty-four. As a young airman, Hal had once volunteered to paint a large water tank at an airfield in the Philippines. The paint used was lead based; Mabel believes this contributed to his early death.

29

Coins

*Third Week of November 1942
Chengdu, Sichuan Province, China, to
Chabua, Assam State, India*

John and I are put on a plane bound for Chungking. We carry the two small brown suitcases that we'd brought with us from Kunming and sit on big green canvas bags of mail. The cases were Daddy's, easily identified because he'd painted his schools' colors—Marlborough's navy blue and dark red and Clare College, Cambridge's black and yellow[1]—in bold stripes across their lids. Mrs. Fenn packs our cases but we no longer can get into these clothes. In the year since we've been away from Mummy and Daddy, we've outgrown everything, so we're both wearing denim overalls that were sent to Mary Frances and Sarah Alice by relatives who live in the American Midwest. I love my overalls because they have lots of pockets. I especially love the big pocket in the bib.

When we arrive in Chungking, Mrs. Gray, who still lives in the house in the compound where we'd lived earlier, invites us to stay with her and the children. The next day we go to visit Mr. Gray's grave, which is behind the house where the three doctors live. Since no flowers are blooming, we pick evergreen branches to place on the grave. In the evening we all play Monopoly; when Brian and Brice want to stop because the game reminds them of their father, we have some hot chocolate and go to bed.

The next day Mr. Sweet, the airline pilot, comes to meet us. He's a jolly man with a round face, a bushy mustache, and only a little hair on his head. He hugs me when we're introduced and gives John a ride on his knee when he sits down to chat with Mrs. Gray. He likes to brush the hair out of my eyes and does this several times while they're talking. He tells Mrs. Gray that we'll be flying the Hump,[2] which is what the Americans call the Himalayan Mountains, and then following the military's South Atlantic ferry route back to the States.[3] I listen closely as he tells her that the route crosses Africa and India and that it's the route the US Army Air Force[4] takes to bring planes and supplies, medical and military, from America to China to help the war effort.

"Isn't crossing the Himalayan Mountains dangerous?" Mrs. Gray says.

"Well, yes," Hal says. "But the pilots are very experienced, and anyway, there's no other way to go. Even before the Japanese captured the Burma Road, which was the only road through the mountains, there were many towns where trucks were stopped and forced to pay a tax just to pass. Not to mention the dangerous driving conditions and other hazards such as thieves and bandits."

The next morning we're rowed out in a sampan to a tiny island, the same bit of land in the middle of the Yangtze River that we'd landed on when we flew from Chengdu. "This is a secret airfield," Hal says—he'd told us when we first met him to call him Hal, not Mr. Sweet. Hal tells us the Japanese have no idea the airstrip exists, even though it's right in the middle of the city.[5] But there's one big problem with it, Hal says. In the rainy season when the river's high, it's completely underwater.

Do you see the narrow strip of land under the bridge? In 1940s Chungking, before this bridge was built, the planes of the China National Aviation Corporation (CNAC) took off and landed on this island in the Yangtze River. The planes' crews and passengers would then be rowed to the north or south riverbank in a sampan. This landing strip was never discovered by the Japanese. John and I arrived and left from here when we came to Chungking from Chengdu to meet Captain Hal Sweet. (Postcard from 1997.)

I look up and down the short runway with respect.

John and I climb up a ladder and into the plane, and Hal follows. As I look around for a seat, Hal points to two parachute packs. We sit.

The plane takes off and banks sharply. "Telephone wires," Hal says, and points out the window.

The rest of the two-hour flight is uneventful until our little plane approaches the airport in Kunming. John and I watch out the window as the plane begins its descent, and we're surprised to see that we're landing between rows of planes unlike any John and I have ever seen before. They have big white eyes and long, sharp teeth painted on their noses. They look fierce, like sharks. Shark planes.

Hal laughs at our astonishment. "Those are the American Flying Tigers,"[6] he says. Then he tells us about the different parts of a plane: the fuselage, the wings, the tail, the rudder, the engines, the landing gear and nose. It's a lot to remember.

While Hal's telling us about the planes, I look through the window at all the activity on the airfield. Carts filled with stones, pulled by little gray donkeys, roll along the side of the runway. Not far from them are rows of men, women, and even children tied by ropes to a huge stone roller; they're pulling the roller over the stones in the airstrip. I realize they're building a new runway, smoothing it out. Or maybe they're repairing an old runway.

As I stand in the open doorway of the plane, waiting for the ladder, a tall man in uniform, another pilot, comes up and says, "Would you like some help, kiddo?" Then, before I have a chance to reply, he lifts me down from the plane.

"Thank you," I whisper as he places me on the runway and turns to lift John out too.

"Where're you kids bound?" the pilot asks as Hal comes up to us.

"They'll be flying to Chabua tomorrow," Hal says.[7] He greets the pilot as an old friend. Hal smiles and shakes the man's hand vigorously. "Great to see you, Bob. It's been a while." He slaps Bob on the back. "I need to find a place to bunk the kids for the night. Any ideas?"

"Oh, no problem; you can have a spot in my hut," the pilot says. "I can stay with some friends."

"That would be great, thanks," Hal says.

"I'm headed to the chow tent now. Join me, and then I can show you my bunking arrangements."

Hal takes John's hand, and he and Bob lead the way to a long tent on the side of the airfield. Inside, men are standing in line to get a tray and their dinner. Bob lifts John up so he can see the big steaming pans of food. A man behind the long counter fills a plate for John and one for me. "There you go," he says. "You're the shortest pilots I've seen in a long time." He smiles and continues to serve up plates for Bob, Hal, and the other men.

The men in line behind us tell jokes and nudge each other. Some look at us, smile, and wave. I guess they don't see children, Western children, very often.

"Have a Life Saver?" a man in mechanic's coveralls says, offering something to me.

"Thanks," Hal says, "but I'd rather they not eat any candy. They've already had a lot of different foods today."

"Aw, shucks," the mechanic says, and puts the roll back in his pocket.

"Here, kid, take this," says a soldier behind us in line, handing John an Indian rupee. Then several other men dig small change out of their pockets and give the coins to John and me—Chinese coins, Indian coins, even British and American pennies. Oh my! John and I turn them over and over in our hands, marveling at the interesting shapes and designs. Then I drop each into the bib pocket of my overalls. "Thank you very much," we both say, then repeat, "Thank you." I know the coins are very valuable, but I have no wish to spend them. Just having them makes me feel special. John and I have never had any money of our own before.

We sit at a table to eat. John and I finish first, and as we sit and wait for Hal and the other men to finish, I notice the colorful lining of a leather jacket lying across the bench next to us. I recognize the Nationalist red-and-blue flag sewn into it. Below the flag are Chinese characters.

"Hal, why is the flag inside that jacket? No one can see it there," I ask.

"Don't ask personal questions, Jennifer," Hal says. "It's not polite." But then he goes on to explain that the flag along with the writing below it is called a "blood chit" and that it will help the pilot if he has to bail out over the jungle; the Chinese characters tells whoever finds him that he's a friend and to take him to the closest American base. "And," Hal adds, "before you ask why it's sewn inside the jacket and not on the outside, that's because the blood chit is a secret. They don't want everyone to see it."

"Oh" is all I can think of to say.

Early the next morning we return to the airfield and board what Hal calls a C-46 for a short flight to a small village, Yunnanyi,[8] about eighty kilometers (49.7 miles) west of Kunming.

As we leave Kunming, we fly over a huge, beautiful, sparkling lake. We look out and see fishermen fishing with cormorants, birds that dive into the water and catch fish but cannot eat them because they have a tight ring around their necks. Daddy told us about this kind of fishing when we were here with him and Mummy and they took us to picnic near Kunming Lake.

Landing in Yunnanyi, we see planes being worked on—repaired, I'm told—and teams of coolies unloading fifty-five-gallon drums from other planes.

John points to a group of Chinese soldiers sitting under the trees. I suppose the soldiers are waiting to get onto a plane. Why else would they be resting there? Hal looks at his watch.

"Hal, are we going with those soldiers?" I ask.

"No, they're going to India for training, I imagine." Hal looks toward the soldiers. "They could also stand fattening up, too," he says. I look at them. They are very skinny.

Hal is right; we're not going with the soldiers. Other than the crew, it looks like Hal, John, and I are the only people boarding the C-47. We climb the ladder and enter the plane. On board, Hal gives us two funny hats he calls masks and tells us these are used if we need oxygen during the flight. He asks if we know what oxygen is, and we both shake our heads. "I'll tell you later," he says. Then he shows us how to put the masks on by placing one on John's head. Hal tells us to keep them nearby, says that he'll signal us if we need to put them on, and points to two parachutes for us to sit on.

The pilots and a third man enter. Hal says this man is the radio operator, and he introduces us. The men smile and nod. "Happy to have you aboard," one says. I realize they're busy, so

I pull John's hand and we head toward our assigned parachute seats. Then we both look back through the open doorway and see coolies loading the last boxes and sacks. "What are those bags?" John asks.

"Mail, going home to America," Hal says. "If you two get tired of sitting on parachutes, go back and sit on those sacks. They're very comfortable." We know, since we've sat on mailbags before.

A few minutes later, we're in the air.

***

"Look." Hal points out the window. "The Mekong River." A silvery ribbon far below snakes between the mountains. "And keep watching. We'll be crossing the Salween River soon."

The plane is extremely cold, but that doesn't seem to bother Hal. He's dressed in a leather jacket and boots. We move from the parachutes and I snuggle down between the bags of mail, but still, I can't keep my teeth from chattering a bit.

After about three hours in the sky, we begin our descent into Chabua—our first stop outside China. We're in India! It's so exciting. I squeeze John's hand.

Out the window I see a soldier sitting in a tall tree, signaling to us.

"That's the Chabua control tower," Hal laughs, "in the tree." He's come to the back of the plane to pull us out from among the bags of mail. "Tomorrow we're going to Dum Dum Aerodrome. That's near Calcutta."

I've already forgotten about the cold.

NOTES

1. Marlborough College, a boarding school for thirteen-to-eighteen-year-old boys, was founded in 1843 on eighty-one hectares (two hundred acres) in Wiltshire, England. Ted was a student there in the 1920s. In 1989 it became coeducational.

2. During World War II, "the Hump" was the name everyone gave to the eastern end of the Himalayas between China and India. In 1942, when the Japanese disabled the only land route, the Burma Road, between these two countries, pilots were forced to "fly the Hump" to bring supplies to support the Chinese war effort, because there were no suitable airfields and no military units trained or equipped to move cargo. Flying this route was extremely dangerous, not only because of the height of the mountains—exceeding twenty thousand feet—and the possibility of attack by Japanese fighter planes, but also because of the erratic air currents, foul weather, and lack of reliable charts and radio navigation towers in the region.

    Hump pilots came from a variety of civilian and military sources, although at the beginning they predominantly were recruited from the China National Aviation Corporation (CNAC). Between April 1942 and November 1945, Hump pilots delivered about 650,000 tons of supplies—armaments, aviation fuel, medicines and medical equipment, and even donkeys for the Chinese army. These deliveries were made at a great cost. By the time the airlift was disbanded, 594 aircraft had been lost and 1,656 personnel, as well as a number of passengers, killed.

    When the Hump flights began, American officials in Washington, DC, believed that CNAC pilots and operations personnel should fly the routes because they were experienced in mountainous and foul-weather flying; however, on the ground in China, Gen. Joseph Stilwell thought these routes should be managed by US military personnel. The American generals in China, Gen. Stilwell and Gen. Claire Chennault, had very different ideas about how the war should be conducted, with Stilwell envisioning a ground tactic and Chennault an airborne one.

These types of disagreements were typical of the situation in the China-Burma-India theater, which was difficult to understand at the time but in hindsight appears to have arisen because each "stakeholder" had a different objective. Generalissimo Chiang Kai-shek, although nominally fighting the Japanese, prioritized the war against the Chinese Communists; similarly, the Chinese Communists' priority was to defeat the Chinese Nationalist government, not the Japanese. Simultaneously, the Americans wanted China to focus on its war with Japan before facing its civil war, so the Chinese would tie up as many Japanese forces as possible and thus keep them away from the areas where the Japanese were engaged with American troops, while the British wanted China to receive just enough support to stay in the war but not enough to build a military force capable of threatening Burma or (rebellious) India, countries they occupied at the time. Since each Allied country had a different objective, it was difficult for the leaders to effect a strategy with the expectation that the other leaders would cooperate.

3. During World War II there were about a dozen air ferry routes around the world, with the major routes crossing the Pacific and Atlantic Oceans; the South Atlantic ferry route was one of the latter. Ferry routes were established to transport planes, personnel, and critical equipment from the United States to wherever they were needed to aid the war effort.

The various military groups that flew these routes included the First Ferry Group, Air Transport Command (ATC); the Army Air Force Ferry Wing; the Tenth Air Force Trans-India Ferry Command Corps; and many ferry squadrons (the Third, Sixth, Thirteenth, Seventy-Seventh, Seventy-Eighth, Eighty-Eighth, Ninety-Sixth, Ninety-Seventh, and Ninety-Eighth). There was even a Navy Ferry Command. All were eventually disbanded when no longer needed.

4. Here is a quick explanation of the evolution of the United States Air Force (USAF): The United States Air Force started in the First World War as the Aviation Section, Signal Corps. On May 24, 1918 it became the United States Army Air Service, and then became the United States Army Air Corp (USAAC) on July 2,

1926. The USAAC became the United States Army Air Forces (USAAF) on June 20,1941. And finally on September 26, 1947, by order of the secretary of defense, all personnel of the USAAF were transferred from the army, and the United States Air Force (USAF) was established.

5. The island (really a sandbar) airstrip in Chungking, on which China National Aviation Corporation (CNAC) pilots landed and took off during World War II, was never discovered by the Japanese. Today it is hardly recognizable, looking like an insignificant, narrow strip of earth under one pillar of a modern bridge over the Yangtze. It's no longer necessary to brave the river's dangerous currents in a sampan in order to go to an airstrip or cross the mighty Yangtze River in Chungking.

6. The First American Volunteer Group (AVG) in China, nicknamed the Flying Tigers, was made up of about thirty pilots from the US Army Air Corps, Marines, and Navy. They were recruited by President Franklin Roosevelt just before the attack on Pearl Harbor. These pilots flew Curtiss P-40 Warhawks and were under the command of Claire Chennault. Their mission was to defend the Republic of China against the Japanese in 1941–42.

7. The air force base at Chabua in the state of Assam, India, was built in 1939 by the Royal Indian Air Force on a former tea plantation. After the Burma Road was cut off during World War II, Chabua was a major supply point for the ferrying of supplies from the United States to the Chinese Nationalist Army in Kunming. It was a hot, muggy, and mosquito-, python-, and scorpion-infested area.

8. The airfield that was built near the village of Yunnanyi, about fifty miles west of Kunming, was first intended for use by the American Volunteer Group (AVG) pilots to train Chinese pilots. Following the loss of the Burma Road, it became the most westerly airfield on the China side of the Hump supply route.

30

The Tonga

End of November 1942
Calcutta, West Bengal State, India

As soon as our plane lands at Dum Dum Aerodrome,[1] John and I are whisked off to nearby Calcutta. What a city it is: carts, cattle, bicycles, cars, and trucks of every description, driving in every direction, not to mention the hordes of people everywhere in the streets. With all its bright colors and air of excitement, Calcutta reminds me of Shanghai. I wish Mummy and Daddy could see it too.

Hal tells us that while we're in Calcutta, we'll be staying at the home of the British ambassador; we've been invited. Hal accompanies us in a jeep to the big, handsome brick house with a flat front and says we'll be here for a few days before we leave on the next leg of our trip. "And for goodness' sake, behave yourselves,"

Hal says. For once I wish I had something other than overalls to wear.

At the door we're met by a gentleman wearing a white turban. He's very stiff and formal and greets us with a bow. He must be a Sikh.

After speaking briefly with the turbaned gentleman and handing him our suitcases, Hal leaves in the waiting jeep. Then the man, whom in my mind I call Mr. Sikh, shows us down a wide hall and up a long flight of stairs to two lovely bedrooms on opposite sides of the hall. As we mount the steps, I glance at the paintings, mostly of men on parade in colorful uniforms, that line the stairs and hall. I find the ones with men on prancing horses the most interesting.

"You'll have time to look at all the paintings, miss," Mr. Sikh says. He asks which suitcase is mine and places our suitcases on stools in our rooms. Then he suggests we bathe before lunch.

From the way Mr. Sikh looks at us and sniffs, I realize we must look, and smell, very untidy. Well, we've been riding around on cargo planes and sitting on big sacks of mail, and it's probably been more than a week since we had a bath. As he closes the door to John's room behind him, a young Indian lady, an ayah,[2] comes down the hall.

"I've come to help you," the ayah says, and smiles. I follow her into the bathroom, where she begins to run water into the tub. I sneak a peek at her—she's not much older than I am—as I hurry to get out of my overalls. I don't need anyone to undress me or bathe me! I shake my head when the ayah picks up the bar of soap and a large round sponge.

"Thank you," I say, reaching for the sponge.

Then she gathers up all my clothes, even the ones in my suitcase, leaving me just one pair of overalls to wear to lunch. She carries them off. *Were they all dirty?* I wonder.

At lunch John and I sit at one end of a long mahogany table in a big room with dark-red velvet curtains and more pictures of soldiers in red uniforms. Mr. Sikh sits bolt upright on a chair at the opposite end of the table, a dark-red leather book open on his lap. Even before the ayah comes in with our first course—soup— he's opened it and started to read to us. It's *The Jungle Book*. Of course, Mummy has already read *The Jungle Book* to John and me, but I don't want to spoil Mr. Sikh's fun, so I thank him. I really enjoy hearing the stories again, anyway. It's a very good book for our visit, and especially since we're in India, I tell myself.

The next course is roast beef, roast potatoes, and Yorkshire pudding. What a wonderful meal; it's like Christmas! Then for dessert we have strawberry jelly and cocoa. Delicious. I'm very naughty because I take a spoonful of the red jelly and drop it in my cocoa. Mr. Sikh pretends not to notice my bad manners. When I spoon the jelly back out, I note that all its corners have melted off.

Mr. Sikh closes the book and says that he has plans for me while John goes into the garden to play in the sandbox.

Plans? What plans?

***

Mr. Sikh, the young ayah, and I go into the street in front of the house. It's a pretty street with wide sidewalks, other elegant houses, and lots of trees. The ayah takes my hand as we walk to the end of the block, where Mr. Sikh starts waving his arm. *"Tonga!"*[3] he calls. *"Tonga!"*

Out of the traffic, a brightly painted pony cart appears and pulls up in front of us. Mr. Sikh opens the door across the back of the little cart, lifts me in as the ayah scrambles in next to me, and gives instructions to the tonga driver; off the pony trots, bells jingling from his harness and hooves clattering on the cobblestones.

I'm delivered to a hairdresser to have a shampoo, accompanied by the ayah.

***

When I get back from my very first visit to a ladies' hairdresser—in Shanghai the barber came to our house to cut everyone's hair—I find John digging in a sandbox in the big green garden. John and I talk about the animals in *The Jungle Book* stories Mr. Sikh read to us at lunch, like the monkeys and the wolves who are Mowgli's family.

The sandbox is big and has lots of sand—a real sandbox. I run the sand through my fingers. It feels good. I look across the wide lawn. The garden's surrounded by a tall, solid brick wall, and growing against the wall is a hedge of red poinsettias, a hedge so tall that it reaches to the top of the eight-foot wall. The bright-red flowers are in full bloom, beautiful. There are small spades and buckets lined up along the rim of the box. I turn to the sand and begin to dig. In the sand John and I find some little cars that have been buried there: one red, one blue, and one green. Toys that must have been buried by other children. We wonder who the other children of the sandbox were. Were they also waiting for their parents to get them?

***

A few days later, Hal picks us up. He tells us we'll be flying to Agra, the airport near New Delhi.

I'm sorry that we didn't get to meet the British ambassador; I guess he's much too busy to meet little children. But I do thank Mr. Sikh and the ayah for taking such good care of us, washing all our clothes and reading *The Jungle Book* at every meal.

NOTES

1.   Dum Dum Aerodrome, first built by the British governor of Bengal in 1929, played an important role during World War II. The United States flew bombing raids over Burma out of Dum Dum, as well as used it as a cargo refueling port and a military communications center.
2.   In India, an *ayah* is a woman hired to care for young children.
3.   A *tonga* is a light horse-drawn vehicle used in India.

31

A Smudge of Planes, Aerodromes, Villages, and Deserts

Early December 1942
Calcutta, West Bengal State, India, to
Khartoum, Khartoum State, Sudan

Now begins a long series of days—weeks—flying from one refueling or layover airport to another. At each stop the plane is serviced, repaired if need be, fueled, unloaded, or loaded. Frequently we change planes. We sit on folded parachutes or piles of mailbags. One plane has a long row of bottom-shapes pressed into long metal benches that run down each side of what I now know is the fuselage. This plane doesn't have windows; it has round portholes, about six inches across, each with a big, round rubber plug in it. Occasionally the planes have a few regular airplane seats.

Sometimes we are the only people on board, and sometimes there are others. Twice we fly with men covered in bandages, most lying on stretcher-beds. There are no seats on these planes; the planes are outfitted to hold the stretchers. I wonder where the wounded soldiers are going—to a hospital, or maybe home? They don't talk much. Some smoke cigarettes. Sometimes, they smile at us.

At night, we stay in all sorts of different places—once we stayed in a very white room in a hospital, another time at an orphanage. At the orphanage we're first blessed with holy water and then we get to run around the yard with the other children. I play hopscotch and jump rope with the girls; John is off somewhere with the boys. Sometimes we stay just one night in a place, and sometimes we stay several nights. Hal says we have to wait our turn, as well as wait for a plane going in the right direction. It's like hitchhiking, he says, only by air. One evening I ask Hal if I can see my passport. When he gives it to me, I see that there are almost no stamps in it to show where we have stopped. I ask Hal about this and he says everyone's too busy to stamp passports and tucks it back in his briefcase. "Remember, there's a war on," Hal says as he snaps the buckle of the briefcase.

We also eat in many different places—the hospital, the orphanage—and sometimes we go with Hal when he visits friends. But mostly we eat in big tents with lots of men in soldier uniforms. That's the most fun, because everyone is chatting and laughing. And especially because the men often give us coins, which we add to our collection.

The men like to talk to us and we like to talk to them. I know we remind them of their children and their families. John enjoys talking with the men a lot. I see him make a special effort to please them, and I feel proud. I don't know why the men like to give us coins, but lots of the soldiers do. They like to give us candy too, even though Hal tells them not to. We now have so many coins that they weigh down the bib pocket of my overalls. When we're alone John and I like to take the coins out and look at them and count them.

***

After our plane leaves Dum Dum Aerodrome, we go to Agra to refuel.[1] Through the plane windows, this part of India looks flat and we see many little villages as we fly over them. At the stop in Agra, we watch planes being unloaded or loaded, usually with the help of elephants. The elephants move big crates and the fifty-five-gallon metal drums that seem to be in every airport, carefully lifting them between their tusks and their trunks. The elephants are usually directed by little boys.

Whenever we get tired of watching the activity on the airfield, all we need to do is look beyond it at other interesting sights. I've seen rows of brightly dressed ladies picking leaves—tea leaves, we're told when we ask—and others pulling plants out of the fields. I watch a man as he makes what I recognize by their curved shape to be roof tiles; he slaps mud into a mold, taps the mold with a stick, and when it comes apart he sets the tiles aside to dry. Next to him are rows and rows of tiles drying in the sun.

Hal tells us that from Agra, we'll fly eleven hundred kilometers (683.5 miles) west to the coast, to Karachi,[2] in British India. He says the airbase in Karachi is very important. When we get to Karachi, there's lots of activity, not just the planes but also many soldiers and other men and women moving back and forth. Here, the air feels different. It's cooler.

After that, we fly over the Arabian Sea to Oman.[3] It's a long flight, with only water, endless water, below us. Hal tells us we're near Saudi Arabia, a name that's familiar because of all the exciting stories we've read about it in books. I look through the window and see long lines of camels with packs on their backs and men in long white robes.

From Oman we take a shorter trip, to Yemen.[4] Then from Yemen we go to Sudan.[5] Although Hal tells us the names of the countries, it's hard to keep them all straight. To me, it's become another day in the air, another long flight.

We land in Khartoum. Thud-thud, thud-thud, thud-thud. John and I hurry to look out of the window but don't see anything that would make the loud thud-thud noise. We see sand, sand in every direction, miles and miles of sand—a desert. I've never seen a real desert before. It's amazing!

We leave the plane and Hal takes us straight to a big tent.

Thud-thud, thud-thud, thud-thud.

"What's that noise?" I ask a heavy gentleman with a sun-tanned face. He's sitting at a table near the entrance to the tent.

"That's the Marston Mats,[6] girlie," the man says.

"Oh" is all I can think of to say. "Thank you."

The man laughs. He can tell I don't know what Marston Mats

are. "They're what the runway's made of. What you hear is a plane taking off," he continues.

Just another plane taking off. All the places, towns, deserts, fields, airfields, soldiers are one big swirl to me, all smudged together. I wonder if we'll get to Mummy and Daddy soon. Or will we be riding around on a plane forever?

NOTES

1. About 1,086 kilometers (675 miles) northwest of Dum Dum Aerodrome, the airfield in Agra, India, was the next refueling stop west on the southern ferry route.

2. The airport at Karachi, British India (now Pakistan), was one of the biggest transshipment bases for US Army Air Force units during World War II. In addition to being used by Air Transport Command (ATC), it was a major supply and maintenance depot. Here planes were received, assembled, and tested before being sent on to the Middle East as well as to China.

3. Masirah Island, about ninety-five kilometers (fifty-nine miles) long and thirteen kilometers (eight miles) wide, stands off the east coast of Oman in the Arabian Sea. During World War II, the British paid the sultan of Muscat a stipend to allow its military on the island, and the US Army had a base there as well. The airport was on the northernmost tip of the island; most of the remaining terrain was mountainous.

4. In June 1940, when Italy declared war on Britain and France, the airport in Aden, Yemen, became an important British base because of its proximity to Italian-occupied Eritrea, just across the Red Sea. The British allowed American transports to refuel there as needed.

5. The military air base Wadi Seidna is twenty-two kilometers (fourteen miles) north of Khartoum, Sudan, and 1.6 kilometers (one mile) west of the Nile River. Its single runway is in the desert.

6. Marston Mats, perforated steel matting, could be laid down on almost any flat surface to form a temporary runway or landing strip and were therefore ubiquitous in the hastily constructed, primitive airports of World War II. The interlocking mats were laid in a staggered pattern for strength. The matting got its name from an airfield in Marston, North Carolina, where it was first used.

32

Are We Almost There?

Second Week of December 1942
Khartoum, Khartoum State, Sudan, to
Ascension Island, South Atlantic Ocean

Hal tells us that the flight from Khartoum to Kano,[1] our next stop, will be a long one. Kano is in Nigeria, and to get there, we'll fly over Chad. The names of these countries don't mean much to me, but I try to remember them. When I look out the window, all I see is endless green countryside with some tiny little dots that Hal says are huts.

We arrive at Kano late in the day, so we eat and go straight to bed, this time sleeping on some trunks stacked up in a shed. Hal tucks us in. Too tired to think, I fall right to sleep.

***

Four days of waiting later, we leave Kano for Lagos,[2] another city in Nigeria. The flight between Kano and Lagos is short. The pilots and radio operator tell jokes and stories about their adventures in Calcutta, laughing and looking at each other in a funny way. I don't understand so I don't bother to listen.

When we arrive in Lagos, Hal takes us to a lady who seems to work for the army. Her name is Mabel. Mabel helps us wash, gives us sandwiches with thick slices of meat she calls Spam, and helps us into bed. This funny meat must be from a local animal, as I don't remember hearing about it in China.

The next morning, I see Hal looking over a map with two other men.

"Our next stop is Accra,[3] in Ghana," Hal says. "Another short hop, only about four hundred kilometers, and then we'll have a long flight to Ascension Island."[4] He points out the route on the map to me. The other men just smile.

"Why is the island in the middle of the ocean?" I ask.

"I don't know," Hal says. "Why do little girls ask silly questions? The island's made by a volcano. And I suppose volcanos can be anywhere. We're lucky to have this island right where it is, halfway between us and Brazil. We couldn't fly all that way in one stretch."

***

We're over the Atlantic Ocean, on our way to Ascension Island. I look out the window; water, water, and water's all I see in every direction.

Two extra pilots are on the plane. I understand by listening to the men as they chat that the pilots will take turns flying when one gets tired.

"Did you hear?" one of the pilots says to his companion. "The scuttlebutt in Natal is that enemy subs in the South Atlantic are sending false radio signals to confuse our flights." I see the men look briefly at each other and then turn away. They don't want me to see. Hal told me last evening that Natal is in Brazil and that's where we're supposed to go after Ascension Island. I look at John, but he's distracted with something on the rack above our heads and hasn't seen the looks on the pilots' faces.

"I'm on top of it; no sweat," the radio operator says. "We'll stick to communications from pilots we can identify."

"Hope we find some," Hal replies. "It's a big ocean."

"And planes are flying at night so that they can navigate by celestial readings."

I don't understand what the pilots and radio operator are talking about, so I decide to play cat's cradle with a piece of string I've been saving. Hal doesn't like me to listen to his or the men's conversations, anyway. He says it's not nice.

The radio operator calls to John and asks his name. He is very thin with a narrow face and hair that's cut very short. "Do you know what a celestial reading is, looking at the stars when you're flying?" he asks John.

John says he has looked at the stars with his friend Dr. Greene and starts to name some of the constellations.

"Well, when you're flying you can use the stars to help you find your way," the radio operator says. "You need a sextant. You check the stars against the exact time in Greenwich, England."

It sounds very difficult, but interesting. *But how does he know the time in England?*

"Of course, you have to be flying at night," the radio operator continues. "During the day we rely on talking to other pilots and signals from land." The radio starts to crackle. The operator winks at John, turns away from us, and puts on his headset. Hal says the radio operator's picked up a signal and spotted Ascension Island, a dot of land off in the distance.

As we approach the runway, we fly high and fast. "I've landed here before," the pilot says. "This is the way to do it if you want to clear the updrafts from those cliffs." He nods to his left. I look out the window and see that the landing strip is between two mountain peaks.

"I've had nightmares about this place," the copilot says.

"Well, you'll sleep well tonight, pal," the pilot replies.

The pilot lands without difficulty. As I start climbing down the ladder from the plane, the nice radio operator lifts me to the ground. This airfield is different from the others; it crunches under my feet and feels funny, different funny, as I walk across it. I look at Hal.

"It's crushed lava," Hal says.

"It feels funny to walk on," I say, glancing up at Hal. He looks tired. "Are we almost there?" I ask.

"Almost," Hal says and rubs his chin.

NOTES

1. Built in Kano, Nigeria, by the British before the country's inde-
    pendence, Kano Airport (now Mallam Aminu Kano International
    Airport) was Nigeria's first airport. It began operations in 1936
    and quickly became an important fuel stop for the long-haul
    planes of World War II.

2. Lagos International Airport, now called Murtala Muhammed
    International Airport, was built during World War II. It's located
    in Ikeja, the capital of Lagos State.

3. Accra International Airport, in Accra, the capital of Ghana, was
    originally a military airport used mainly by the British during
    World War II. Now called Kotoka International Airport, it was
    handed over to civilian authority after the war.

4. Sixteen hundred kilometers (one thousand miles) west off the
    coast of Africa and 2,250 kilometers (fourteen hundred miles)
    east off the coast of Brazil, Ascension Island is an isolated
    eighty-eight-square-kilometer (thirty-four-square-mile) volca-
    nic island in the middle of the South Atlantic Ocean. Discovered
    by a Portuguese navigator in 1501, the island was an inhospitable
    bit of barren land that remained uninhabited until 1815, when
    British soldiers were stationed there at the time Napoleon was
    exiled. Ships used it as a supply depot; they dropped off goats,
    rabbits, and other animals in hopes that they would multiply and
    provide a future food supply.

    In 1836, Charles Darwin visited Ascension Island on his
    second *Beagle* voyage. In 1843, he was followed by botanist and
    explorer Joseph Hooker, who with Darwin's encouragement ini-
    tiated a forestation project there. The British Royal Navy, among
    others, transported trees, plants, and grasses from London's Kew
    Gardens, which helped capture rain and improve the island's
    soil. Subsequently, botanical gardens in Argentina, Europe, and
    South Africa contributed to the project also.

    During World War II, Ascension Island was an important
    naval and air station, providing antisubmarine warfare bases. It
    is governed by the British as a part of their Overseas Territories.

33

America

Mid–December 1942
Ascension Island, South Atlantic Ocean,
to Florida, United States

Early the next morning we walk over the crunchy surface again. We're off, this time on another long leg, even longer than the last flight, to Natal.[1] It's our first stop in Brazil, Hal says. What I say to myself is that we're getting closer to Mummy and Daddy. I close my eyes and dream of seeing Daddy, of him playing with us, reading to us, taking us for walks, hugging us, and holding my hand. I think about the walks we took in the park in Shanghai and of climbing on the big metal bell in the park. How I miss him. It seems like a long time since I've seen him. I know John feels the same way, although we do not talk about it.

It's late when we arrive in Natal. John and I are asleep on the mailbags when Hal wakes us. We stumble sleepily off the plane. The airport building is small and almost deserted. I see two men working at the other end. They're speaking a language that's new to me. I look at Hal. "Portuguese," he says. "It's the language spoken here in Brazil."

"It sounds like singing," I reply. Hal leads us to a low building where the off-duty pilots relax. He talks to some of the men and finds a spot for us, and we hasten off to bed.

Another long flight the next day. Hal says we're going to Belém,[2] another town in Brazil. When we land, I realize the town must be on the coast. The air smells good, fresh, salty—of the sea. On this trip I've learned how to recognize when we're near the ocean by sniffing the air.

It's very dark, no streetlights, no lights in the houses. Hal whispers to us that there's a blackout because no one wants the German U-boats to see the city, especially the airport. I don't know why he's whispering. Can the U-boats also hear us? What are U-boats, anyway? I decide to ask Hal tomorrow. We are all very tired and go to a small hotel near the airfield. John and I share a bed, sleeping at opposite ends.

***

At the next airport, in Guiana,[3] the airstrip runs beside a wide river. It's raining and very hot. Hal asks one of the men in uniform if he can give us a ride into town. The driver agrees to take us and says the town's about forty kilometers (24.9 miles) away.

As we speed by elegant brick buildings down wide boulevards, the jeep's windshield wipers beating back and forth in rhythm, I ask where we're going. Hal says we need to find a place for the night.

"Oh, you and the kids need to stop overnight, do you?" the driver asks. "I'll take you to the BOQ—the bachelor officers' quarters. They'll be able to fit you in, I'm sure."

"Thank you very much," Hal says and leans back in the seat. "Does it rain like this all the time?"

"Only in monsoon season, the end of November until January," the driver says. "Actually, we have two rainy seasons. The other is mid-May till mid-July."

"Georgetown certainly has its share of water," Hal says. "Is that a problem?"

"Not really. We have a good system of drains and dikes. They're very important; the whole city's below the high water-mark at high tide."

***

As we walk toward the BOQ, I see something shining in the grass and stoop to pick it up. It's a piece of metal, the lid of a sardine can that someone must have discarded here. I slip it into my pocket. I don't know exactly why I'm saving it. It just seems that it might be useful. Later, when we're alone, I'll show it to John. He'll have an idea of what we can use it for. "You'd better not show it to Hal," John says after dinner as we admire its shiny sharp edges.

Hal says that our next stop is a short hop to Port of Spain, in Trinidad. He says we're getting close to the end of our trip. It seems like we've been flying forever. Almost every morning we get up and get on another plane. One more plane, one more big tent with lots of men standing in line, one more place to sleep, one more. One more.

That evening John and I take out our coins and spread them on the floor. We put the ones that look the same together in little stacks. There are a lot of different kinds. "John, we have seventy-six coins," I say. "I counted them twice." He smiles at me as I drop them back in the bib pocket of my overalls, one by one.

***

The next morning as we walk away from the big breakfast tent, I happen to look down in the grass and see a little coin. What good luck! That's coin number seventy-seven.

"John, I just found number seventy-seven."

"What's that all about?" Hal asks.

"We have seventy-seven coins," I say proudly.

"Jennifer, I'm tired of you kids begging for coins," Hal says. "Give them to me."

Something shifts inside me, and without thinking I whip the piece of sardine can out of my pocket. The edge is sharp. I'll cut Hal before I give him any of our coins. "No!" I say.

Hal's eyes widen.

"We're going to give this money to Mummy and Daddy so they won't leave us again," I say in a firm tone.

Hal looks at me for a long moment and then away and doesn't say anything. Silently he ushers us up the rolling stairway that's been pushed up to the plane. No more is said about the coin collection. Neither is anything said about the sardine-can lid.

*∗∗

We're in Trinidad.[4] The airport's very busy. Men in uniform are everywhere. It's lovely and warm. I look at the beautiful sea and all the palm trees and greenery growing near the airfield. I wish I were wearing shorts and not these old overalls. They're getting hot.

We get on an unusual plane; its wings are high above the fuselage. Hal tells us it's a Catalina,[5] a special plane because it can land on water. *Land on water?* I think. *I've got to see this!*

We fly all day, most of the time over the sea, on our way to a place called Florida in America. The view out the window is interesting because there're many islands below us. Hal tells us the islands are Haiti and the Dominican Republic, which are really just one big island. The little waves under us look pretty. It's nice to be flying closer to the land and the sea, not high above the big ocean, which seems to worry the pilots. They don't say anything, I just get that feeling when I look at them and how they sit.

We arrive in West Palm Beach.[6] The plane circles, then descends closer and closer to the water, until splash—the plane lands! Water splashes up over the wings, and fish fly past the windows. How lovely it all is, how exciting. The plane taxis a little and stops. One of the pilots waves to a man in a motorboat, who turns the boat toward us. All the while the pilot anchors the plane. Then Hal, John, and I—and lots of big green bags of military mail—get a lift in the motorboat to the shore.

Hal tells us we're in America now. Tomorrow we have one last flight to take; we're going to Washington, DC.

Finally. *Finally.*

Mummy and Daddy will be there.

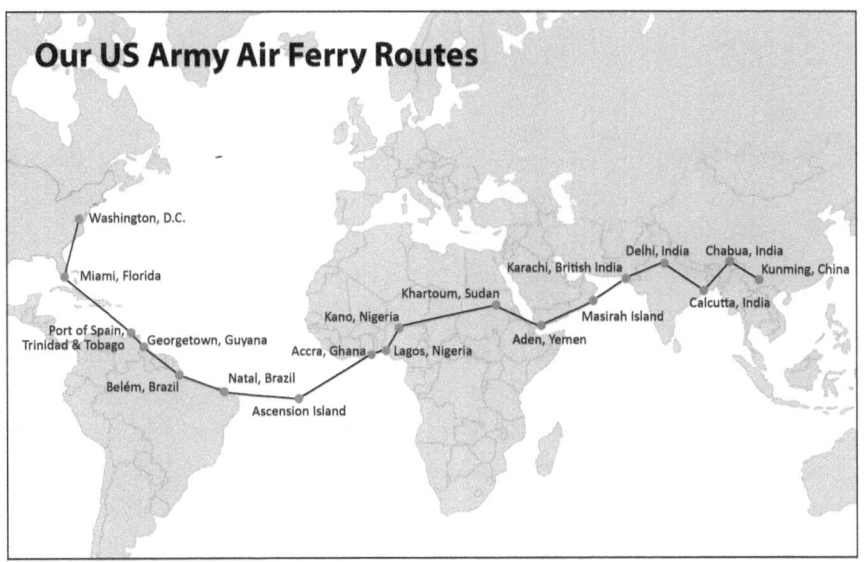

Our US Army Air Ferry Routes

AUTHOR'S NOTE

During World War II, US Military Commands established air ferry routes that crossed the Pacific and Atlantic Oceans, as the need for them became apparent. Thus planes, military matériel, and personnel were transported to battlefronts around the world. Returning planes carried the wounded, mail, and goods not available in the United States. In our case, John and I caught flights returning on the South Atlantic air ferry route and on other routes across Africa, India, Burma, and China. At each stop, we waited to continue west.

NOTES

1.   Before World War II, Parnamirim Airport, which served Natal,
     Brazil, was a combination land and marine airport used not only
     by Brazil and the United States but also by several European
     countries. When Pearl Harbor was attacked, the British Secret
     Service no longer allowed the Italian airlines to use the airport.
     It became a strategic base for aircraft flying between South
     America and West Africa, used by the Brazilian Air Force, the
     US Army and Navy, the British Royal Air Force, and commer-
     cial airlines; maintenance and security were provided by the US
     Army. The airport is now called Augusto Severo International
     Airport.

2.   In 1934, Brazil's director of military aviation ordered an air-
     field be built on a site near Belém; a hangar, a parking area for
     military aircraft, and a courtyard were also constructed. When
     World War II broke out, sites along the coast of Brazil became
     extremely important, and after negotiations with the United
     States, Brazil built two runways and other facilities to meet US
     Air Transport Command (ATC) needs. Thousands of American
     and Canadian planes, personnel, and equipment destined for
     North Africa passed through this facility. After the war, the air-
     port was returned to civilian use. It is now called Val de Cans /
     Júlio Cezar Ribeiro International Airport.

3.   Before the Japanese attacked Pearl Harbor in 1941, American
     public sentiment about entering a foreign war had been primarily
     anti-involvement—so much so that in 1935, Congress passed the
     Neutrality Acts, which banned the sale of arms to any combatant
     nation. However, by mid-1940 during World War II, Germany
     had defeated France, and it appeared that little stood in the way
     of Germany's also conquering Great Britain. Although President
     Roosevelt's hands were somewhat tied politically, he managed to
     effect a destroyers-for-bases deal with Great Britain whereby the
     United States exchanged fifty mostly mothballed World War I
     destroyers for land rights on British possessions.

     Georgetown, British Guiana, was one of these possessions. In

June 1941, the American army surveyed land near Georgetown for a bomber airfield, after which forest was cleared, hills were levelled, and a concrete runway and weather station were built. The airfield opened in June 1941 with the mission of protecting the colony against German U-boats, and it quickly became a major refueling and transshipment site for Air Transport Command (ATC). In addition, antisubmarine detection and bombing runs were conducted there before these activities were turned over to the US Navy.

4.   Trinidad is an island of about 5,180 square kilometers (two thousand square miles) that lies eleven kilometers (seven miles) northeast off the coast of Venezuela. Its capital, Port of Spain, is located on a large bay on the island's west coast. The airport, which opened in 1931, is thirty kilometers (nineteen miles) east of the downtown area. During World War II, the airport was used by both the US Army and the US Navy as a transport airfield and to launch antisubmarine patrols. After the war it was returned to civilian use.

5.   The PBY Catalina was an amphibious aircraft designed in the United States and manufactured in both the US and Canada just before the outbreak of World War II. Originally designed as a patrol bomber (hence the PB in its name), the Catalina was slow but had endurance; it was able to cruise a distance of over four thousand kilometers (twenty-five hundred miles) at two hundred kilometers per hour (125 miles per hour) and had an operating ceiling of more than 4,572 meters (fifteen thousand feet). Under optimal conditions, the Catalina could stay in the air for twenty hours. A typical crew was made up of nine men.

An extremely versatile aircraft, this seaplane was used in the Pacific, Atlantic, Mediterranean, Arctic, and Caribbean theaters of the war. Although the armed forces of many countries possessed Catalinas, the US Army and Navy, the British Royal Air Force, and the Royal Canadian Air Force had the most. The aircraft was used for reconnaissance, to hunt for submarines, to protect convoys and merchant ships, to undertake search-and-rescue operations, and even to drop mines. After World War II, the use of the Catalina rapidly declined because the construction of numerous airstrips made the ability to land on water less important.

6.   With the outbreak of World War II, a massive defense buildup began in the United States, including the search for a suitable location for the Army Air Corps's military base. The commissioners of Palm Beach County, Florida, anticipating that the project would provide relief from the recent depression, offered a tract of land. Funded by the Works Progress Administration (WPA), a base was built that included everything the Army Air Corps required—barracks, a kitchen, hangars, a hospital, a chapel, and runways—to supplement the small existing facility.

The first military personnel arrived at Morrison Field in February 1941. Although it was initially planned as a training base, it quickly became obvious that the location was ideal as an embarkation location for the US Air Corps Ferrying Command, later the Air Transport Command (ATC). Here planes and personnel were processed before leaving for overseas. In 1959 the airfield in West Palm Beach was converted to a civilian facility.

PART II

THE USA

34

Who's That Lady?

December 17, 1942
Washington, DC, United States, to
Pennsylvania, United States

The plane descends toward the runway at National Airport in Washington.[1] It's December 17, 1942, a month since we left China. The sky is dark and it's raining lightly—cold, but not cold enough for snow. The airfield looks deserted. There's no one to be seen on the wide expanse of tarmac except a man holding two flags to direct the landing.

It seems like we've been flying forever, but now that we're coming to our last stop, I feel confused and don't know why. I wonder how John feels but say nothing. I reach up and touch the lump that's our coin collection in my bib pocket. It, at least, is solid and reassuring. A gift for Mummy and Daddy.

The plane rolls to a stop in the middle of the glistening tar-mac, and a set of stairs is pushed across the airfield by two men in overalls and rain ponchos. They hunch their shoulders against what must be chilly, damp air as they position the stairs against the side of the aircraft.

One of the pilots opens the door. Hal directs us to get off ahead of him; he'll follow with our suitcases. John and I step out onto the top of the stairs. I look across the airfield. No men in uniform. No crowds moving boxes, barrels, and bags. Not even other planes on the airfield.

Then a lone woman appears, walking resolutely across the wide, wet tarmac. She's dressed in black and wears a small black hat with a black veil stretched over her face. She advances steadily across the asphalt toward the plane. She's almost here.

John and I wait on the top of the rolling stairs. Drizzle hits our faces. I look at John.

"Who's that lady?" I ask.

There's no reply.

We start down the stairs. Then John hurries to the bottom step, leaving me behind. He runs up to the lady and throws his arms around her legs, hugging her. Only then do I realize the lady must be our mummy. I look at her. She looks different from how I remember her. In China she didn't wear black, and I don't remember her ever wearing a veil on her face.

John lets go of her legs and looks up at her. "Where's Daddy?" he asks.

There's a long pause. "He's dead," Mummy says.

Silence.

He's dead. He's dead. He's dead. The words rattle around and around in my head. I don't look at Mummy; I can't look.

We walk away from the plane. I stumble along, led by the hand. I don't hear if John says anything, or asks anything, or if anything more is said at all.

We reach the terminal and walk through the deserted building and out onto the street. Mummy hails a taxi. I'm in a daze. The driver opens the door and we get in.

The taxi drives to a big train station—Union Station,[2] Mummy calls it—and we get on a train. I sit by the window. I am numb.

He's dead. He's dead. He's dead.

Mummy reaches into a bag and pulls out a toy boat—it's red with a white sail—and puts it on the seat next to John. She gives me a soft doll, its body made of light-blue cloth. Only its head and hands are hard. The little doll doesn't make me feel any better. *Dead. Dead. Dead.* The word ricochets around in my head.

I place the doll on the seat beside me and look out the window of the train. It's still raining steadily. The train starts moving; it leaves the station. I'm silent. John is silent. He holds his sailboat on his lap with both hands and sits silently. I watch as the drops of rain slide down the glass windowpane, pushed by the wind as the train picks up speed. The rain cries. It cries for John. It cries for me. But it cries mostly for Daddy.

The train moves along, faster and faster. After a while it stops and people get off and other people get on. The people shuffle down the aisle but I don't look at them. I cannot look at them. I cannot look at John. I take the little blue doll from the seat next to me and hold it.

After a while we arrive at another station. Mummy tells us that this is 30th Street Station in Philadelphia,[3] and it's our stop. We climb off the train; Mummy carries our suitcases. We go up a staircase and walk through a white marble hallway with tall columns and a very high ceiling. Mummy walks ahead. John and I follow.

Suddenly John stops. Beside us, on the left, is a statue of an angel holding a man in her arms. We both stare in amazement. "Mummy, look. The angel is carrying Daddy up to heaven," John says.

John, age seven, now in America, 1943.

Me, age nine, now in America, 1943.

NOTES

1. The first airport in Washington, DC, National Airport, opened in 1926, was privately owned. It was located near the current site of the Pentagon. A street crossed its single runway, and a guard had to stop traffic for each takeoff or landing. Although the need for a better airport was recognized, a congressional statute prohibited the building of airports. This statute was lifted in 1938, and President Roosevelt allocated funds for the construction of the current National Airport, now called Ronald Reagan Washington National Airport. It opened in 1940.

2. Union Station, in Washington, DC, is a train station that opened in 1907 at 50 Massachusetts Avenue, NE. At the height of World War II, as many as two hundred thousand people passed through the doors of Union Station daily.

3. Located at 2955 Market Street, Philadelphia, Pennsylvania, 30th Street Station was built from 1929 to 1933. It has a neoclassical exterior and art deco–detailed interior and is considered one of the last remaining grand train stations in the United States. It was placed on the National Register of Historic Places in 1978.

    The statue we saw in 30th Street Station, of a soldier in the arms of an angel, was a World War I memorial sculpted by a participant in the Works Progress Administration (WPA). The WPA was an American New Deal agency designed to employ millions of (mostly) not formally educated men to construct roads, bridges, airports, and public buildings. One of its most famous adjuncts, named WPA Project Number One, employed writers, musicians, artists, actors, and directors to research and transcribe historical surveys and create works of literature, drama, music, and art. This sculpture was placed in 30th Street Station temporarily—the statue and its creator as ethereal as the angel it depicts.

35

Christmas 1942

Last Week of December 1942
Pennsylvania, United States

A week passes. It's almost Christmas, and Mummy takes us by train from Wayne, Pennsylvania, where we live with our grandmother and Uncle Thos at 518 West Beech Tree Lane, to see the shops in Ardmore. I don't care whether we see shops. Ever since Mummy got us, I've felt lost. John looks lost too; I think he feels the same way. Both of us just do what we're told and go where we're told, without thinking. Like ghosts.

Mummy hasn't talked to us about Daddy. She never even mentions his name. How did he die? Where did he die? Granny tells John and me that he died in the war, but I want to know everything and Mummy tells us almost nothing. The only thing she says about the war is that when she arrived in America, she was very thin and weighed eighty pounds. Granny says that's true and tells us that when Mummy can't sleep at night, she goes to the kitchen and opens the door of the refrigerator and looks at all the food. Mummy smiles when Granny tells us this story.

Mummy goes to Philadelphia on the train every day. She's studying so that she can get a job and help win the war. She comes home late every evening and is always tired. Sometimes we even have to go to bed before she gets home. Big brother Teddy is here but he doesn't pay much attention to us. He doesn't play with us. He goes to Haverford School and does lots of homework. Maybe he thinks I'm just a girl and John's too young. I think he's sad about Daddy too, but since no one talks about Daddy he doesn't talk much about him either. He did once tell me how he learned that Daddy was dead; one morning while Uncle Thomas (who we call Thos) was driving him to school, Thos stopped the car on the side of the road and told him Daddy'd been killed in the war. And after that he took him on to school.

Katie—Gran—helps win the war by knitting gloves and scarves for sailors. She gets other ladies to knit too. The ladies come to our house; they have a knitting club called the Navy League.[1]

Gran talks to us, takes us shopping when she buys groceries, and watches us do our homework. The best thing she does is help us remember our life in China. She tells us stories about the fun things she did in Peking and Shanghai: sledding and ice skating in winter when our mummy was a girl; hiking, camping, and picnicking in summer; and going to the beach at Beidaihe.[2] She reminds us of our summer house on the top of Candlin Hill in Beidaihe, where we climbed trees and rode little gray donkeys to get from the house down to the beach to swim. She talks about China.

Donkeys were brought to meet us when we arrived in Beidaihe by train each summer. Here, we children are on our way to the beach by donkey transport. No cars, not even a road, go to our hilltop summer house. Great-Grandmother Mary Candlin (Katie's mom) has her own transportation—a sedan chair, which is stored above the porch rafters when not in use.

Since no one speaks about the war, I don't speak about it either.

On the day we go to see the shops in Ardmore, we get off the train after a few stops. I don't hate trains but they are sad for me, so I'm glad we're not on board for long.

We walk down the steps from the train station and into a place with lots of stores. Mummy calls it the Suburban Square shopping center.

I gasp and think, *Wow!* The shop windows, Best & Co.,[3] are wonderful. Blinking red, blue, and yellow lights, toys and more toys, even a Christmas tree. The shop windows are different from anything I've ever seen.

Next to me, John stands transfixed. After a few moments, he turns and says, "Ferfer, this is like when Dorothy stepped out of her house into Munchkinland."

I know what he means. China was a sad, gray country, and America is all bright, happy, and full of colors.

NOTES

1. The US Navy League, a civilian nonprofit organization, was founded with the help of Teddy Roosevelt in 1902 to support all US sea service members and their families.

2. Beidaihe is now a popular seaside resort, but in 1895, when my great-grandfather G. T. Candlin rode there in an oxcart to find a retreat for his family from Peking's hot summers, it was a sleepy fishing village. He purchased a twenty-seven-acre rock-strewn hill that the farmer who sold it to him said was only good to graze goats on, and imported a thousand pine trees from Scotland and had them planted with locust trees to shade the saplings. Now the trees are tall, and the hill, in appreciation of these trees, is a city park. The stone house that Great-Grandfather had built on top of the hill had a wide central hall with several large rooms on each side. A veranda, the family's gathering place, curved around two sides. Coolies carried water to a cistern on the roof, from where it was piped down to the bathtub. Leaves shed by the surrounding trees often arrived with the bathwater; I called them tea leaves. In those years, Great-Grandmother's sedan chair was stowed in the rafters of the veranda when not in use. There was a separate servants' quarters and a stable where little gray donkeys were kept for transportation. The house was later demolished, but the huge rock formation that was behind it still stands.

3. Best & Co., a beloved American department store founded in New York in 1879, had many branches in suburban shopping areas around the United States. It initially specialized in classical children's clothing, accessories, and toys. When the store in Ardmore, Pennsylvania, closed in the late 1940s, devoted customers cried.

36

Moving On

December 1942 to August 1945
Pennsylvania, United States

Christmas is different this year without Daddy. But then again, *everything* is different. We are no longer a small family in a large house, but a large family in a small house: Mummy, Granny, Uncle Thos, Teddy, John, two dogs, and me.

One day Kate Smith calls on the telephone and asks us to be on her radio program. She tells Mummy that she wants to ask us about our trip to America and how it felt to see our mother for the first time after a year. Mummy takes John and me into Philadelphia on the train. Then we ride to the offices of radio station KYW in a taxi. When we arrive at the studio, we're given a script that we practice reading while in the waiting room and then answer Miss Smith's questions, reading into a phone. Two weeks later, when we tune in to the broadcast, we discover that the voices on the radio are not our voices at all; apparently, they've been dubbed over. I'm sad but not surprised. It's like everything in this new country, where I don't really know who I am. A country where I'm living from a new script and my voice isn't my own.

The war rages on. Like the other children from school, we collect old newspapers and metal, flatten tin cans by jumping on them in the basement of our house, use our weekly twenty-five-cent allowances to buy war-bond stamps sold at school,[1] and paste them into little green booklets that we eventually exchange for war bonds. We plant a victory garden—carrots and green peppers in neat rows—in the vacant lot beside our house. On schooldays, John and I walk to the elementary school in Wayne. It's a long walk from our house on West Beech Tree Lane, but we enjoy the freedom of walking on our own.

We don't see much of our mother. She's now working as a draftsman in a factory,[2] drawing airplane parts, and every day she takes the train to her job in the city and returns after dark. When we do see her, she's different. She's not fun, as she used to be. She no longer reads to us at bedtime. We learn to read to ourselves.

One morning at breakfast, Thos and Gran seem to have forgotten I'm there and start to talk about Mummy. Thos says that when she arrived in America, she was a penniless widow with no employable skills, and Gran says it must have been sobering for her to be transformed from a Shanghai flapper who loved parties and dancing, with servants who took care of everything—including us—to *this*. "All in less than a year," Gran adds. "It must be devastating for her, poor thing. A handsome, loving husband, gone. The future as she knew it, gone. Her lovely house reduced to a single little room in the attic."

I picture Mummy's bedroom—up a narrow staircase from the second floor, fashioned out of the attic, surplus furniture and suitcases stacked out of sight behind four wallpapered panels across one side. Light streams in from two tiny windows that flank the chimney as it comes up through the floor from the living room below to pass through the roof.

Mummy still doesn't tell us anything about Daddy; she doesn't talk to us much at all. Does she miss Daddy? I want to ask her, but I don't think she wants me to talk about it. I want to tell her that I miss him, but I stay silent. Her silence gives me the idea that she thinks we shouldn't talk about how we feel. Maybe it's not something you're supposed to do.

The war drags on.

The following year, we all move to a larger house in Haverford. I have a room of my own on the third floor next to Mummy's. Teddy now goes to boarding school in Delaware, John goes to Haverford School, and I go to Haverford Friends School. We play on the nearby college grounds, sledding in winter, running in summer. One day while swinging on the rings in the college gym, I discover blood running down my leg. I'm glad there's no one else in the gym that day. I run home, thinking I've cut myself. Gran draws a box of Kotex out from under the old bathtub with little feet, which is in the bathroom next to her room, and tells me I'm growing up.

In April 1945, President Roosevelt dies, and the entire nation cries. We hadn't been told how sick he was and so his death comes as a great shock to everyone. We're still at war when he dies, but just a few weeks later, in May, the war in Europe ends, followed by V-J Day in August 1945.

The world takes a moment to rejoice, then starts licking its wounds, trying to recover from the past six ghastly years.

Marlene Miller (second from right) and I share a birthday, so we shared a birthday party when we were twelve in 1946. This is the entire fifth grade that year at Haverford Friends School in Haverford, Pennsylvania, from left to right: Bridget Hamilton, Helga Pfund, Betty Jane Davis, me, Babs McCabe, Felicia Forsythe, twins Stephanie and Janet Hetzel, Marlene, and Laura Comfort. Mrs. Vickers (not pictured) was our teacher.

NOTES

1. US victory bonds, or war bonds, were government debt sold to fund military operations during World War II. The lowest-denomination bond sold for $18.75 and was redeemable in ten years for $25.00. More than eighty-five million Americans bought these bonds, raising $185.7 million at an interest rate of 2.9 percent.

2. During the war, my mother worked at Sikorsky Aircraft, an American company founded in 1923 that designed and manufactured both landplanes and seaplanes.

37

Bad

October 1946 to September 1952
Pennsylvania, United States, to New Jersey, United States

In 1946, Mother marries Fred Metcalf. He was part of the reason Mummy was almost never home. Gran doesn't like him. We move to Philadelphia, leaving Gran in Haverford.

After we leave Gran's house, I turn bad. Often I stay out past the time I'm told to be home, inviting Fred's ire; red welts left by his belt across my hips last for several years. Once my screams result in a neighbor calling the police. When an officer arrives, Fred reaches out a clenched fist to him, and the officer silently leaves.

Alice Dobbs Metcalf, 1947.

John continues at Haverford School, now riding back and forth on the train on weekdays. I'm not trusted to go that far, so I take the streetcar to a public school twenty-seven blocks west of our midtown apartment near Rittenhouse Square. Every day I'm given fifteen cents, just enough for the round-trip trolley fare to and from school, and every day I walk the twenty-seven blocks each way to save the fifteen cents. I'm saving up to take the train from Philadelphia's 30th Street Station to Haverford to visit my grandmother.

Finally, the day arrives when I've saved enough for the ticket. I even have a little left over. I arrive at the train station in Haverford. I have just enough money left after the train ticket to either take a taxi or buy a Sunday *Philadelphia Inquirer* newspaper for my grandmother.

With the bulky newspaper under my arm, I leave the station and start off toward Gran's house. A car that I haven't noticed behind me pulls up to the curb; it's Fred and my mother, who demand that I get in. I run, determined to get to my grandmother's. But at thirteen, I'm not clever enough to evade adults bent on grabbing me. I'm captured and forced into the car. Fred turns the car and we drive back to the city.

On that day I promise myself that I won't plan an escape again until I know that I'll succeed.

**

In June 1952, three days after receiving my high school diploma, I pack a few things and take a bus to Ocean City, New Jersey. Along with a hundred other recently graduated high school girls, I've been hired to wait tables at the Flanders Hotel for the summer.

I never live with Mother and Fred again.

3 8

Good

After I leave home, I build myself a life, as people do. I put myself through college in Maryland by working as a waitress at the Jersey Shore each summer. Part of the reason I select Washington College in Chestertown, Maryland, is because my grandmother lives close by in Oxford.

A year after graduating from college I travel to Europe with a friend. While there, I meet a couple in Frankfurt, Germany, whose young son attends a Montessori School. I'm so impressed by the little boy that I return to the States and get a job in New York City in order to finance my return to Italy, where I train as a Montessori teacher in Bergamo and Perugia, Italy.

I return to the United States to take my first teaching position, near Philadelphia. After that I help establish and manage several additional Montessori preschools: recruiting students, ordering teaching materials from Italy, locating, designing, and setting up classrooms, hiring teachers, and eventually creating and presenting a teacher-training program. In Philadelphia, I meet Mahmoud Shaalan, a pathologist who's recently emigrated from Egypt. We marry in 1969, and two years later our beautiful son, Sherief, is born.

Mahmoud is offered the post of chief pathologist at the hospital in a small town, so we move to northern Mississippi. I quickly find a suitable building and open a Montessori preschool. Mahmoud is one of twenty-eight doctors in town, and we shortly acquire the income, house, and car enjoyed by those in such a position. Our social life consists of an endless round of parties with the same twenty-seven other couples; the bartender who's hired for every party knows the favorite drink of each of the fifty-six doctors and their wives.

Mahmoud and I enjoy a pleasant enough life together but eventually divorce. After the divorce, I stay in Corinth. My house is close to Mahmoud's, so Sherief can walk back and forth between the two. Still, it's a sad time for me. I've lost my position as a doctor's wife, and my pretty house and swimming pool, the cocktail parties and fancy dinners. And, surprisingly, I'm snubbed by several local shops. I presume the thinking is that my income is probably no longer adequate. But I've adapted to change in the past, and I can do it again. If there's one thing I know how to do, it's to adapt.

***

I go to graduate school and then work for a freight airline in their international training department, where I can use my knowledge of German and Italian and travel to Hong Kong, Taiwan, and mainland China, among other countries.

John, high school senior, Glassboro, New Jersey, 1955.

John grows up to be a scientist, earning a BS in mechanical engineering, an MS in physics, and a PhD in particle physics. He conducts extensive research in the areas of particle physics and engineering, authors a number of articles that are published in peer-reviewed journals, and is issued thirty-one patents. For his professional efforts, he's featured in three issues of *Who's Who in Science and Engineering*, seven editions of *Who's Who in the East*, and eight editions of *Who's Who in the World*.

Big brother Teddy (Edward C.) graduates from Harvard in 1952 and, after a tour of duty with the Marines, joins the multinational insurance company American International Group (AIG). His first post is in Cuba, followed by posts in Venezuela, Argentina, and Brazil. After being responsible for much of AIG's business in South America, he becomes vice president for Africa and much of the Middle East before retiring. He dies in 2016.

The last picture taken of us together, Ted's three children, 1998.

My mother dies in 1982, never having mentioned my father since that day on the tarmac in Washington, DC. In 1998, I take my mother's ashes to scatter in Beidaihe, China, the country of her birth, which I know she loves as I do.

As for my father, his body is never found.

At some point during these years, I realize that I've never said goodbye to my dad. And that I need to. That not saying goodbye means I'm holding on to the fairy-tale life, the dream of China. I realize this quite unexpectedly one day while wandering around in a bookstore in Florence, Alabama. After divorcing and not being able to find a decent job in Corinth, Mississippi, I'm in Florence attending graduate school at the University of North Alabama. It's between classes, so I have time to go into town. I stroll aimlessly between the bookshelves—picking out a book, reshelving it, and then picking up another, not looking for anything in particular.

As I round a corner, a beam of sunlight slips along the shelves in front of me, lighting up the titles. The beam strikes a middle shelf and lingers on a book, a title: *Learning to Say Good-Bye.* I take the book off the shelf but don't open it. The sheer force of the title hits me so hard that I dissolve onto the edge of a protruding shelf. I hug the book gently. Speaking softly so none of the other customers in the store can hear, I whisper, "Goodbye, Daddy, I love you. Goodbye."

***

One day John tells me that even now, he sometimes finds that he's furious with our father. Why didn't he leave Hong Kong when the Japanese attacked? Why didn't he take Mummy back to Kunming, back to us? But then, he continues, he remembers something that happened in one of the little towns we stopped in along the Burma Road.

He and Daddy were strolling around the village. They had just passed an alleyway when a huge brown dog jumped out at them, barking and snarling. Holding John's hand, Daddy turned the two of them around to face the dog, then quietly said, "This dog is on a chain, but if you ever encounter a dog that's not on a chain, you must face him and stand your ground. If you run, he will surely catch you and bite you. If you stand your ground and show no fear, there's a chance you won't get bitten."

John takes a deep breath. "I guess that's what Daddy was doing in Hong Kong. Standing his ground. Taking a chance that he wouldn't get bitten."

EPILOGUE

Christmastime, 2002
Memphis, Tennessee, United States

"Mom, where should I put the decorations after I take them off the tree?" Sherief calls from the living room. It's New Year's Day and I want to make full use of his help before he returns to Pittsburgh, Pennsylvania, where he's teaching.

"Oh, I'll bring the box the decorations are stored in," I say, happy to have him home. I see so little of him these days. "And there's some Bubble Wrap for the angel."

"Don't worry, Mom, I'll take care of everything."

"And please put the box back in the attic when you're finished."

"In the back corner. I know."

***

An hour later Sherief descends from the attic and meets me in the kitchen. "Yes, Mom, I remembered to turn off the light," he says as he watches me dry my hands on a dish towel. "And don't worry, I put the ornaments back in the corner. By the way, why do you still have that old wooden box up there? It's taking up a lot of space." He brushes his dark, curly hair out of his eyes. "What's in it, anyway?"

"Letters and documents from when I was a child in China, I believe." I look at Sherief and think how much he resembles his father. "I should probably take a look at them. There might be some information about what happened to my family during World War II."

"Like what?"

"Well, for one thing, did I ever tell you my mother was a POW in Hong Kong?"

"Grandma was a prisoner of war!" Sherief says.

I nod. "After my father was killed. What happened was, we had to leave China and . . . well, I'll tell you about it someday." I hang the dish towel back on its hook at the end of the kitchen counter. "In fact, I might write a book about our experiences living in Shanghai and traveling up the Burma Road during the war. They were exciting times."

Sherief looks at me and smiles. "I hope you do, Mom. I hope you do."

ACKNOWLEDGMENTS

Thank you, Daddy, for inspiring this story. You lingered close by and silently pushed me to dredge up the feelings I'd tried for years to forget, then you steered me to my laptop—a tool that didn't exist when you were alive!

And thank you, beloved brother John, who never tired of answering my incessant questions, reminding me of details, and helping me remember. You were always ready, always there, always helpful.

Sincere thanks to my editor, Jackie Freimor, who tirelessly kept me on track with her insight, knowledge, suggestions, unwavering professionalism, and friendship.

And many thanks to the friends who encouraged me throughout the years: Donald Owings, whom I first met in the mid-1950s and who never stopped telling me to record this story; Gerda von Witte, who helped me daily during the last two years of concentrated effort; and Nancy Warren, who helped find buried information and encouraged me with her steadfast faith. Without these loyal friends, this story would not have materialized.

Sincere thanks to Dawnn Blalock of Blalock Imaging in Memphis, Tennessee, for the lovely job of preparing the many pictures for *Lost in China*.

And last, many thanks to my wonderful team at Girl Friday Productions, led most ably by Kristin Duran. This team of editors, mapmakers, artists, and publicists, each an expert in their field, have put up with my many iterations and demands and produced this beautiful volume. Thank you very much for realizing my dream.

ABOUT THE AUTHOR

Jennifer Dobbs's experience of being lost in China led her to study Montessori teaching methods in Bergamo and Perugia, Italy. As a Montessori teacher, Dobbs helped open five schools in Pennsylvania and Mississippi. She holds a bachelor of arts in English, a bachelor of science in psychology, and a master's in school counseling. After years of working with children, Dobbs joined the FedEx operations and sales training departments and worked in China when the company first initiated service there.

Dobbs is now dedicated to animal rescue. She incorporated a group called Petmatchmaker Rescue South, which cares for and places hundreds of dogs and cats each year. Dobbs currently lives in Memphis, Tennessee. *Lost in China* is her first book.

www.ingramcontent.com/pod-product-compliance
Lightning Source LLC
Chambersburg PA
CBHW030354130626
46549CB00004B/1494